VOL. 12
VIZ Media Edition

Story and Art by
RUMIKO TAKAHASHI

English Adaptation by Gerard Jones

Translation/Mari Morimoto
Touch-Up Art & Lettering/Wayne Truman
Cover and Interior Graphics & Design/Yuki Ameda
Editor (1st Edition)/Julie Davis
Editor (VIZ Media Edition)/Avery Gotoh
Supervising Editor (VIZ Media Edition)/Michelle Pangilinan

VP, Production/Alvin Lu
VP, Publishing Licensing/Rika Inouye
VP, Sales & Product Marketing/Gonzalo Ferreyra
VP, Creative/Linda Espinosa
Publisher/Hyoe Narita

INUYASHA 12 by Rumiko TAKAHASHI
© 1999 Rumiko TAKAHASHI
All rights reserved.
Original Japanese edition published in 1999
by Shogakukan Inc., Tokyo.

Printed in Canada

Published by VIZ Media, LLC
P.O. Box 77010
San Francisco, CA 94107

1st Edition Published 2002

VIZ Media Edition
10 9 8 7 6 5 4 3
First printing, June 2004
Third printing, March 2009

PARENTAL ADVISORY
INUYASHA is rated T+ for Older Teen
and is recommended for ages 16 and up.
This book contains violence.
ratings.viz.com

www.viz.com

store.viz.com

INUYASHA

VOL. 12   VIZ Media Edition

STORY AND ART BY
RUMIKO TAKAHASHI

CONTENTS

Long ago, in the "Warring States" era of Japan's Muromachi period (*Sengoku-jidai*, approximately 1467-1568 CE), a legendary doglike half-demon called "Inu-Yasha" attempted to steal the Shikon Jewel—or "Jewel of Four Souls"—from a village, but was stopped by the enchanted arrow of the village priestess, Kikyo. Inu-Yasha fell into a deep sleep, pinned to a tree by Kikyo's arrow, while the mortally wounded Kikyo took the Shikon Jewel with her into the fires of her funeral pyre. Years passed.

Fast-forward to the present day. Kagome, a Japanese high-school girl, is pulled into a well one day by a mysterious centipede monster, and finds herself transported into the past, only to come face to face with the trapped Inu-Yasha. She frees him, and Inu-Yasha easily defeats the centipede monster.

The residents of the village, now 50 years older, readily accept Kagome as the reincarnation of their deceased priestess Kikyo, a claim supported by the fact that the Shikon Jewel emerges from a cut on Kagome's body. Unfortunately, the jewel's rediscovery means that the village is soon under attack by a variety of demons in search of this treasure. Then, the jewel is accidentally shattered into many shards, each of which may have the fearsome power of the entire jewel.

Although Inu-Yasha says he hates Kagome because of her resemblance to Kikyo—the woman who "killed" him—he is forced to team up with her when Kaede, the village leader, binds him to Kagome with a powerful spell. Now the two grudging companions must fight to reclaim and reassemble the shattered shards of the Shikon Jewel before they fall into the wrong hands...

THIS VOLUME Sango's love for her little brother is the motivation behind her betrayal of Inu-Yasha and the others, while Kikyo, meaning only to help the sick, is taken prisoner by the demon Naraku.

CHARACTERS

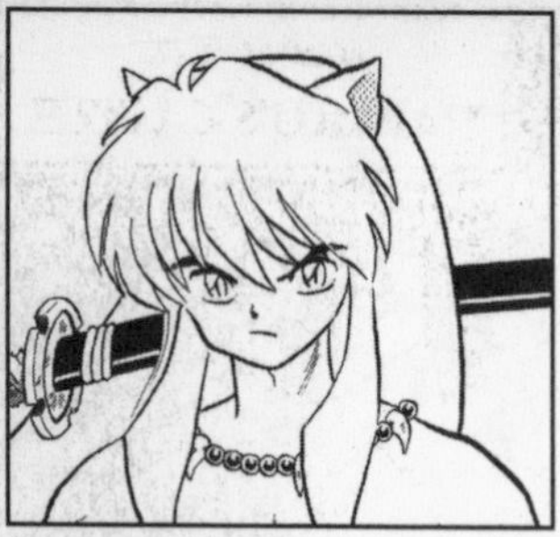

KAGOME
Modern-day Japanese schoolgirl who can travel back and forth between the past and present through an enchanted well.

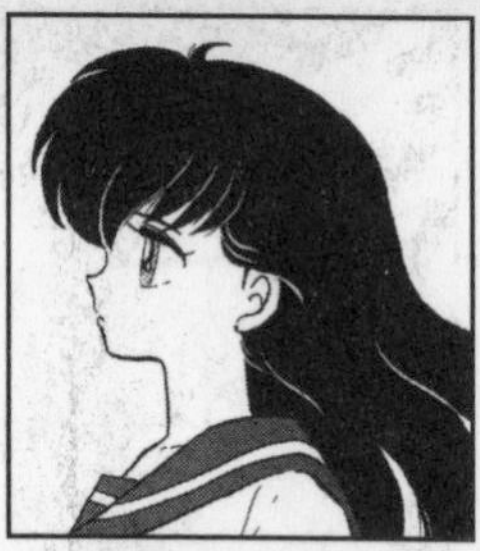

INU-YASHA
Half-demon hybrid, son of a human mother and demon father. His necklace is enchanted, allowing Kagome to control him with a word.

KIKYO
Powerful priestess who died protecting the Shikon Jewel, now resurrected to a kind of "life" by equally powerful magic.

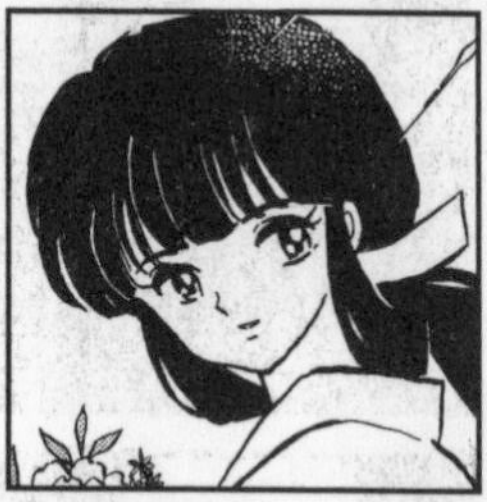

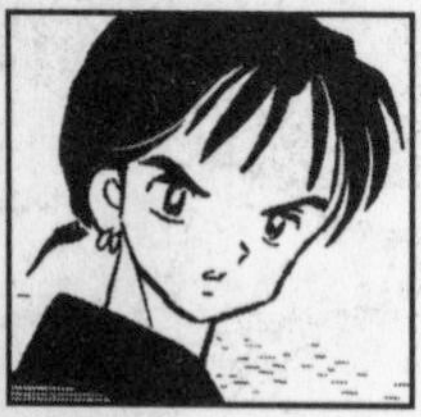

MIROKU
Lecherous Buddhist priest cursed with a mystical "hellhole" in his hand that's slowly killing him.

KAEDE
Kikyo's "little sister," now 50-plus years old. It was her spell that bound Inu-Yasha to Kagome with the spoken word, "Sit!"

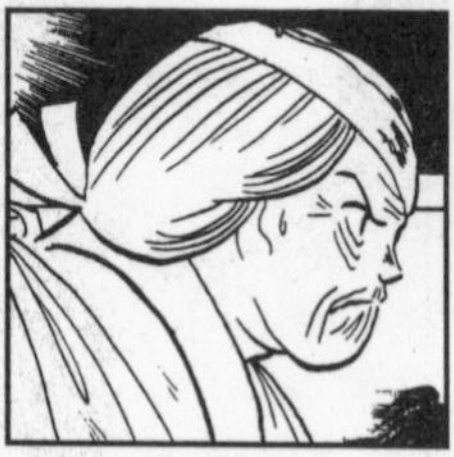

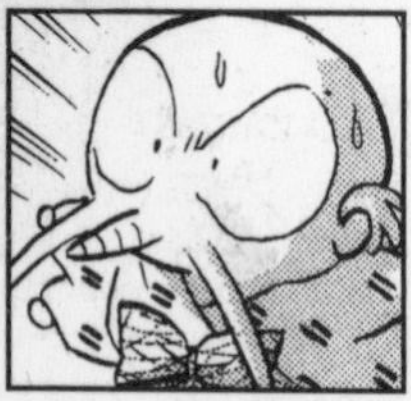

MYOGA
Tiny flea-demon and servant to Inu-Yasha. A pain in his master's side...and not just because of the bloodsucking.

SHIPPO
Orphaned young fox-demon who likes to play shape-changing tricks.

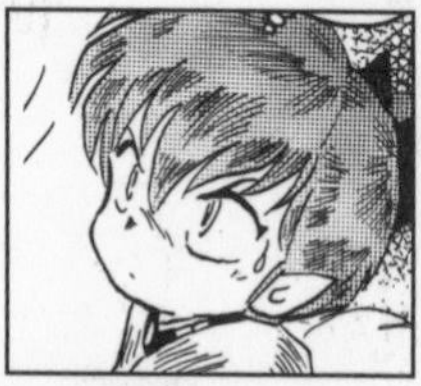

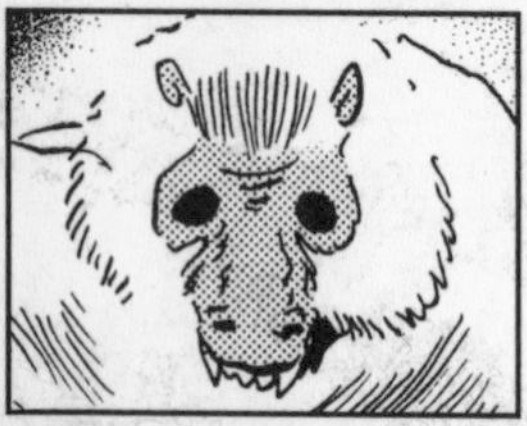

NARAKU
Enigmatic demon-mastermind behind the miseries of nearly everyone in the story.

SANGO
"Demon Exterminator" or slayer from the village where the Shikon Jewel was first born.

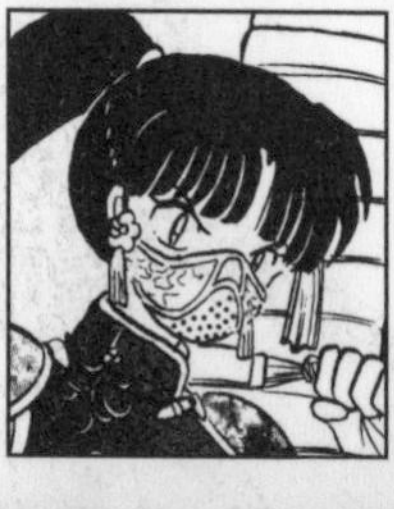

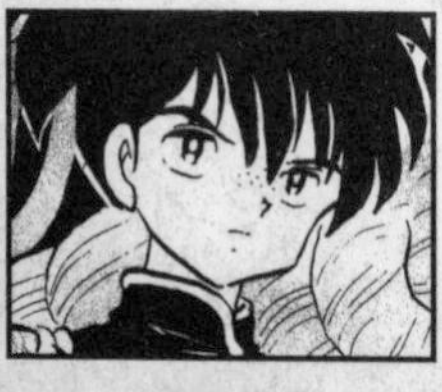

KOHAKU
Killed by Naraku—but not before first slaying both his own and Sango's father—now he's back again in a newer...if somewhat *slower*...form.

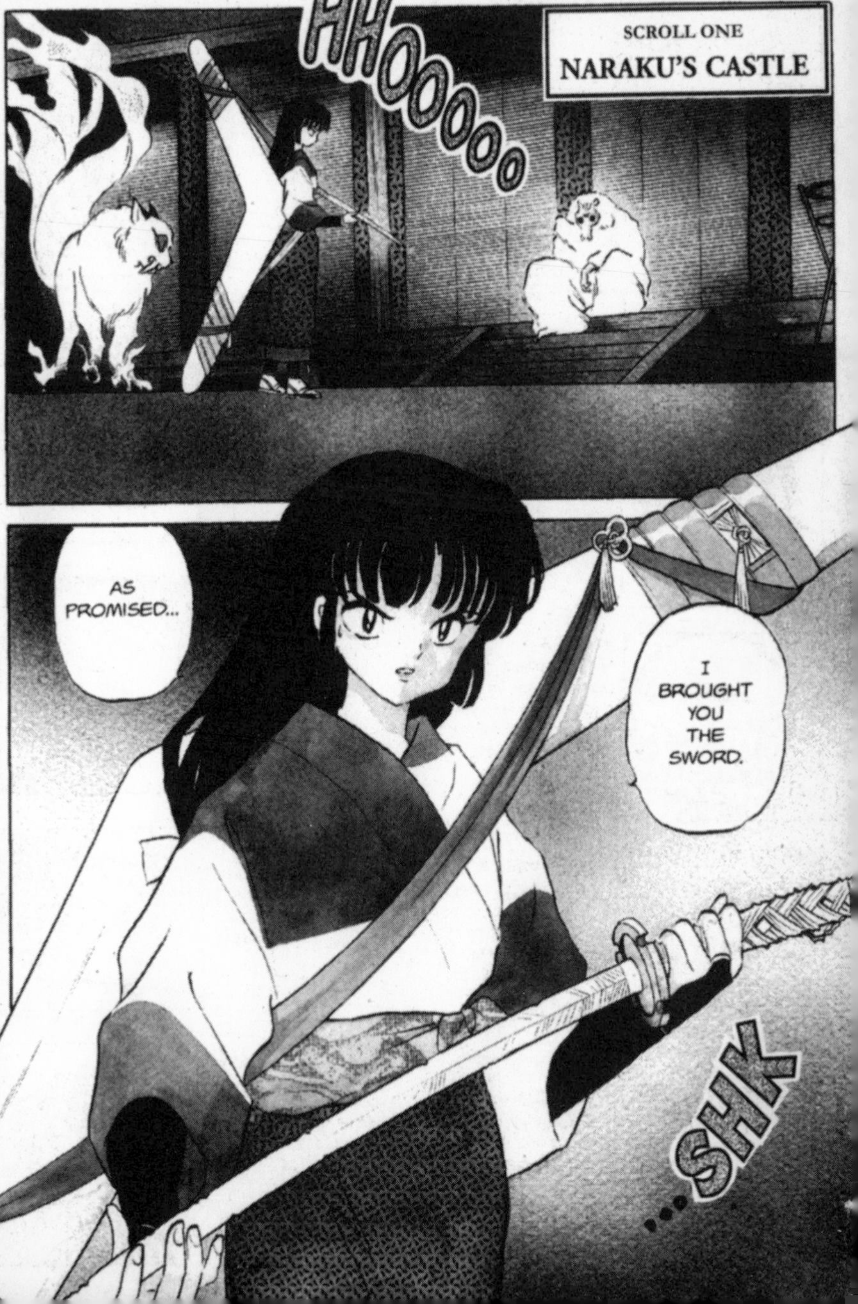
HHOOOOO
SCROLL ONE
NARAKU'S CASTLE
AS PROMISED...
I BROUGHT YOU THE SWORD.
...SHK

SCROLL ONE
NARAKU'S CASTLE

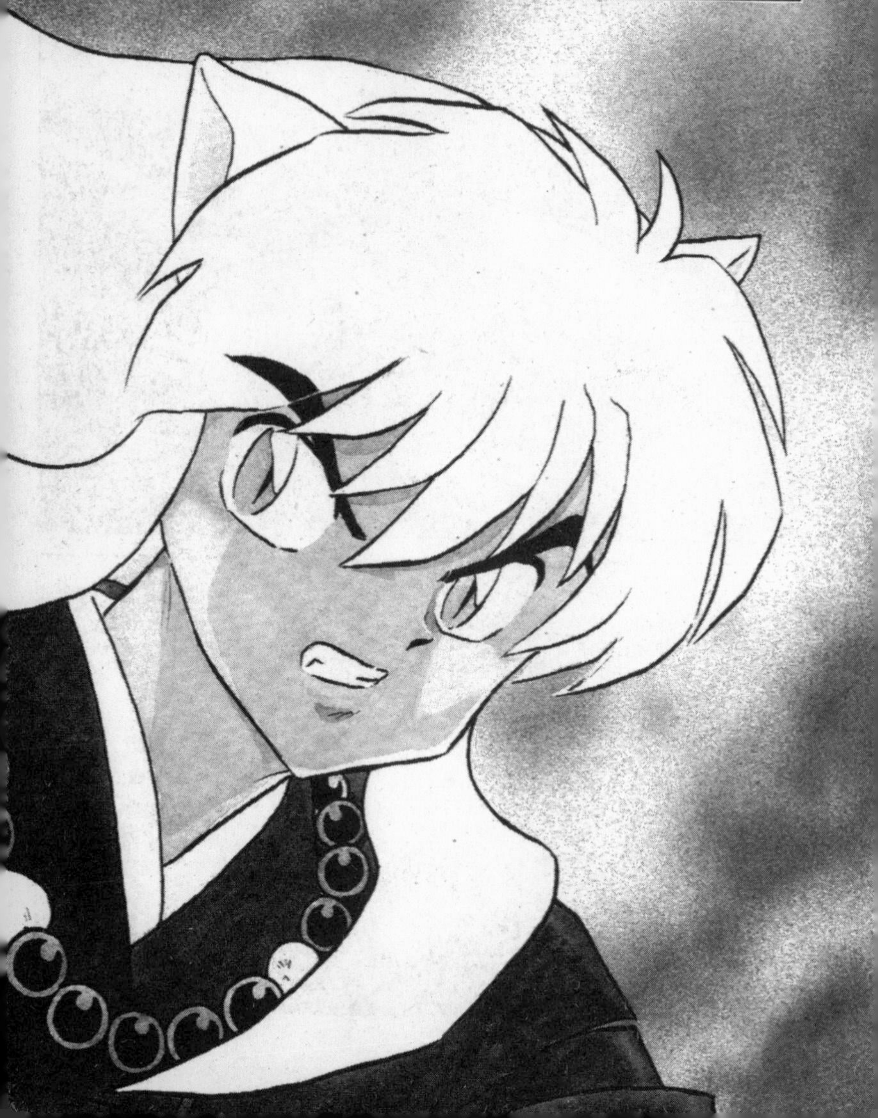

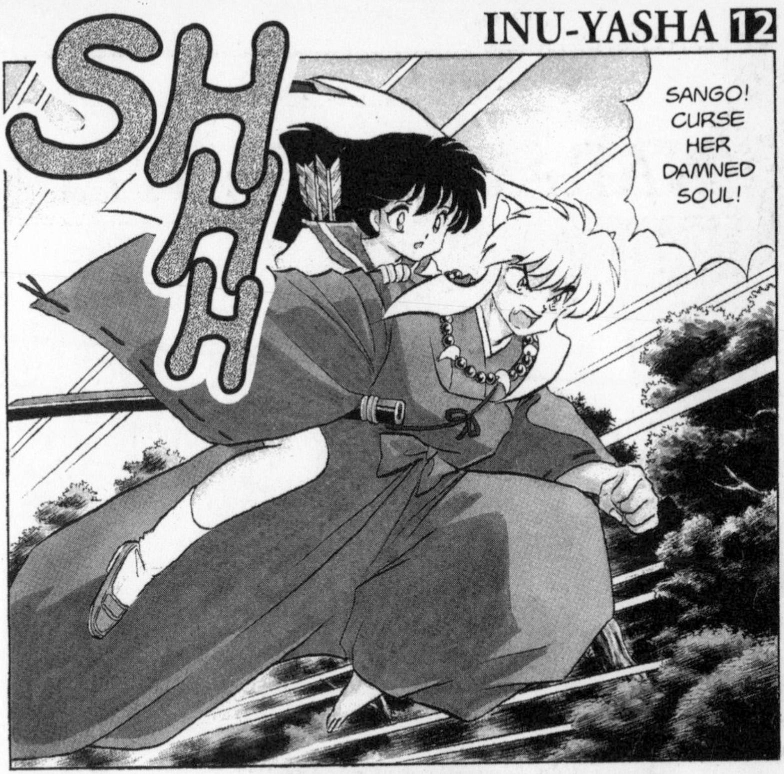
SHHH
SANGO! CURSE HER DAMNED SOUL!

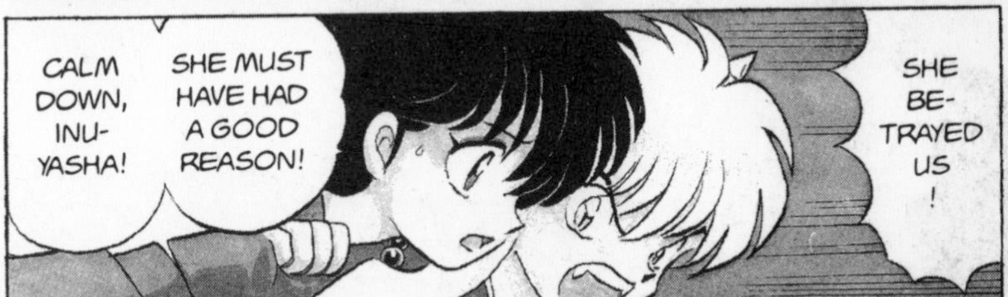
CALM DOWN, INU-YASHA!
SHE MUST HAVE HAD A GOOD REASON!
SHE BE-TRAYED US!

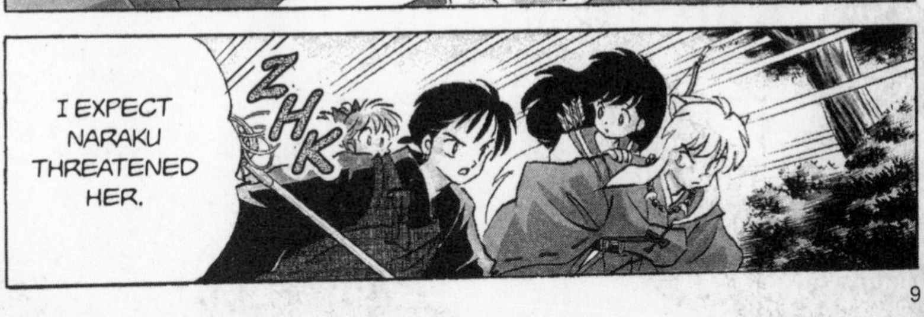
I EXPECT NARAKU THREATENED HER.
ZHK

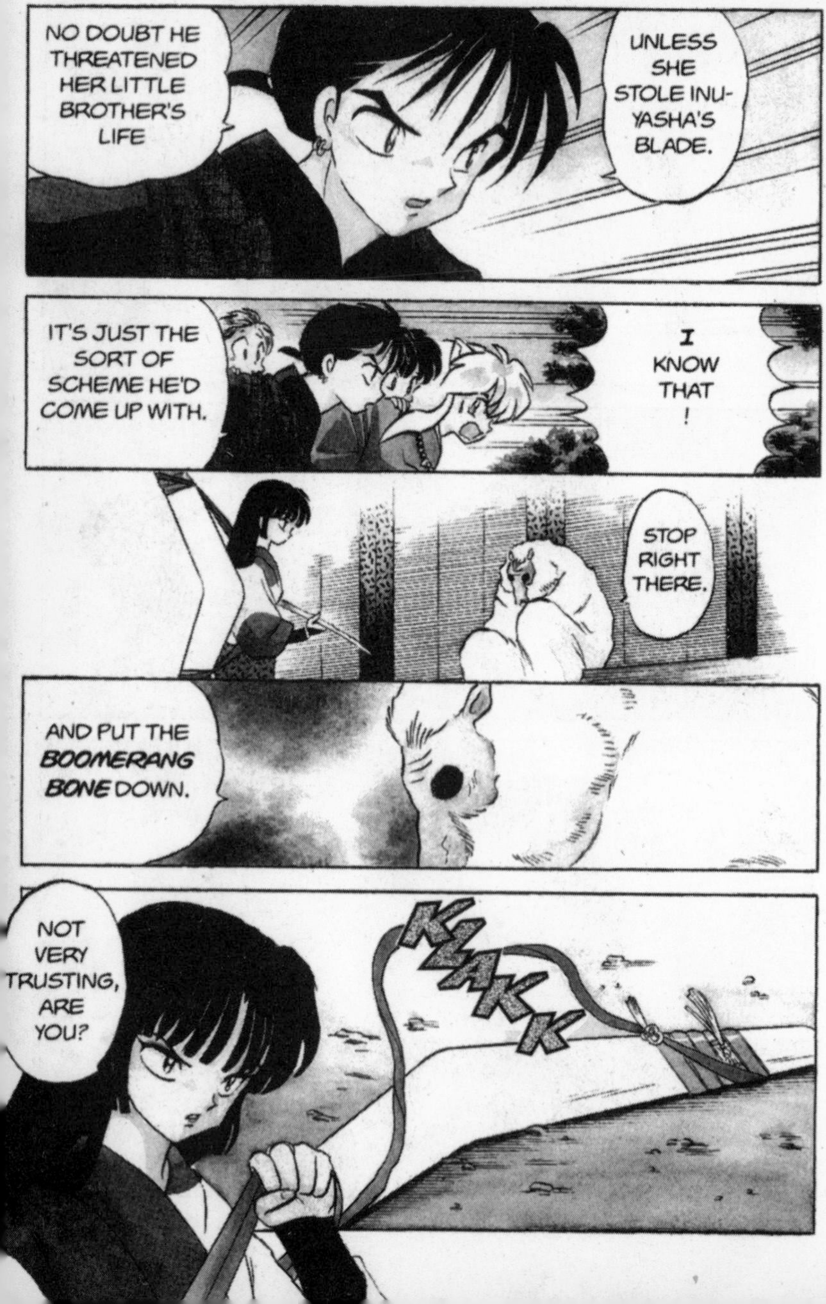
NO DOUBT HE THREATENED HER LITTLE BROTHER'S LIFE
UNLESS SHE STOLE INU-YASHA'S BLADE.
IT'S JUST THE SORT OF SCHEME HE'D COME UP WITH.
I KNOW THAT!
STOP RIGHT THERE.
AND PUT THE ***BOOMERANG BONE*** DOWN.
NOT VERY TRUSTING, ARE YOU?
KLAKK

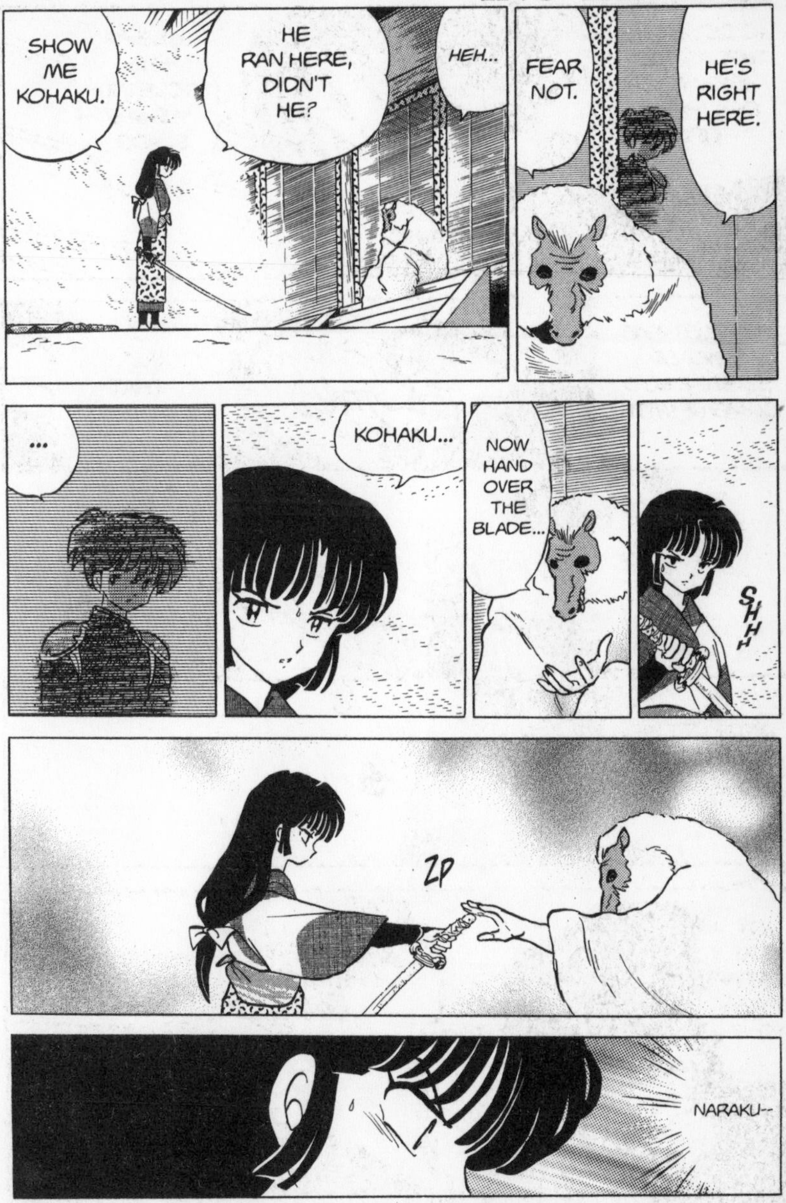
SHOW ME KOHAKU.
HE RAN HERE, DIDN'T HE?
HEH...
FEAR NOT.
HE'S RIGHT HERE.
...
KOHAKU...
NOW HAND OVER THE BLADE...
SHHH
ZP
NARAKU--

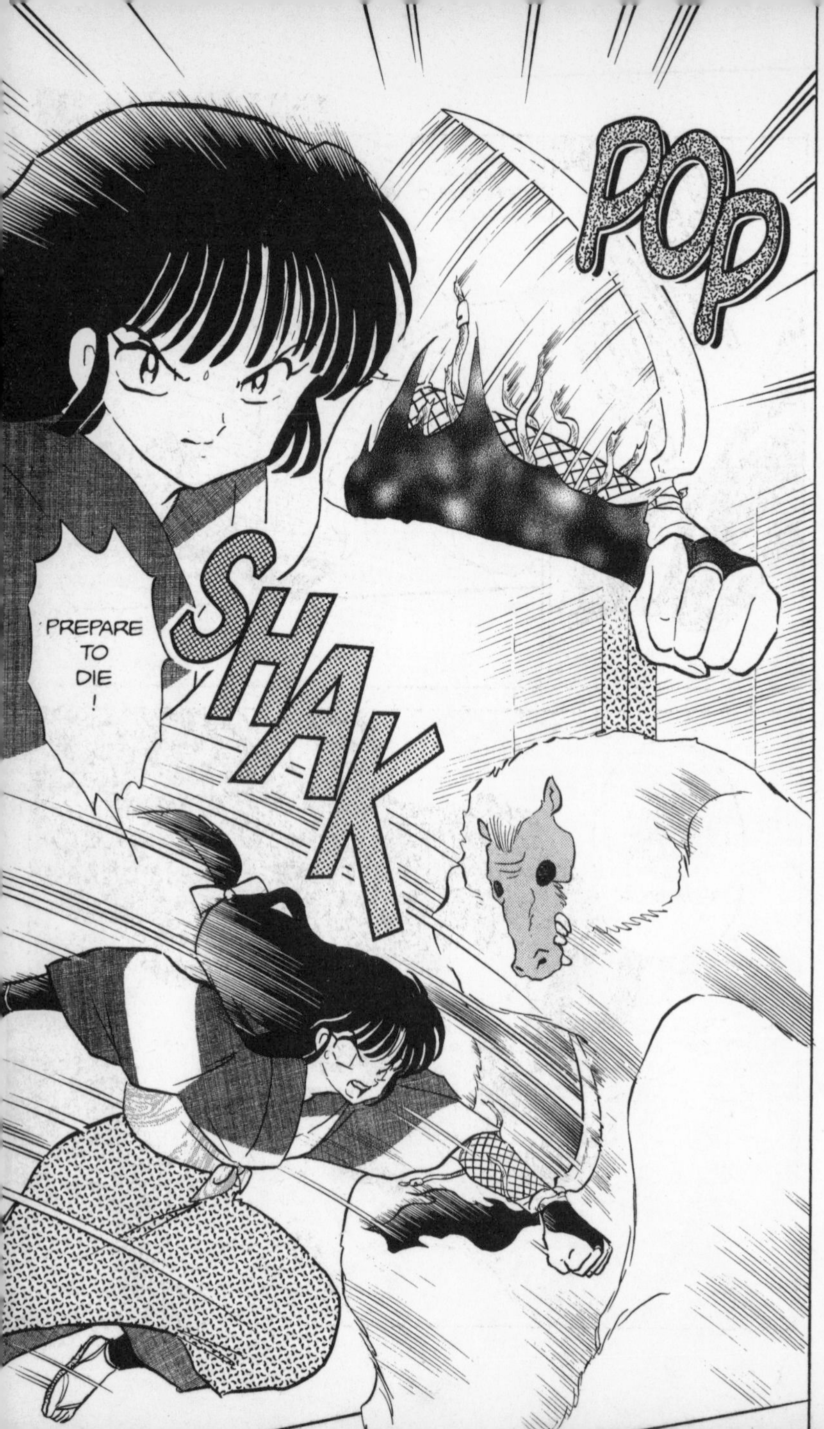

POP
PREPARE TO DIE !
SHAK

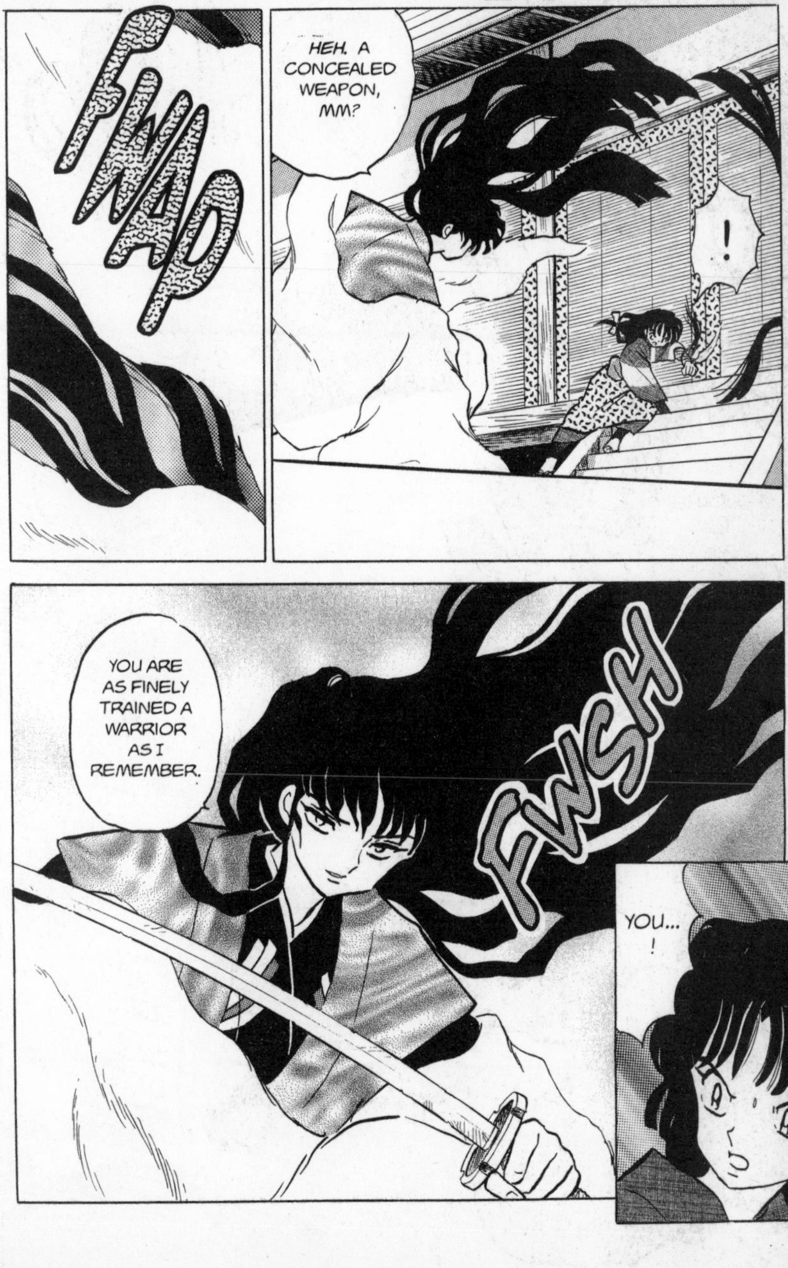
FWAP
HEH. A CONCEALED WEAPON, MM?
!
YOU ARE AS FINELY TRAINED A WARRIOR AS I REMEMBER.
FWSH
YOU... !

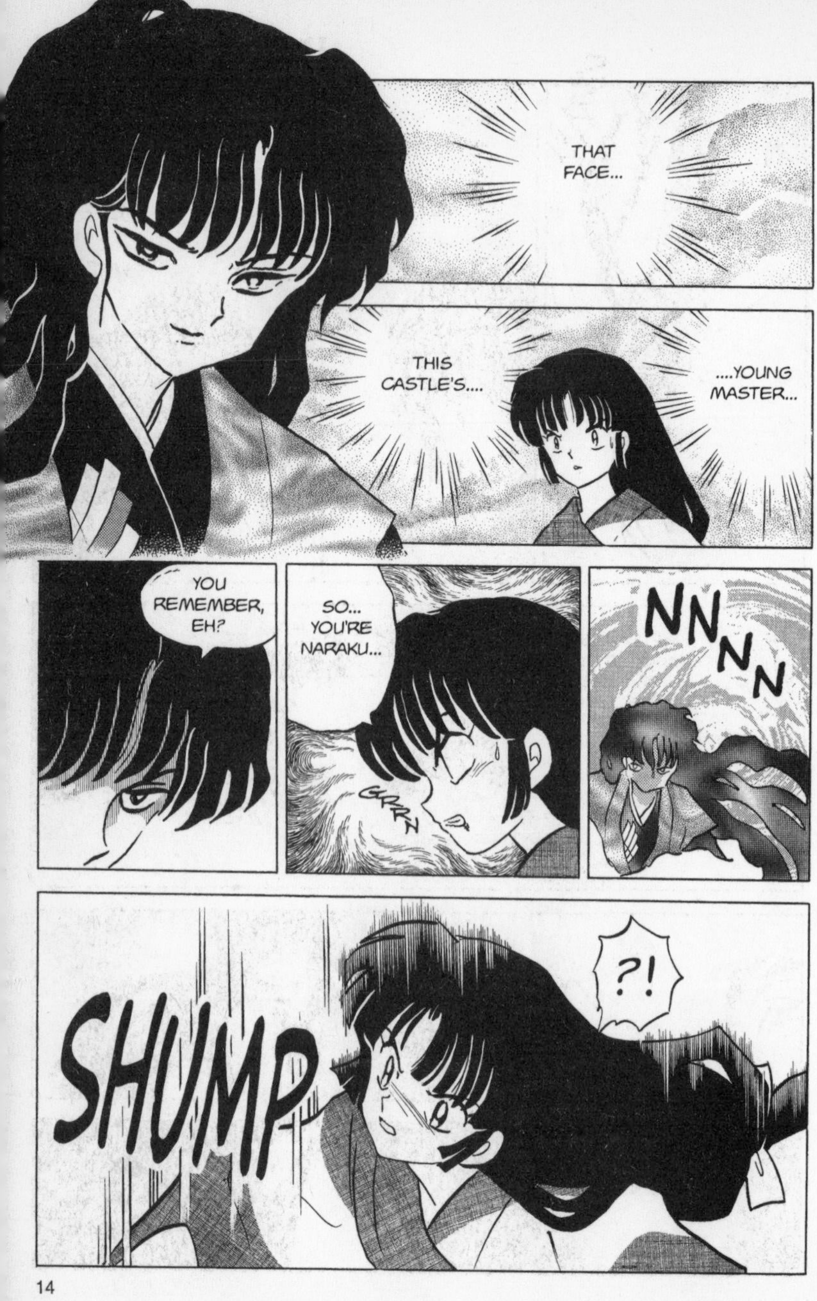
THAT FACE...
THIS CASTLE'S....
....YOUNG MASTER...
YOU REMEMBER, EH?
SO... YOU'RE NARAKU...
NNNNN
SHUMP
?!

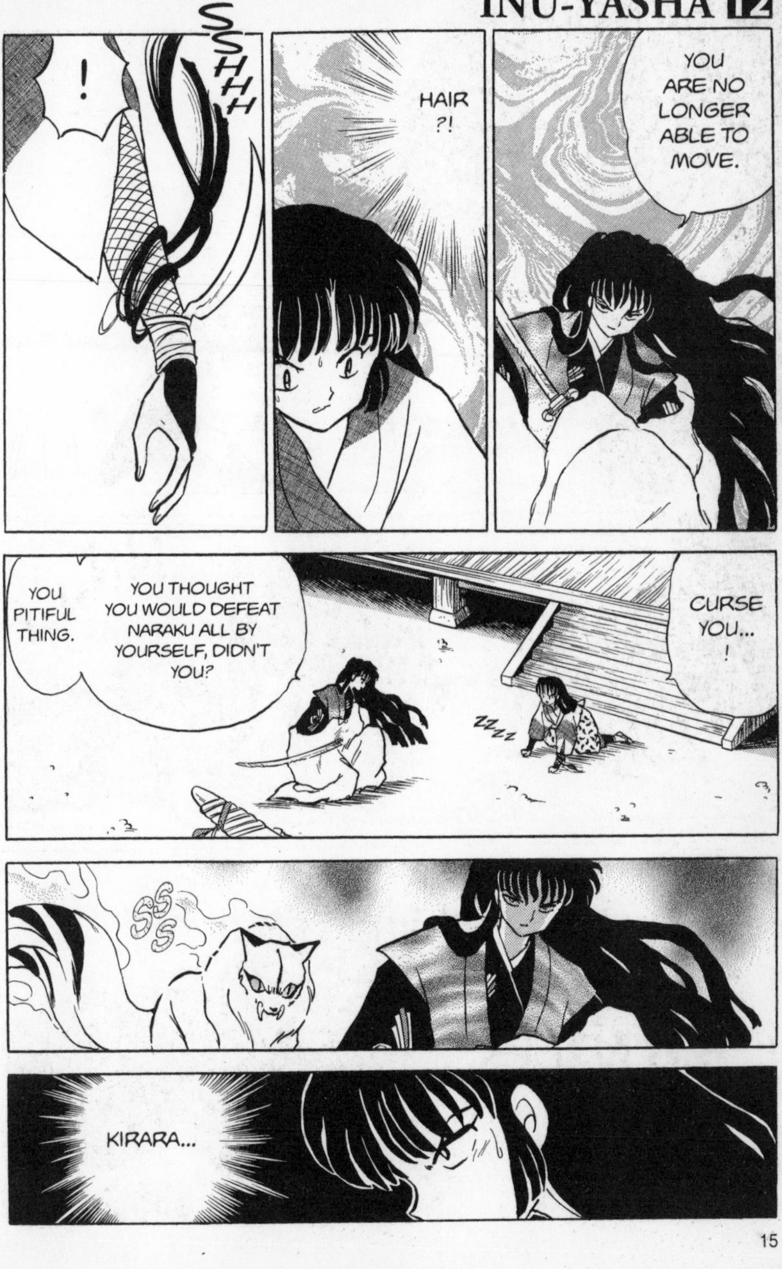
!
SSHHH
HAIR ?!
YOU ARE NO LONGER ABLE TO MOVE.
YOU PITIFUL THING.
YOU THOUGHT YOU WOULD DEFEAT NARAKU ALL BY YOURSELF, DIDN'T YOU?
ZZZZ
CURSE YOU... !
SSS
KIRARA...

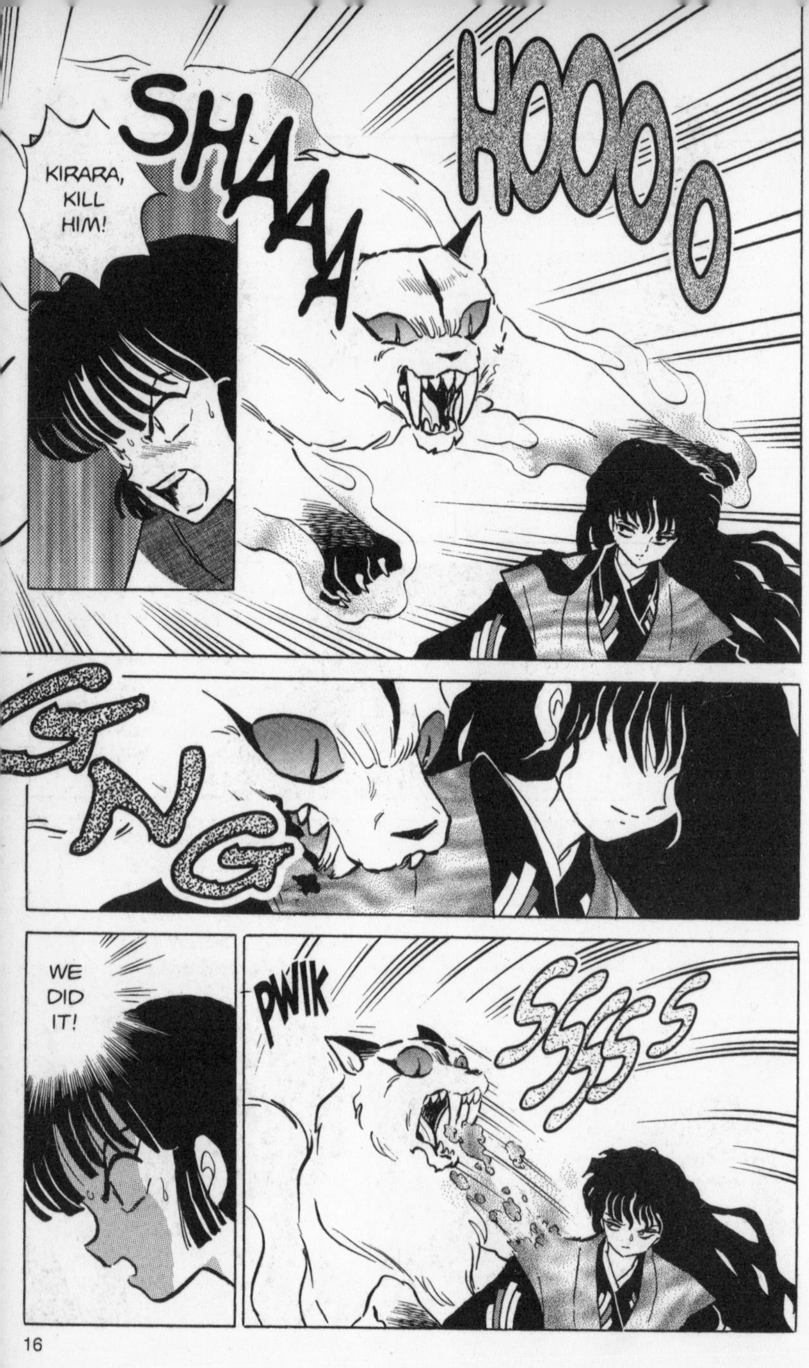

KIRARA, KILL HIM!
SHAAAA
HOOOOO
GNG
WE DID IT!
PWIK
SSSSS

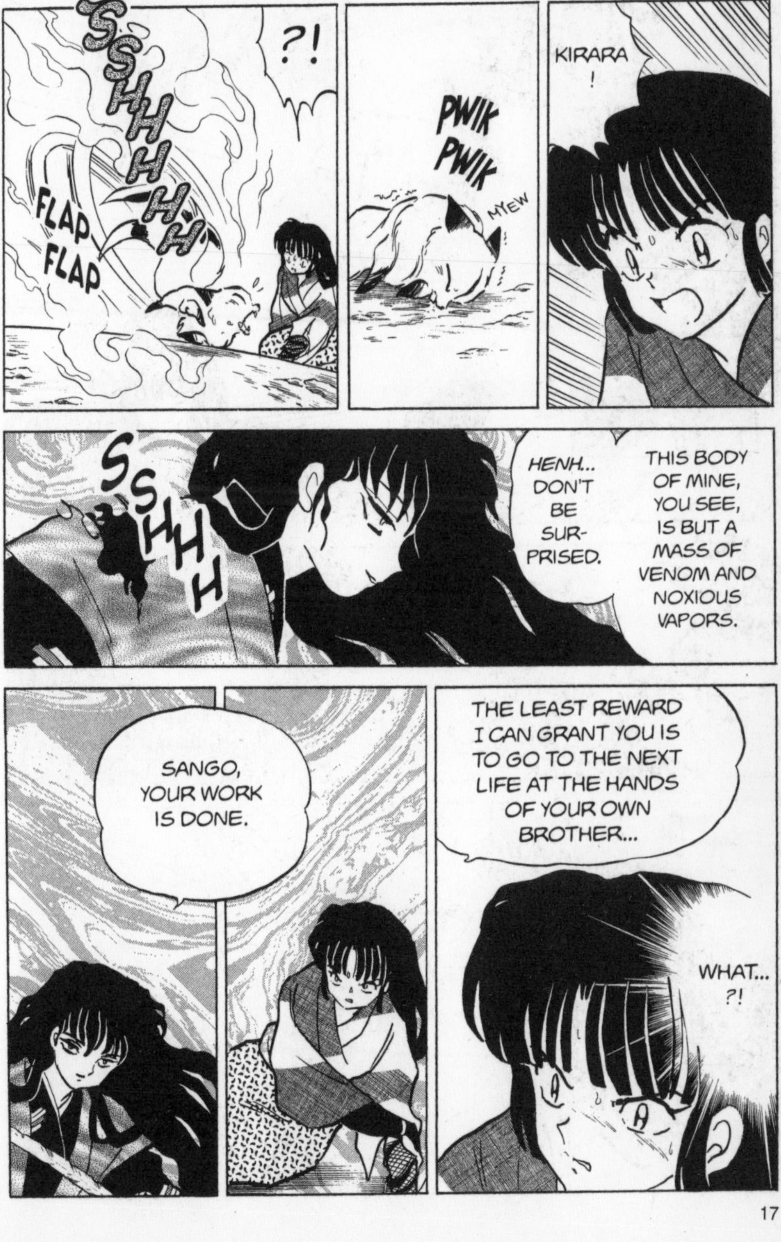
SSSHHHHHH
FLAP FLAP
?!
PWIK PWIK
MYEW
KIRARA !
SSHHH
HENH... DON'T BE SUR-PRISED.
THIS BODY OF MINE, YOU SEE, IS BUT A MASS OF VENOM AND NOXIOUS VAPORS.
SANGO, YOUR WORK IS DONE.
THE LEAST REWARD I CAN GRANT YOU IS TO GO TO THE NEXT LIFE AT THE HANDS OF YOUR OWN BROTHER...
WHAT... ?!

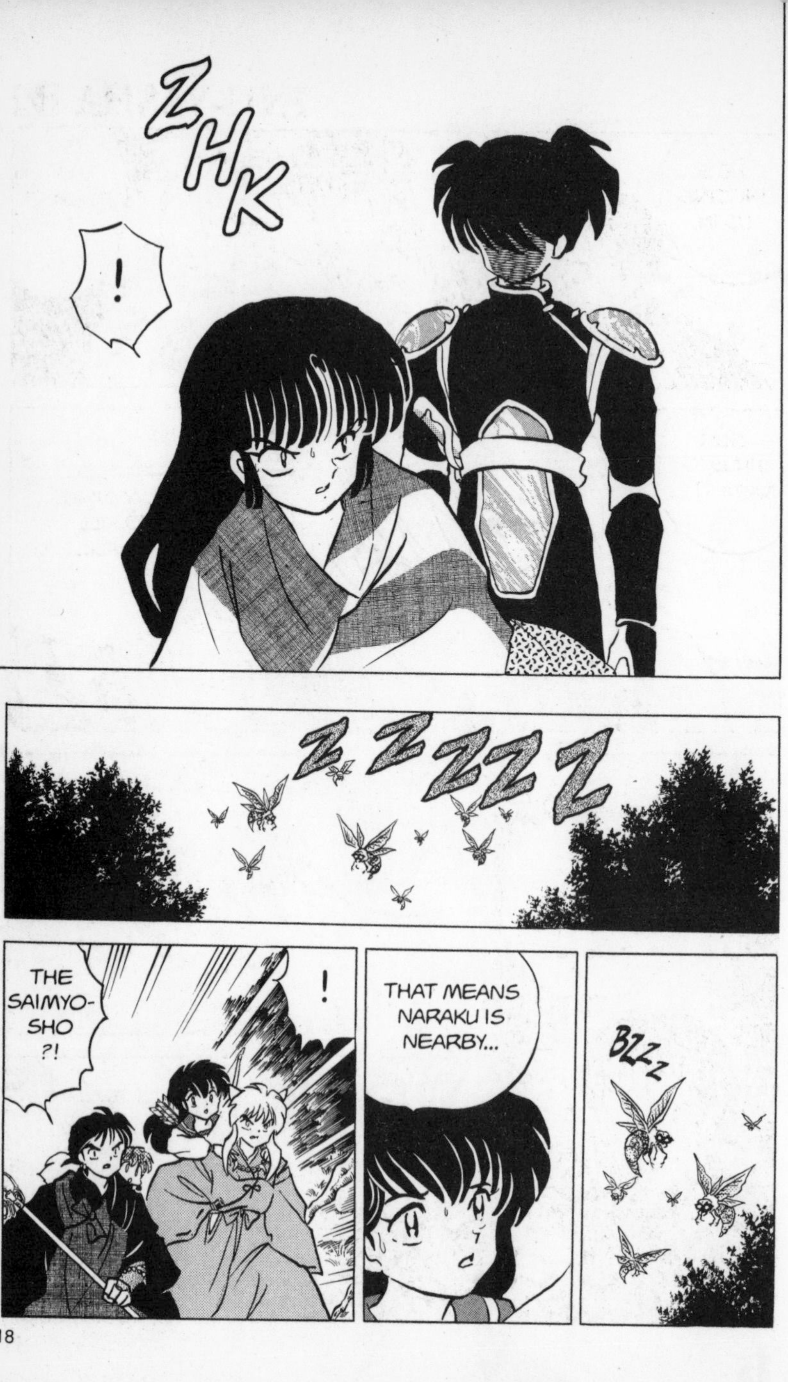
ZHK
!
ZZZZZZ
THE SAIMYO-SHO ?!
!
THAT MEANS NARAKU IS NEARBY...
BZZZ

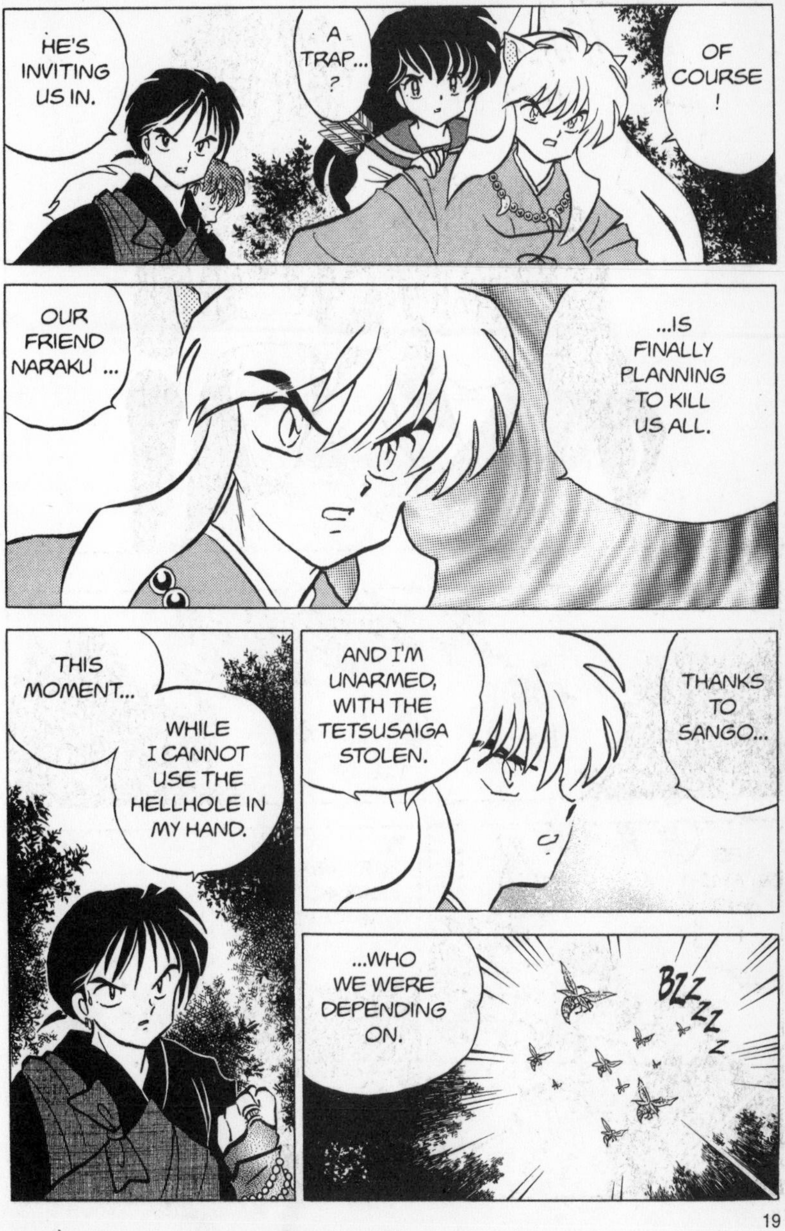
HE'S INVITING US IN.
A TRAP... ?
OF COURSE !
OUR FRIEND NARAKU ...
...IS FINALLY PLANNING TO KILL US ALL.
THIS MOMENT...
WHILE I CANNOT USE THE HELLHOLE IN MY HAND.
AND I'M UNARMED, WITH THE TETSUSAIGA STOLEN.
THANKS TO SANGO...
...WHO WE WERE DEPENDING ON.
BZZZZZ

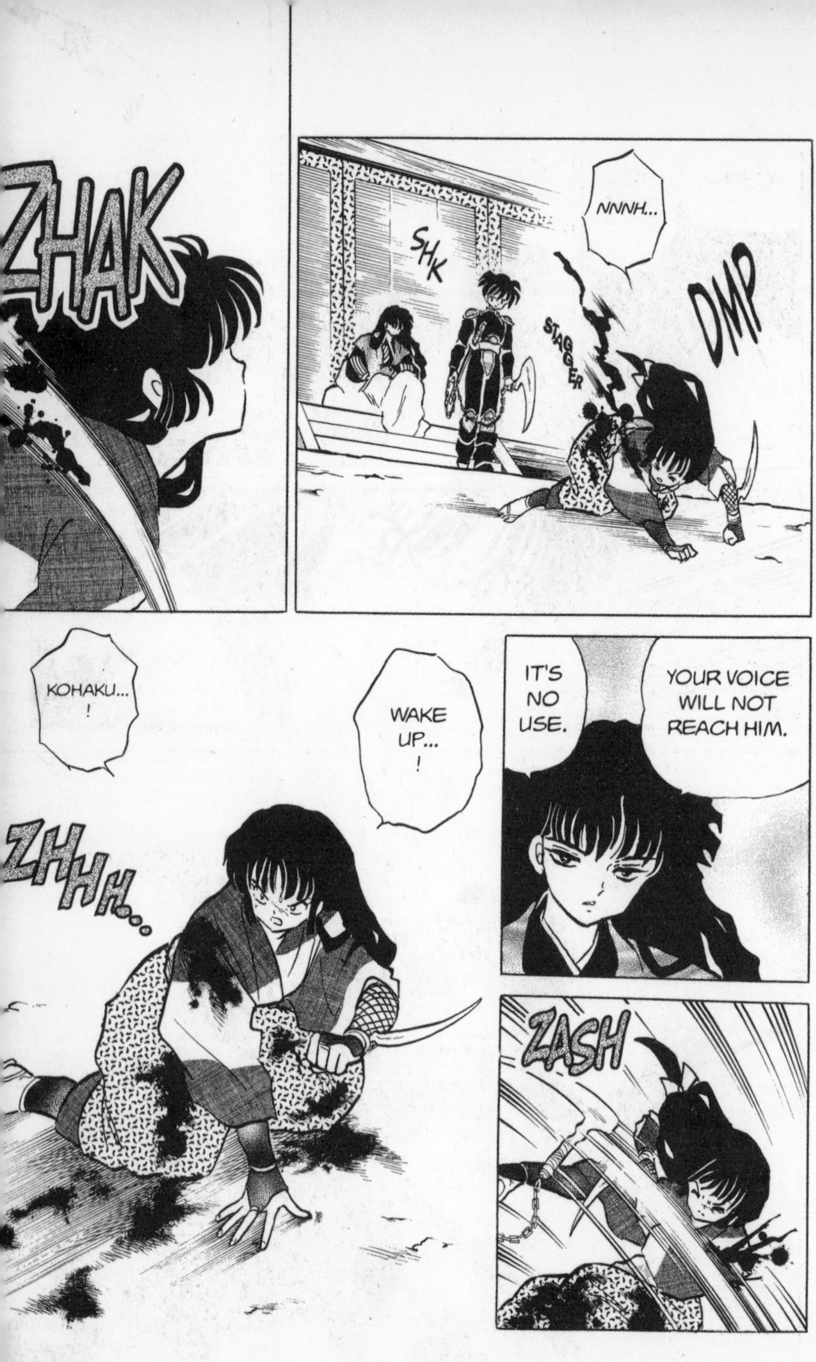
ZHAK
SHK
NNNH...
STAGGER
DMP
KOHAKU... !
WAKE UP... !
ZHHH...
IT'S NO USE.
YOUR VOICE WILL NOT REACH HIM.
ZASH

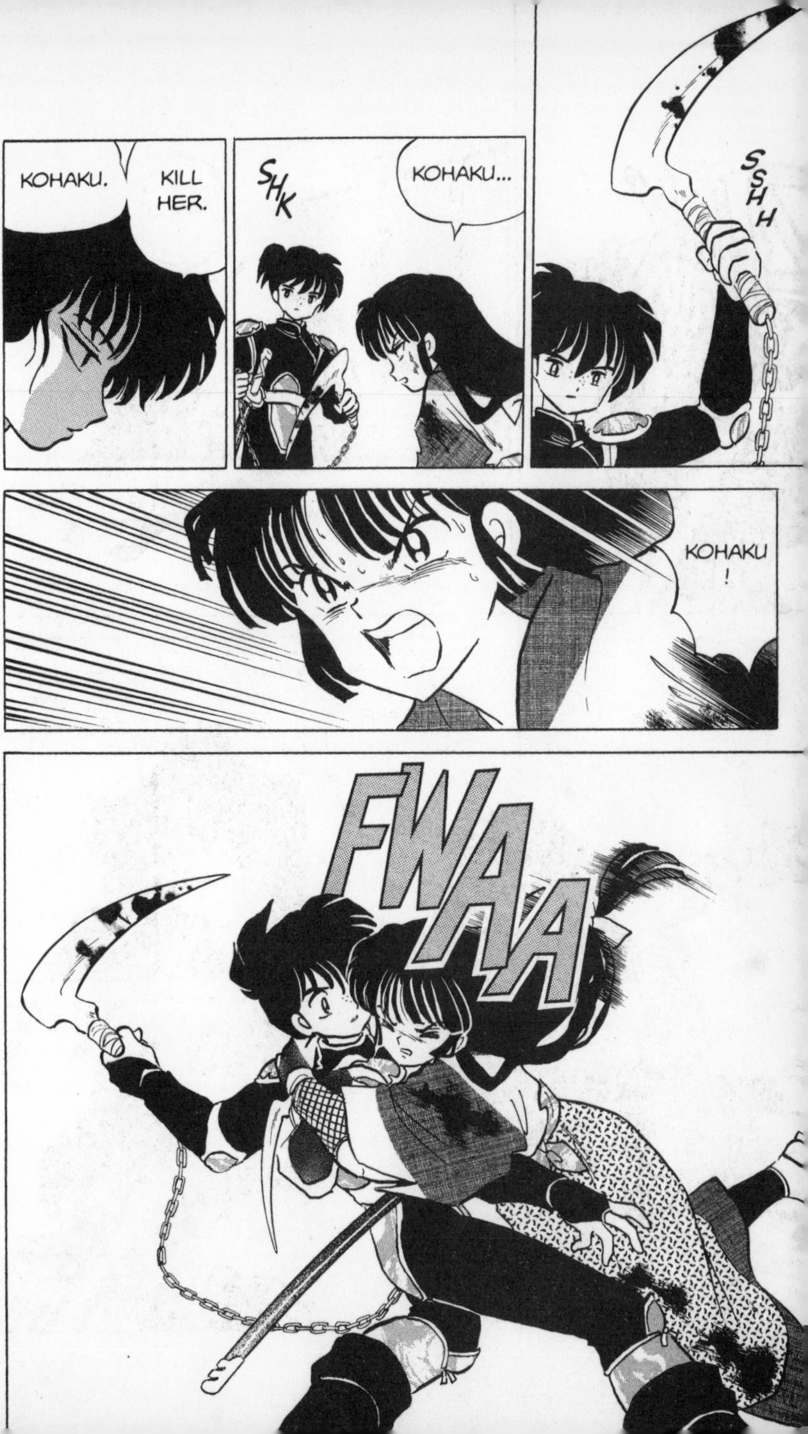
KOHAKU.
KILL HER.
SHK
KOHAKU...
SSHH
KOHAKU!
FWAA

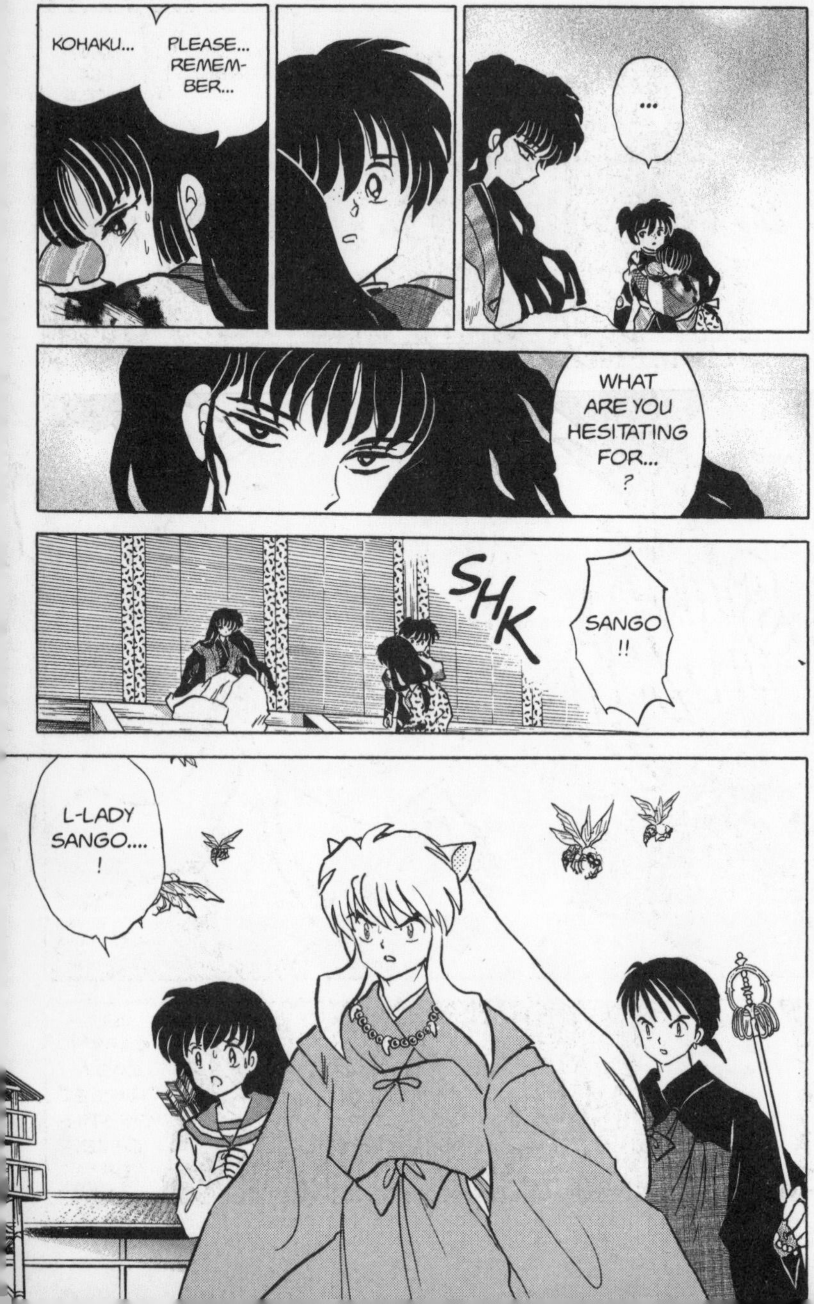
KOHAKU...
PLEASE... REMEMBER...
...
WHAT ARE YOU HESITATING FOR...?
SHK
SANGO!!
L-LADY SANGO....!

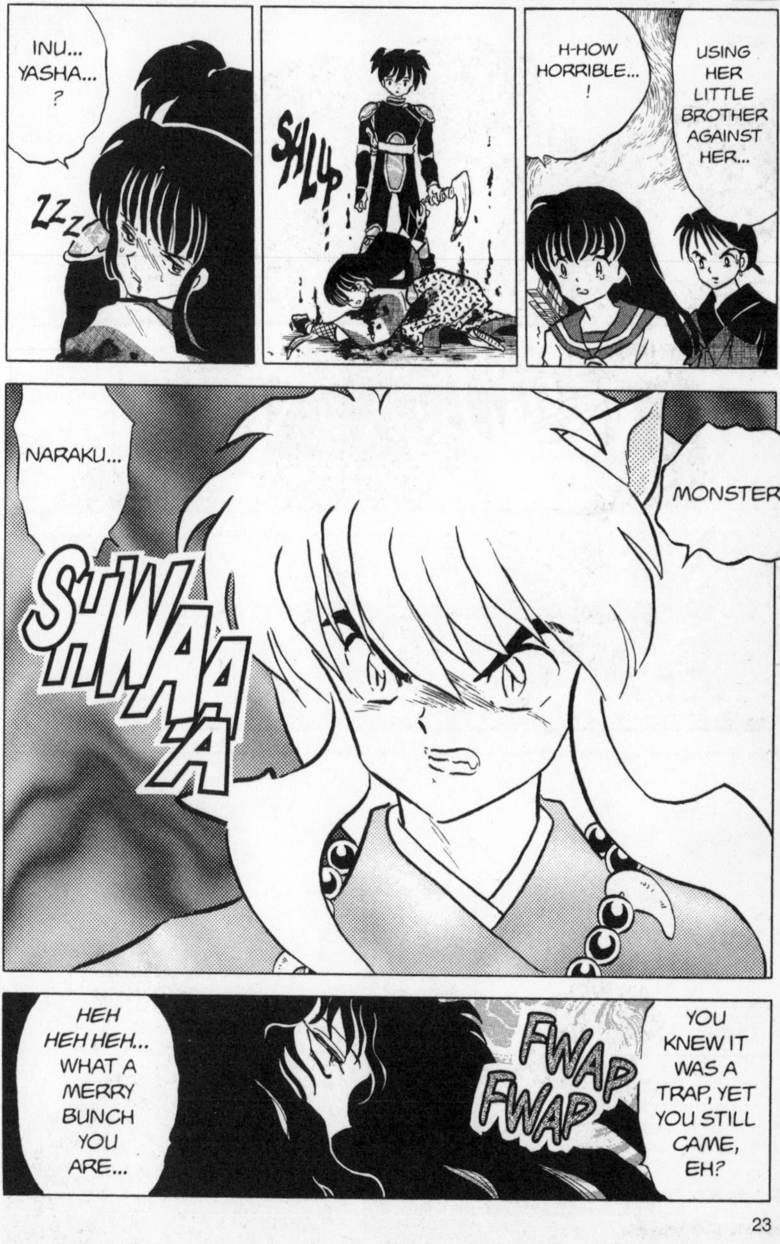
INU... YASHA... ?
ZZZ
SHLUP
H-HOW HORRIBLE... !
USING HER LITTLE BROTHER AGAINST HER...
NARAKU...
SHWAAA
MONSTER...
HEH HEH HEH... WHAT A MERRY BUNCH YOU ARE...
FWAP FWAP
YOU KNEW IT WAS A TRAP, YET YOU STILL CAME, EH?

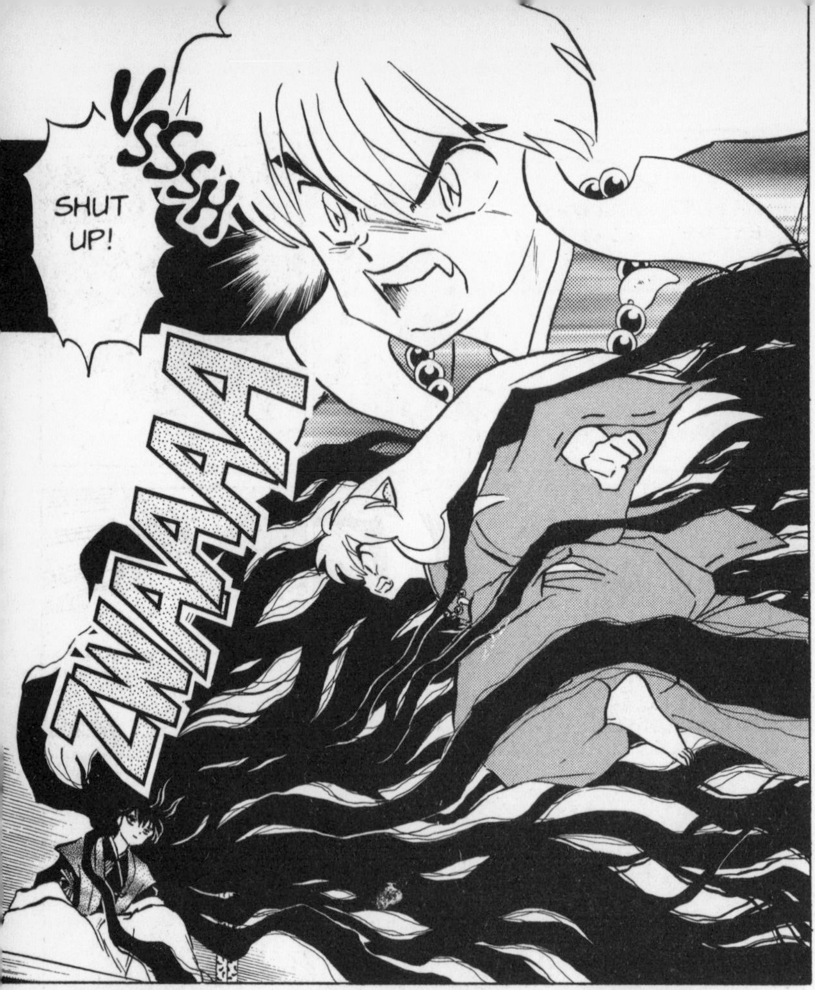
VSSSH!
SHUT UP!
ZWAAAA

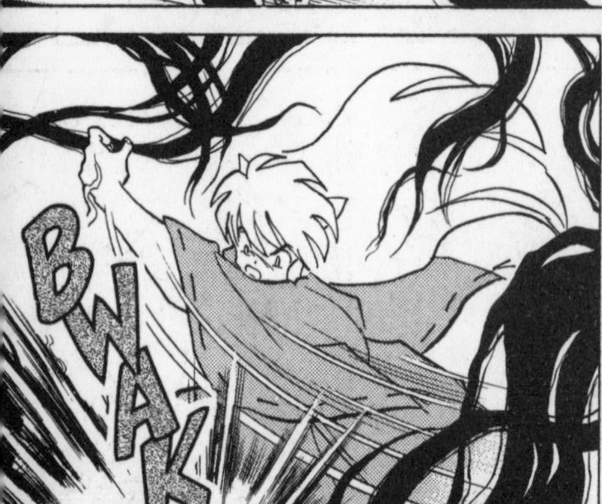
BWAK

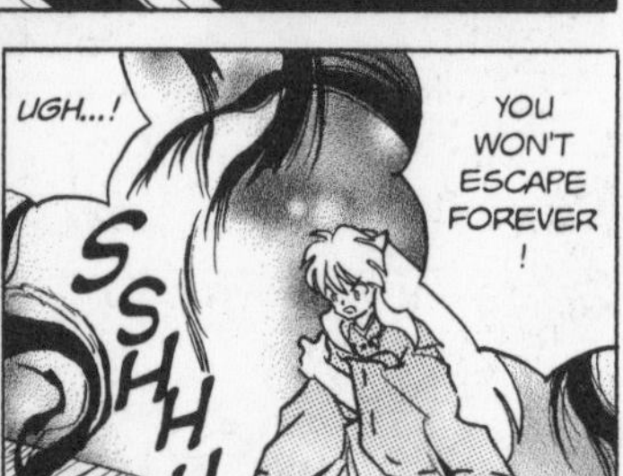
UGH...!
YOU WON'T ESCAPE FOREVER !
SSHHHH

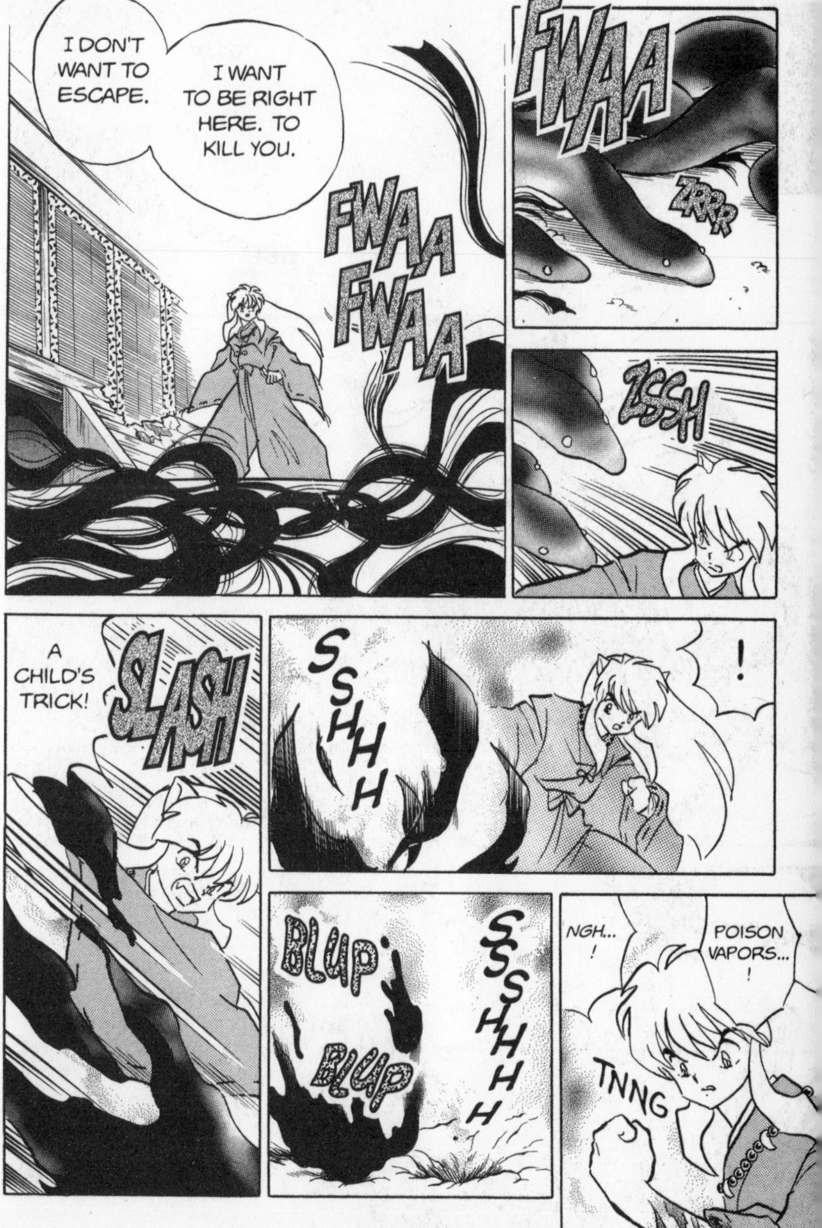
I DON'T WANT TO ESCAPE.
I WANT TO BE RIGHT HERE. TO KILL YOU.
FWAA FWAA
FWAA
ZRRR
ZSSH
A CHILD'S TRICK!
SLASH
SSHHH
!
BLUP
BLUP
SSSHHHH
NGH...!
POISON VAPORS...!
TNNG

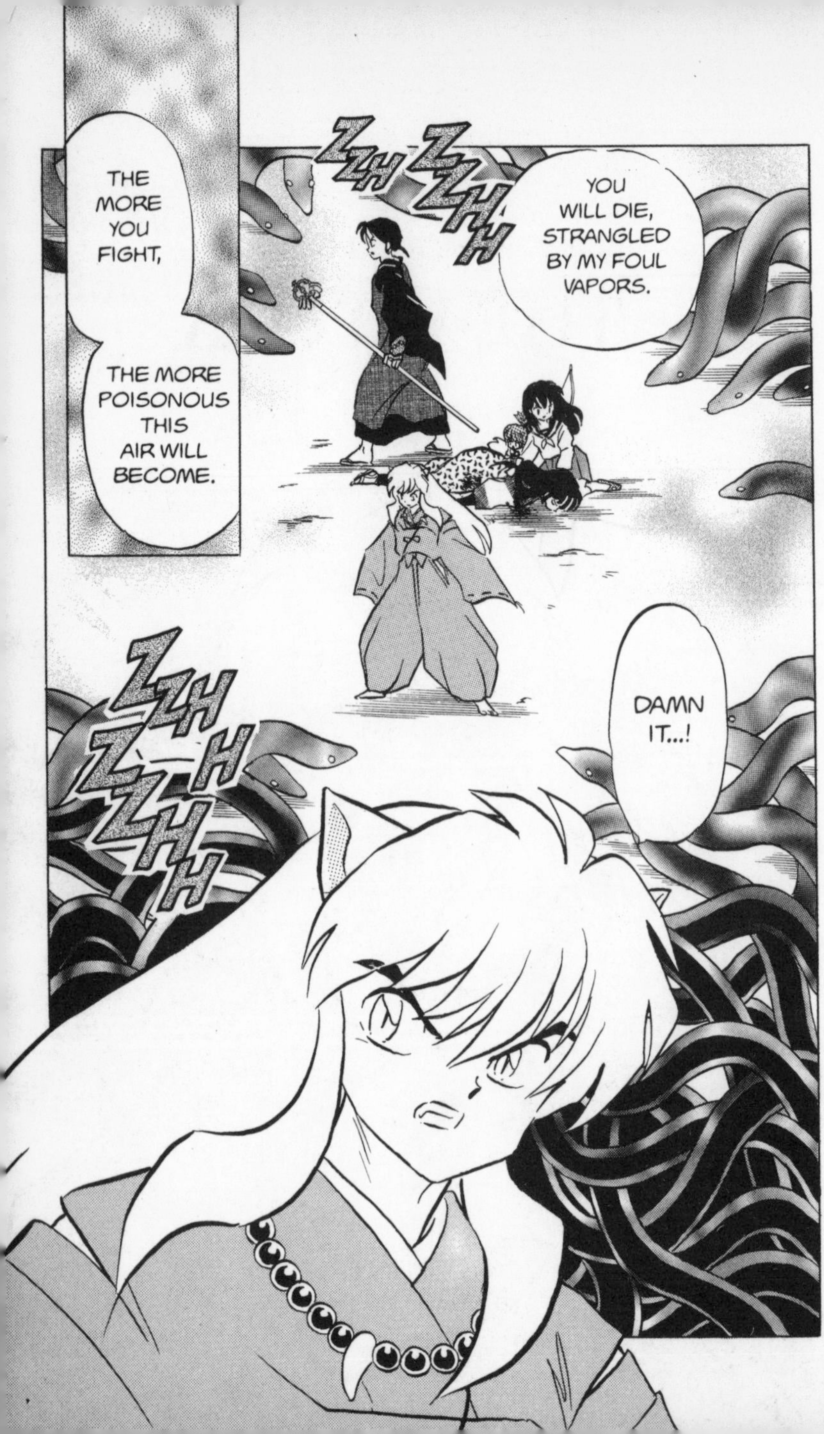
THE MORE YOU FIGHT,
THE MORE POISONOUS THIS AIR WILL BECOME.
ZZH ZZHH
YOU WILL DIE, STRANGLED BY MY FOUL VAPORS.
ZZHH ZZHHH
DAMN IT...!

SCROLL TWO

THE VAPORS

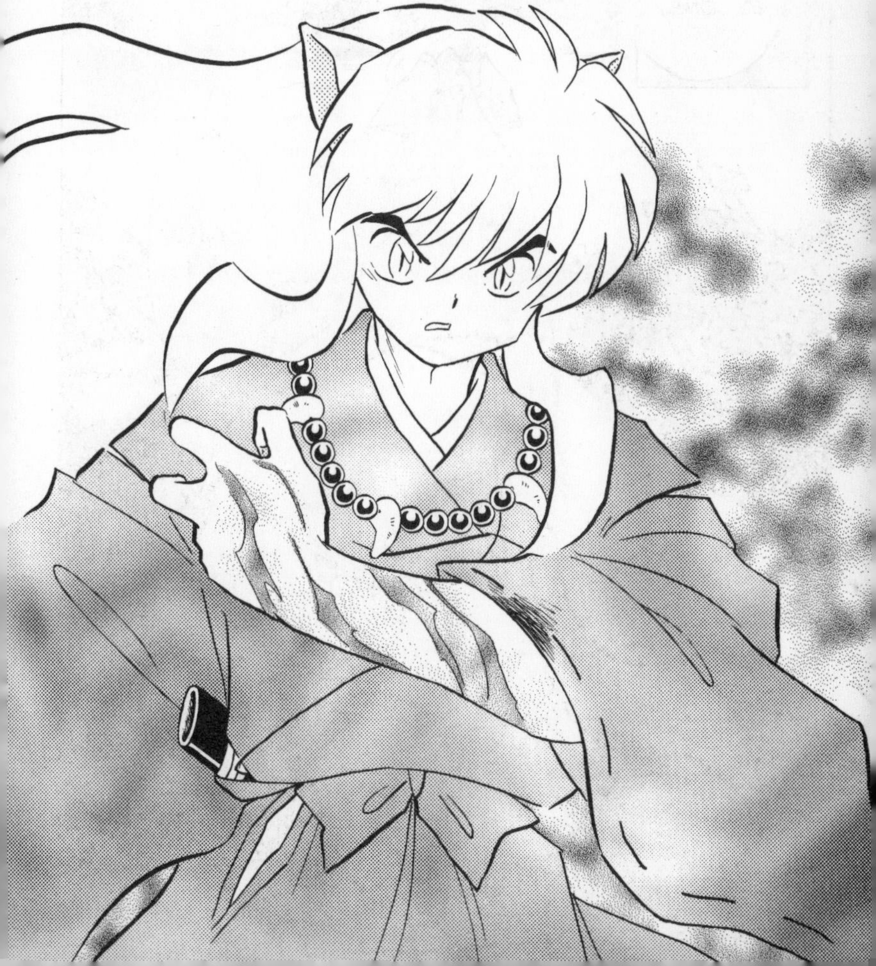

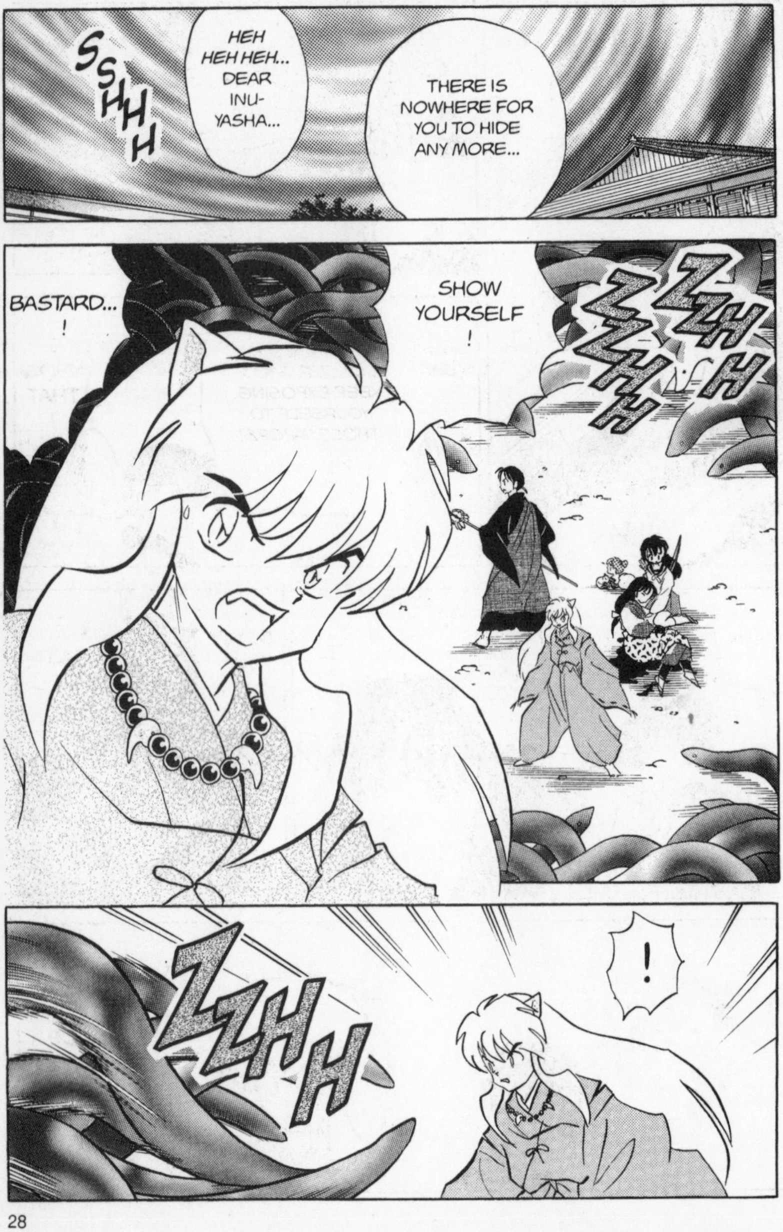
SSHHH
HEH HEH HEH... DEAR INU-YASHA...
THERE IS NOWHERE FOR YOU TO HIDE ANY MORE...
BASTARD...!
SHOW YOURSELF!
ZZHHH
ZZHHH
ZZHHH
!

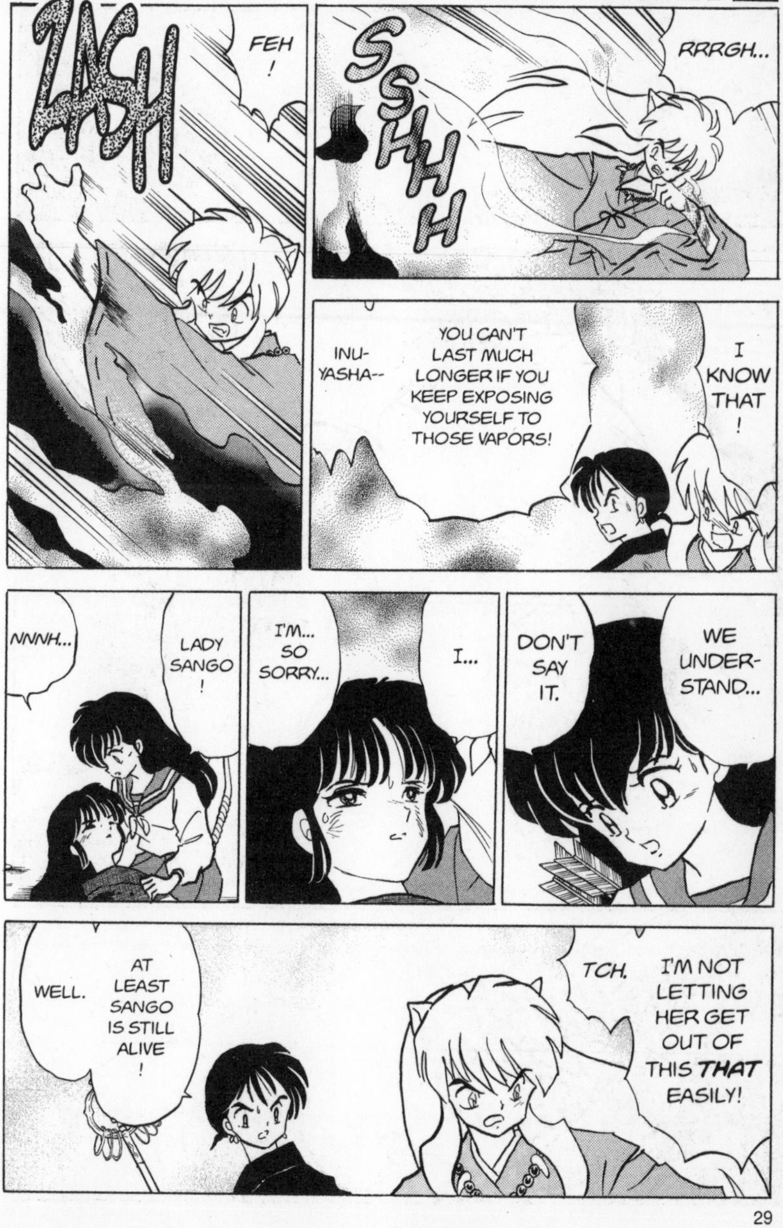
ZASH
FEH!
SSHHH
RRRGH...
INU-YASHA--
YOU CAN'T LAST MUCH LONGER IF YOU KEEP EXPOSING YOURSELF TO THOSE VAPORS!
I KNOW THAT!
NNNH...
LADY SANGO!
I'M... SO SORRY...
I...
DON'T SAY IT.
WE UNDERSTAND...
WELL.
AT LEAST SANGO IS STILL ALIVE!
TCH.
I'M NOT LETTING HER GET OUT OF THIS THAT EASILY!

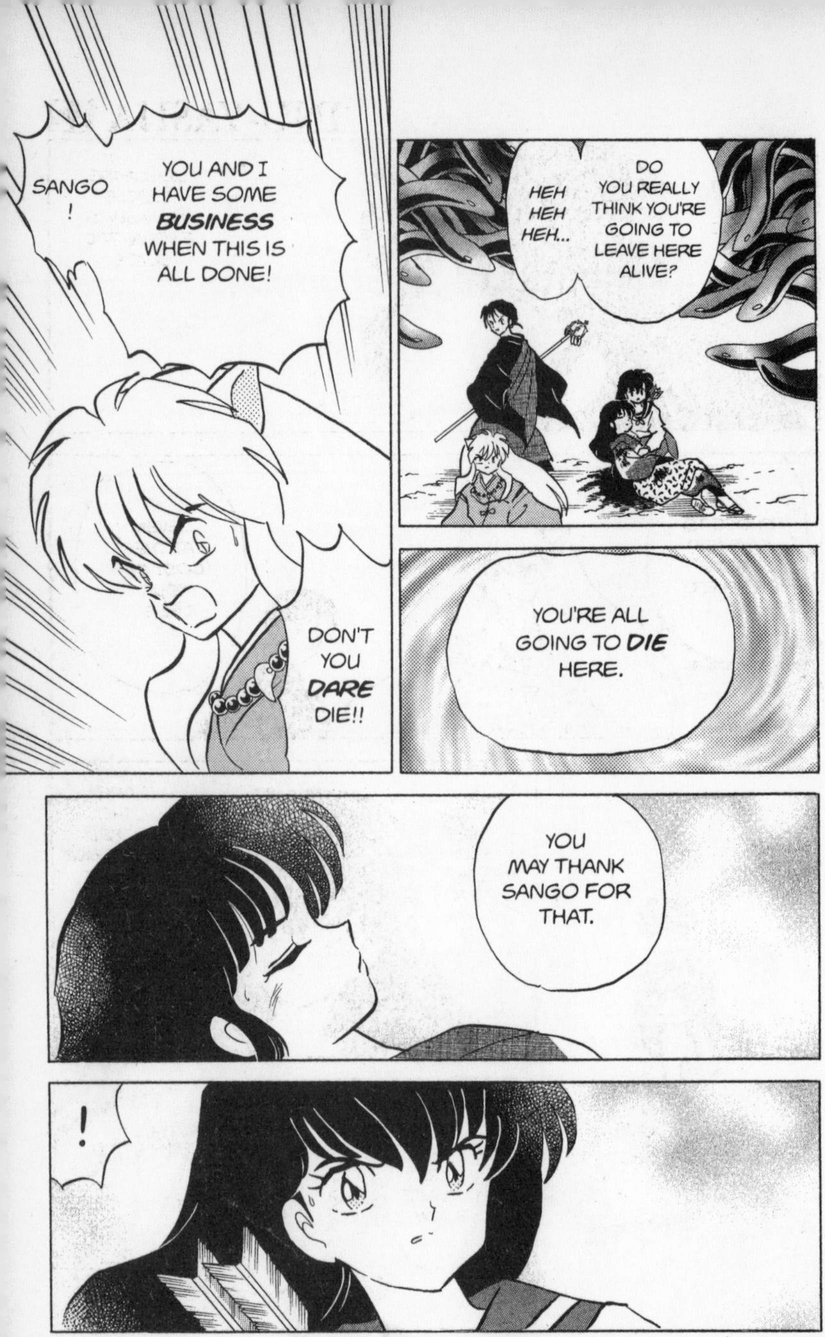
SANGO!
YOU AND I HAVE SOME **BUSINESS** WHEN THIS IS ALL DONE!
DON'T YOU **DARE** DIE!!
HEH HEH HEH...
DO YOU REALLY THINK YOU'RE GOING TO LEAVE HERE ALIVE?
YOU'RE ALL GOING TO **DIE** HERE.
YOU MAY THANK SANGO FOR THAT.
!

HE'S RIGHT... IT'S ALL BECAUSE OF ME....

...BECAUSE I STOLE INU-YASHA'S ENCHANTED BLADE.

SANGO CHOSE TO SAVE HER LITTLE BROTHER...

...EVEN AT THE COST OF YOUR LIVES.

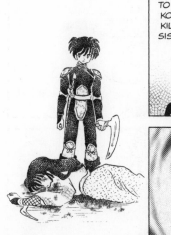

HE TRIED TO MAKE KOHAKU KILL HIS SISTER...

...WHEN SHE RISKED EVERYTHING TO SAVE HIM.

IF YOU WISH TO PLACE BLAME...

...THEN BLAME SANGO'S PETTINESS.

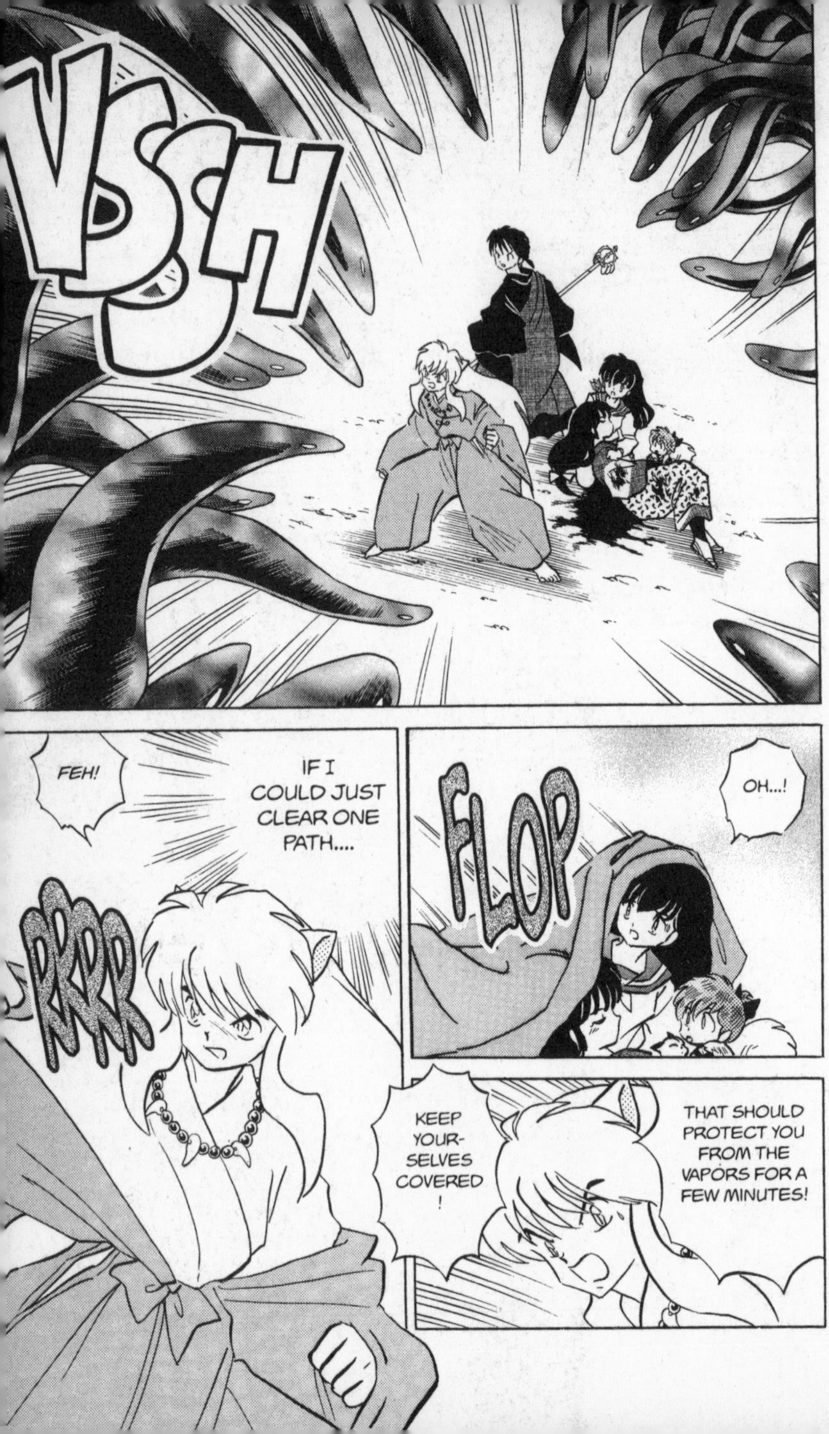
VSH
FEH!
IF I COULD JUST CLEAR ONE PATH....
RRRR
FLOP
OH...!
KEEP YOURSELVES COVERED!
THAT SHOULD PROTECT YOU FROM THE VAPORS FOR A FEW MINUTES!

EXORCISING CLAWS OF STEEL!

ZASH

ZNNN

BLUP
BLUP
SSSHHH

GUH!

INU-YASHA!

HHOOOO

IT'S NO USE!

THERE'S NO END TO IT...!

HAKK

ZZZZZZ

33

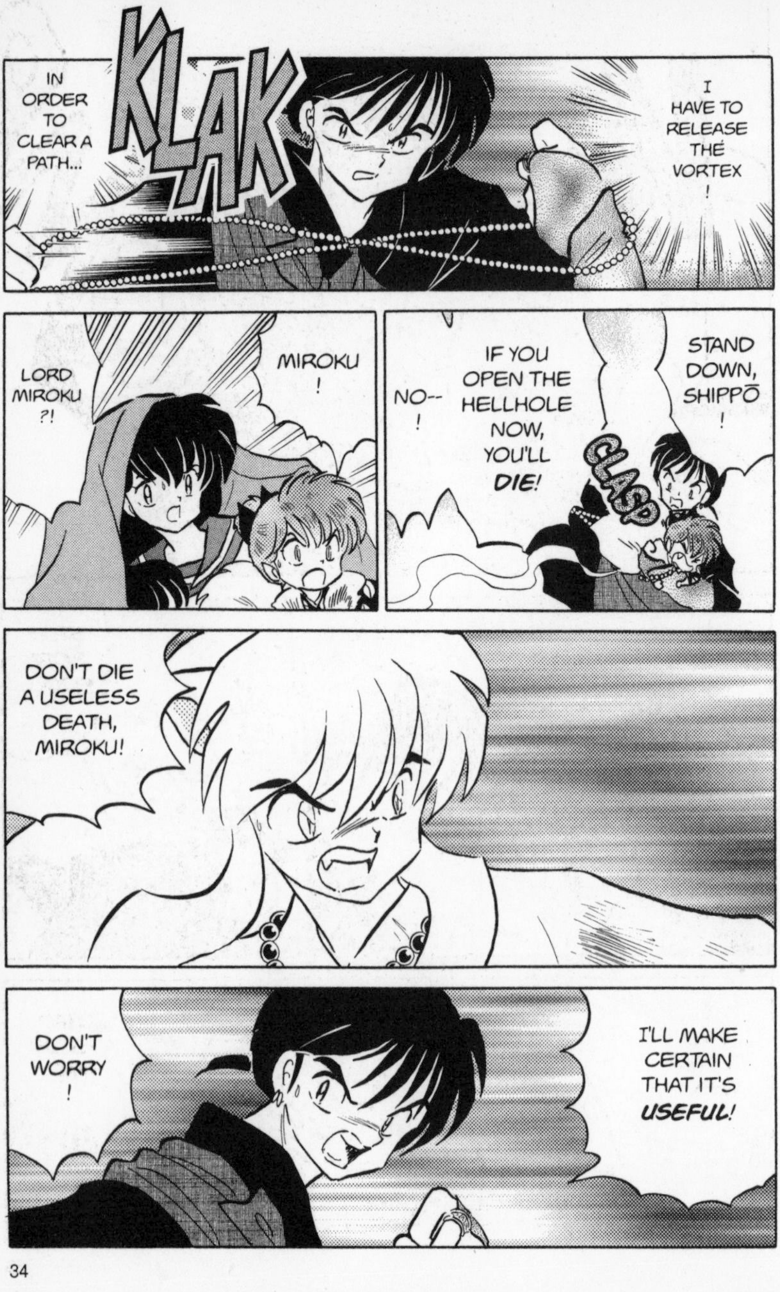

IN ORDER TO CLEAR A PATH...
KLAK
I HAVE TO RELEASE THE VORTEX!
LORD MIROKU?!
MIROKU!
NO--!
IF YOU OPEN THE HELLHOLE NOW, YOU'LL DIE!
STAND DOWN, SHIPPŌ!
CLASP
DON'T DIE A USELESS DEATH, MIROKU!
DON'T WORRY!
I'LL MAKE CERTAIN THAT IT'S USEFUL!

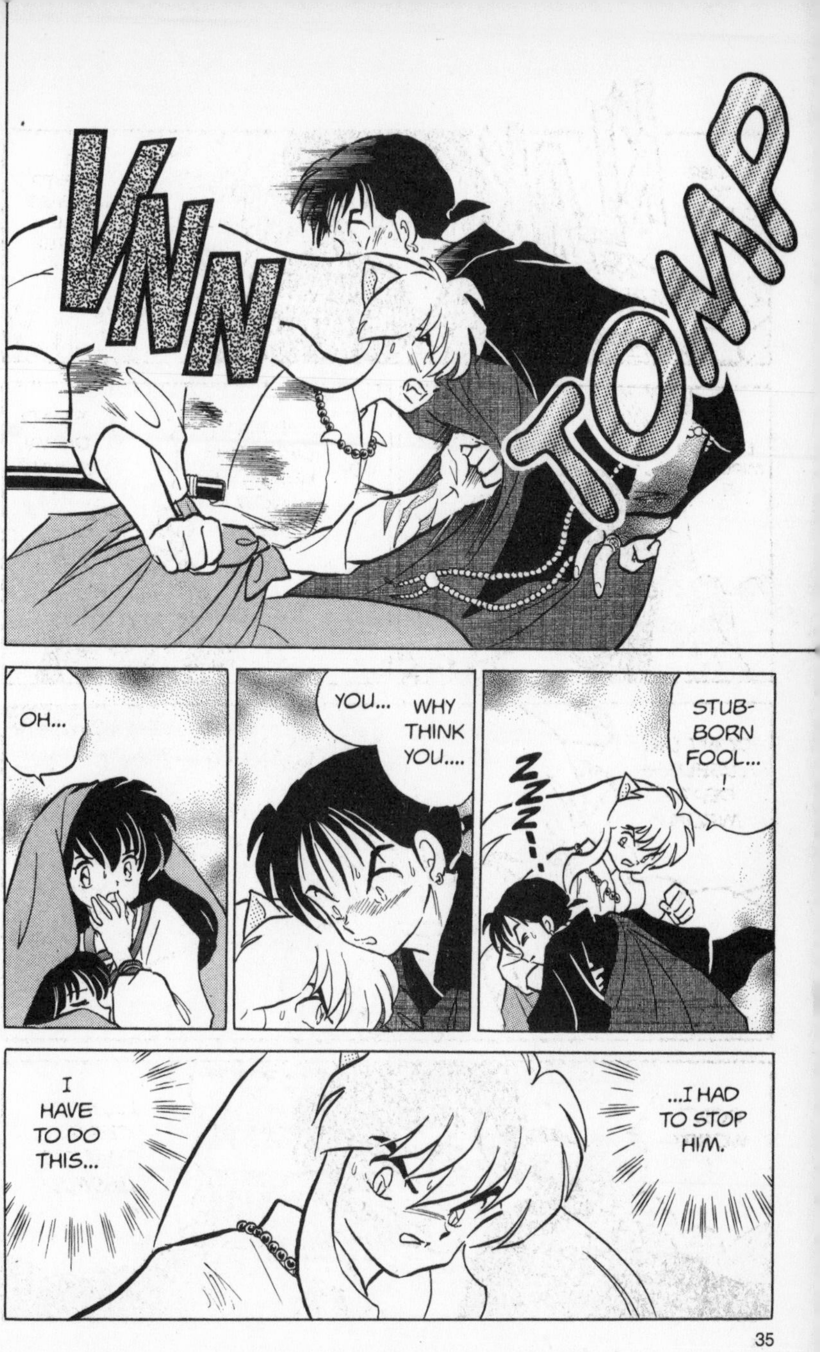
VNN
TOMP
OH...
YOU... WHY THINK YOU....
ZZZ...!
STUB-BORN FOOL...!
I HAVE TO DO THIS...
...I HAD TO STOP HIM.

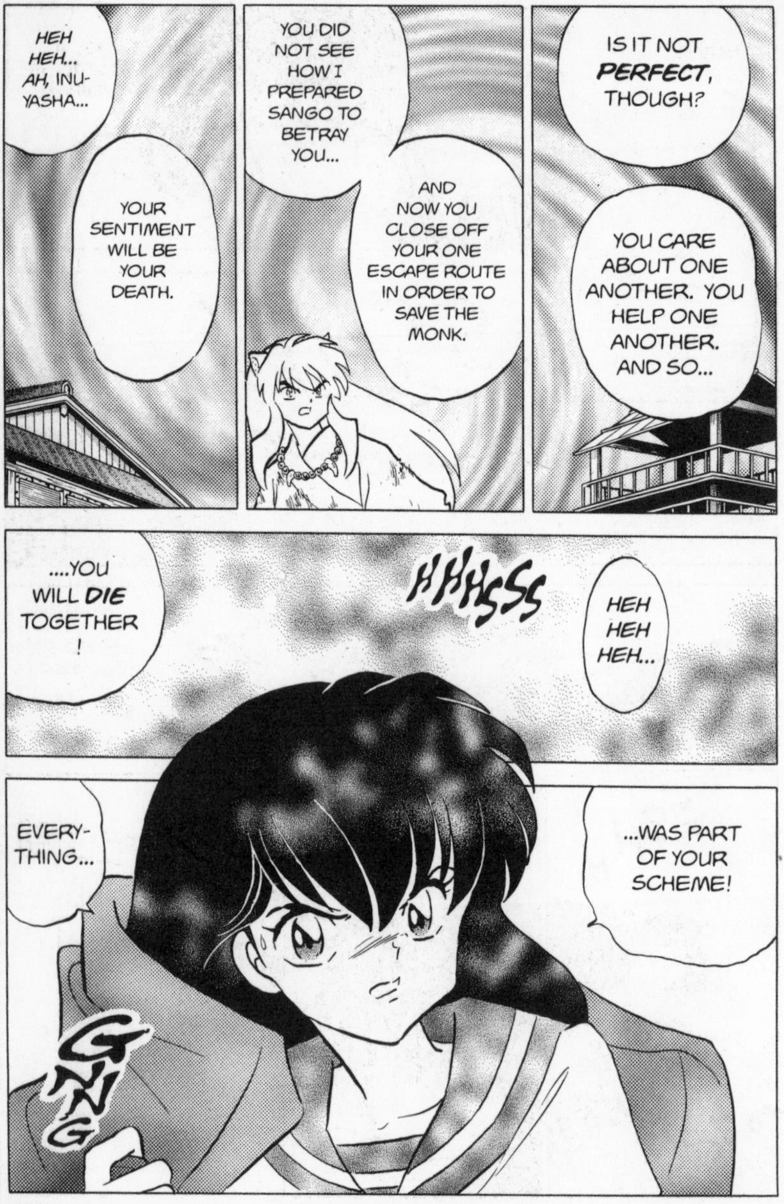
HEH HEH... AH, INU-YASHA...
YOUR SENTIMENT WILL BE YOUR DEATH.
YOU DID NOT SEE HOW I PREPARED SANGO TO BETRAY YOU...
AND NOW YOU CLOSE OFF YOUR ONE ESCAPE ROUTE IN ORDER TO SAVE THE MONK.
IS IT NOT **PERFECT**, THOUGH?
YOU CARE ABOUT ONE ANOTHER. YOU HELP ONE ANOTHER. AND SO...
....YOU WILL **DIE** TOGETHER!
HHHSSS
HEH HEH HEH...
EVERY-THING...
...WAS PART OF YOUR SCHEME!
GNG

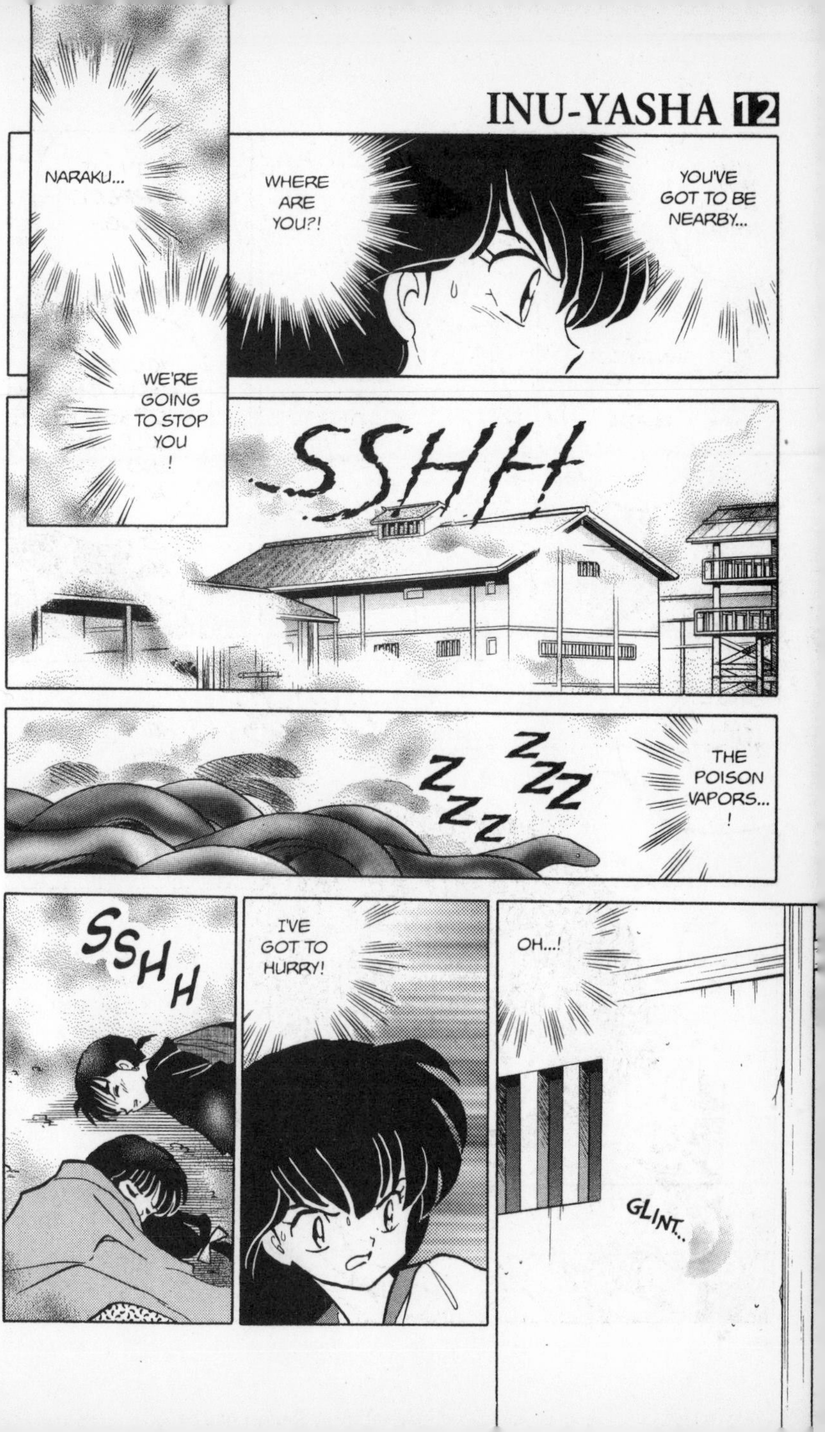
NARAKU...
WHERE ARE YOU?!
YOU'VE GOT TO BE NEARBY...
WE'RE GOING TO STOP YOU!
SSHH!
ZZZZZZ
THE POISON VAPORS...!
SSHH
I'VE GOT TO HURRY!
OH...!
GLINT...

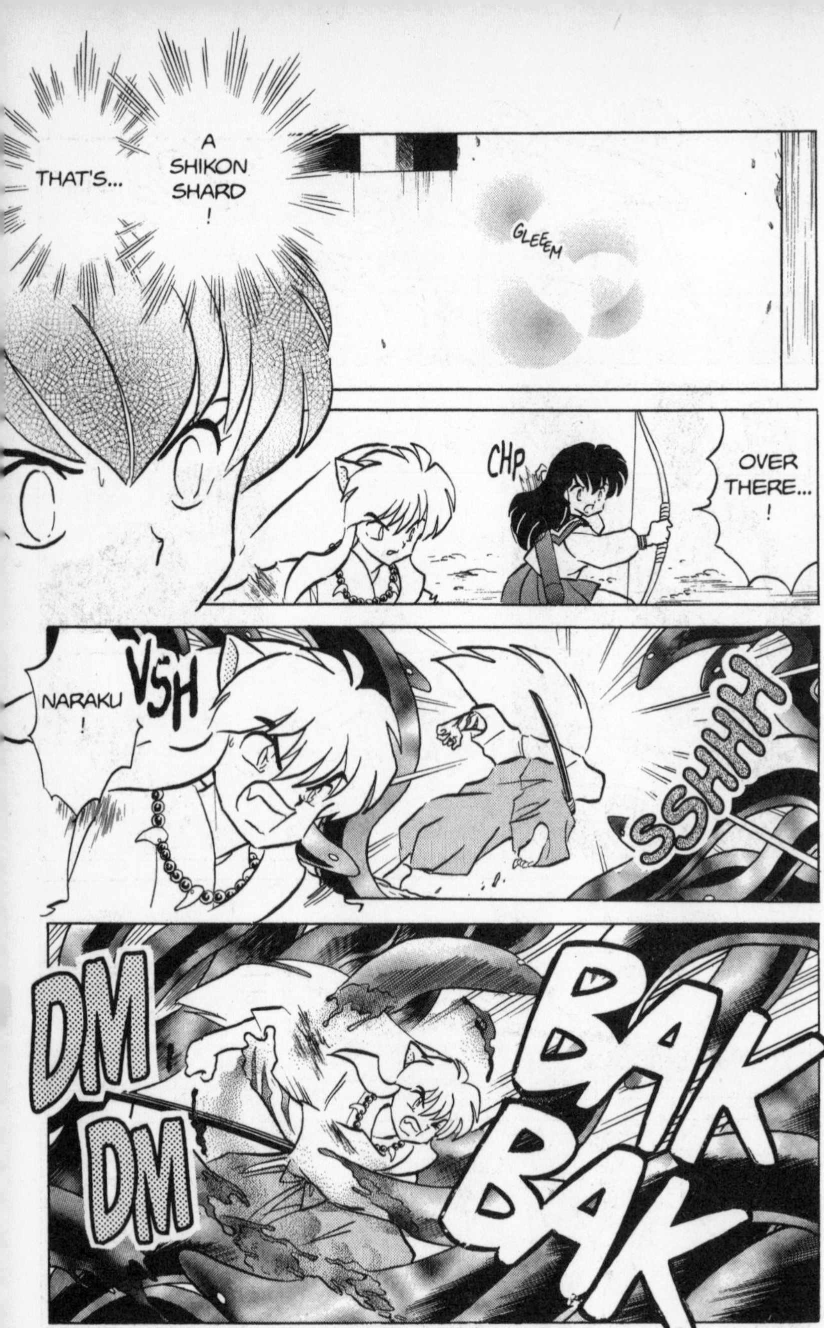
THAT'S...
A SHIKON SHARD !
GLEEEM
CHP
OVER THERE... !
NARAKU !
VSH
SSHHH
DM DM
BAK BAK

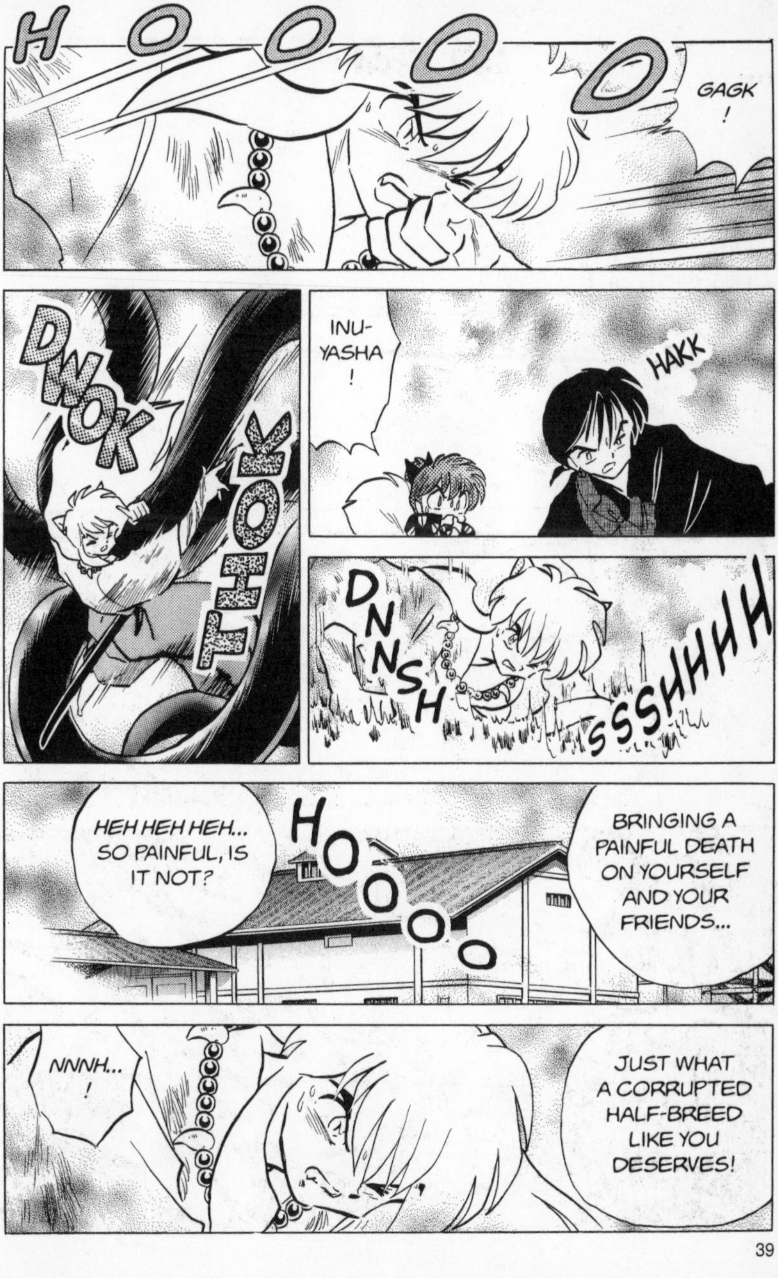
HOOOOO
GAGK !
DWOK
THOKK
INU-YASHA !
HAKK
DNNSH
SSSHHHH
HEH HEH HEH... SO PAINFUL, IS IT NOT?
HOOOOO
BRINGING A PAINFUL DEATH ON YOURSELF AND YOUR FRIENDS...
NNNH... !
JUST WHAT A CORRUPTED HALF-BREED LIKE YOU DESERVES!

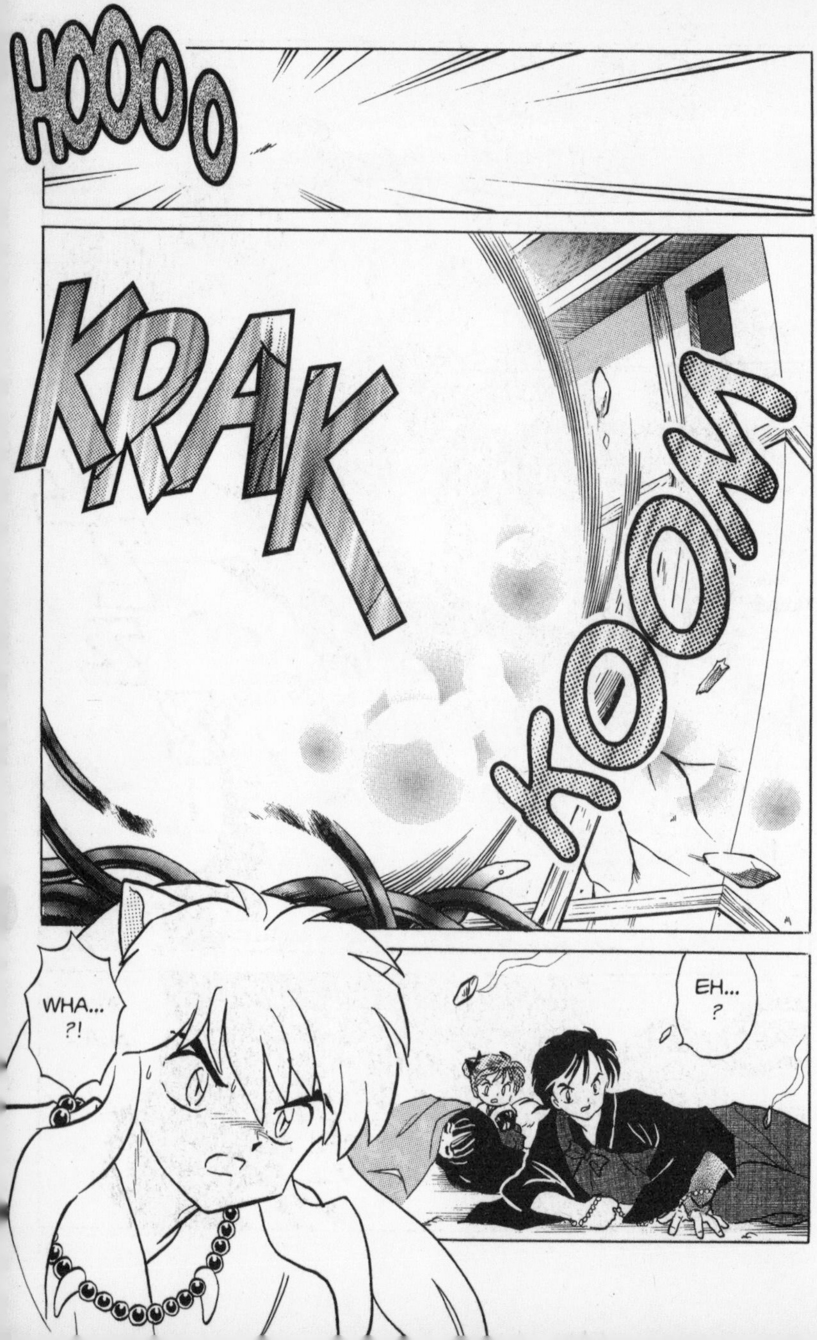
HOOOO
KRAK
KOOM
WHA... ?!
EH... ?

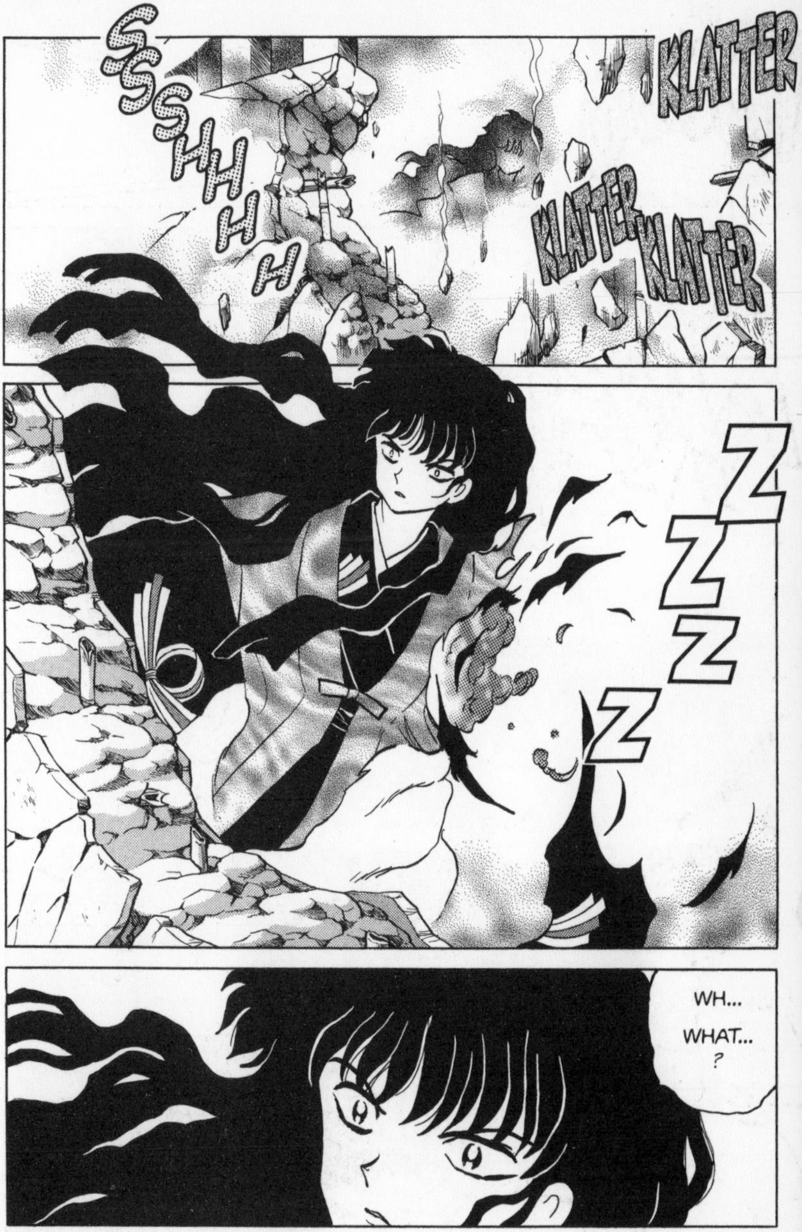
SSSHHHHH
KLATTER
KLATTER KLATTER
ZZZZ
WH...
WHAT...
?

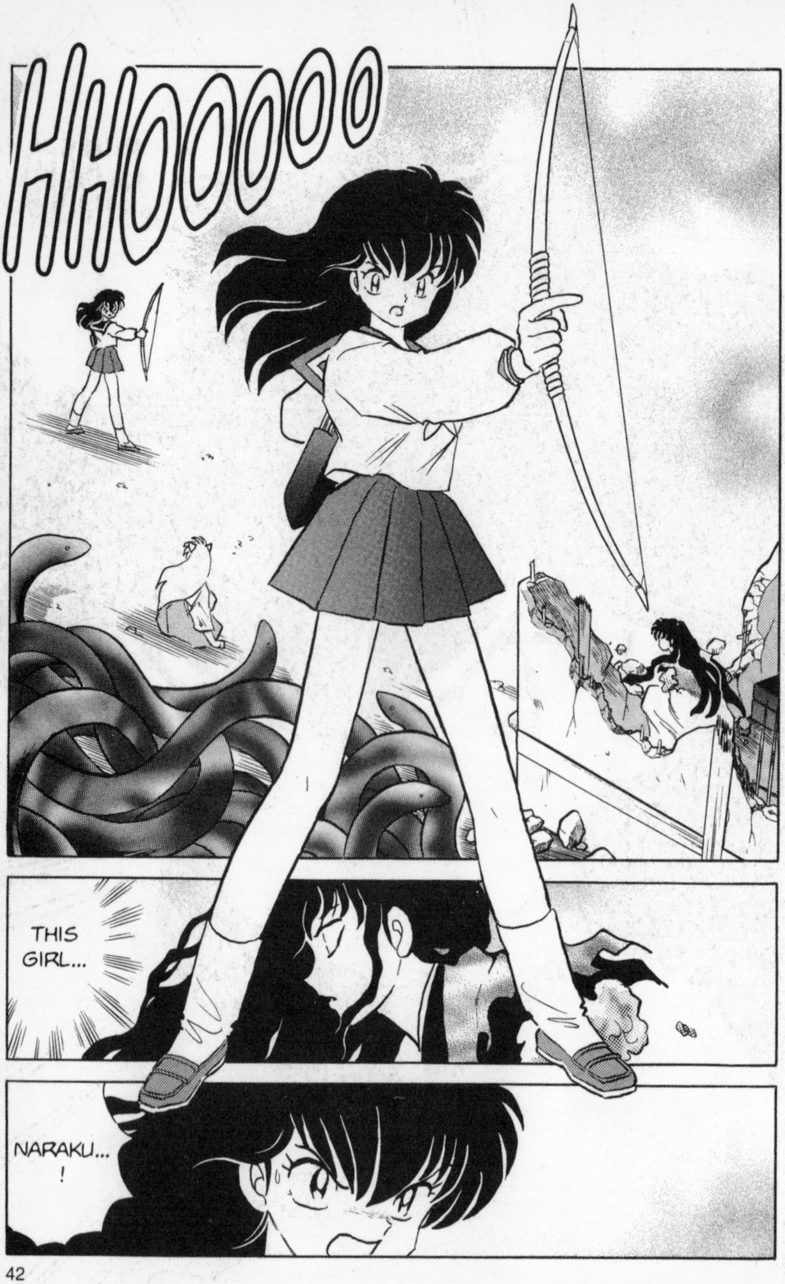
HHOOOOO
THIS GIRL...
NARAKU... !

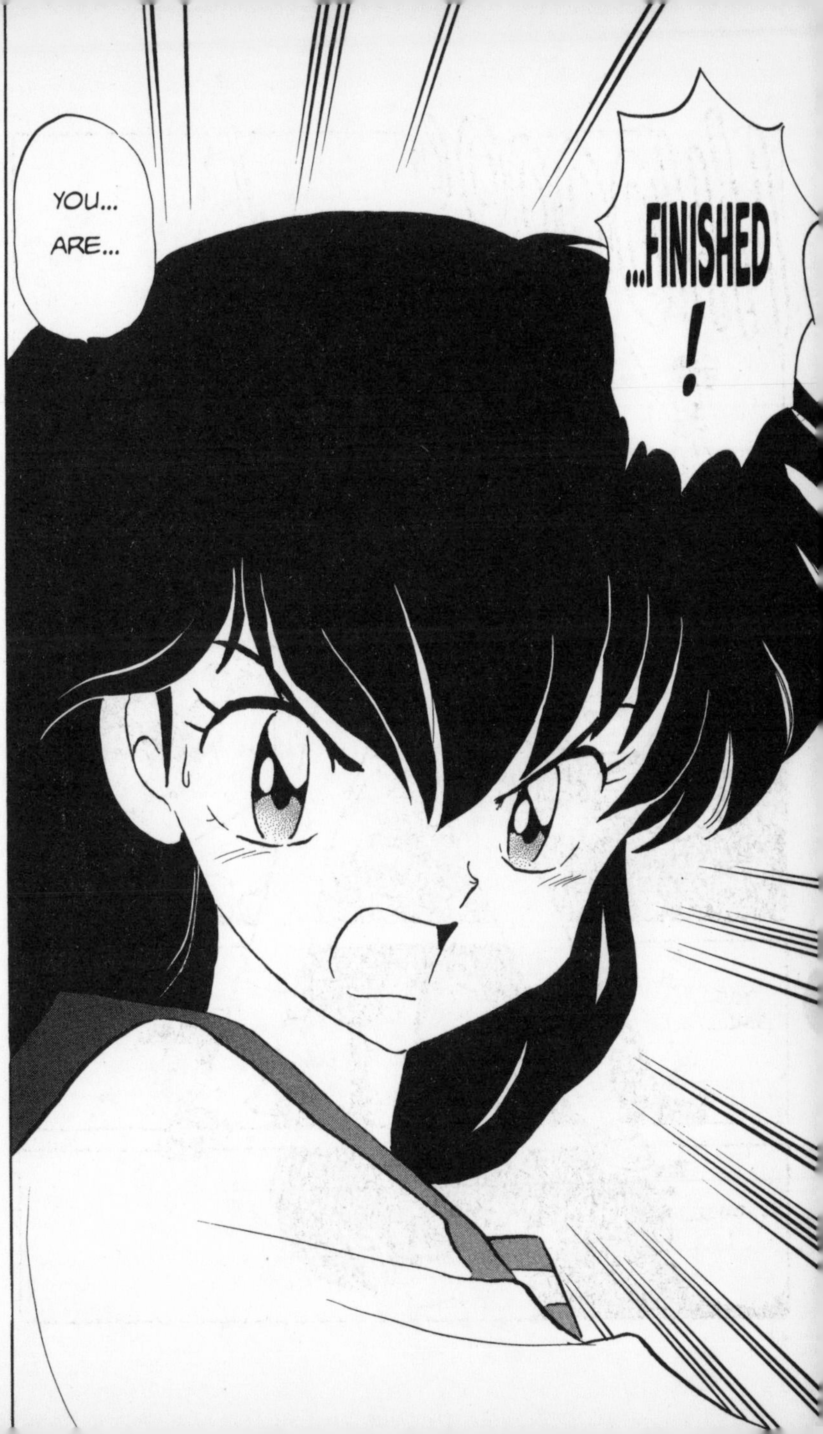
YOU... ARE...
...FINISHED!

HHSSSHHH SSSHHH

THE VAPORS... THEY'RE DISSIPATING!

IS THIS... SOME- HOW ... LADY KAGOME'S DOING... ?

KAGOME... ?

I'M NOT GONNA LET YOU GET AWAY!

CHK

WHAT... ?

WHAT *IS* THIS GIRL'S POWER.... ?!

SCROLL THREE

PURIFICATION

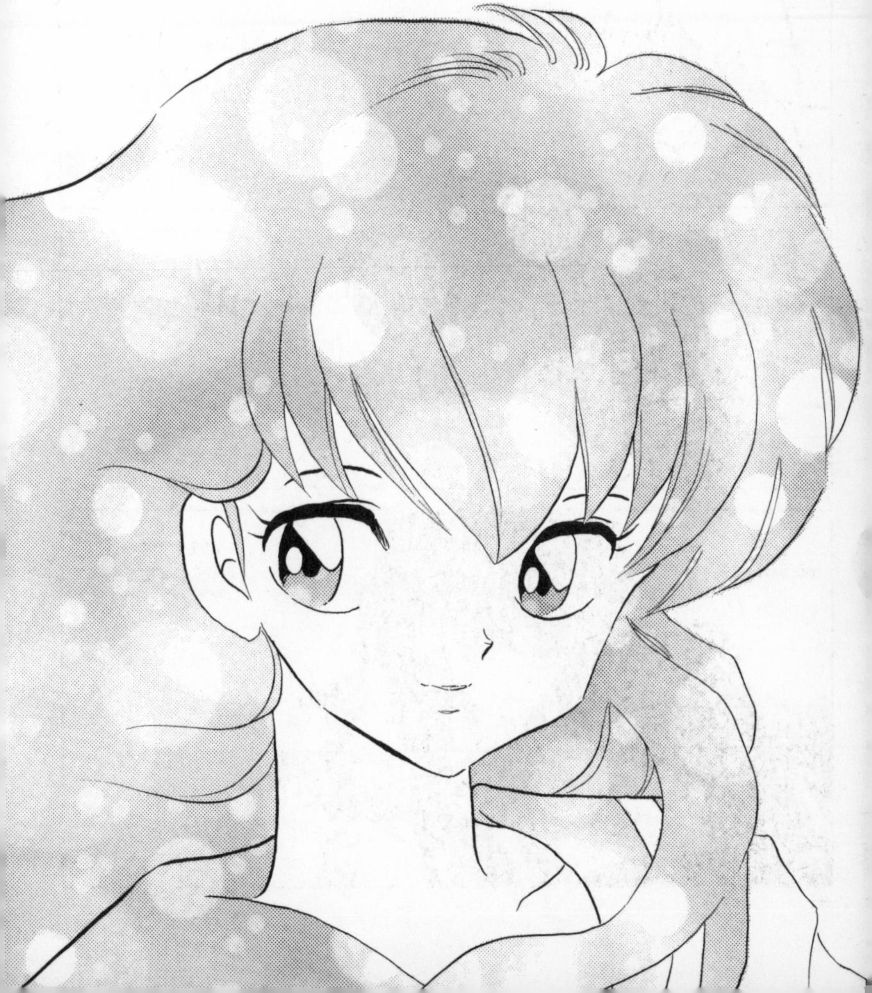

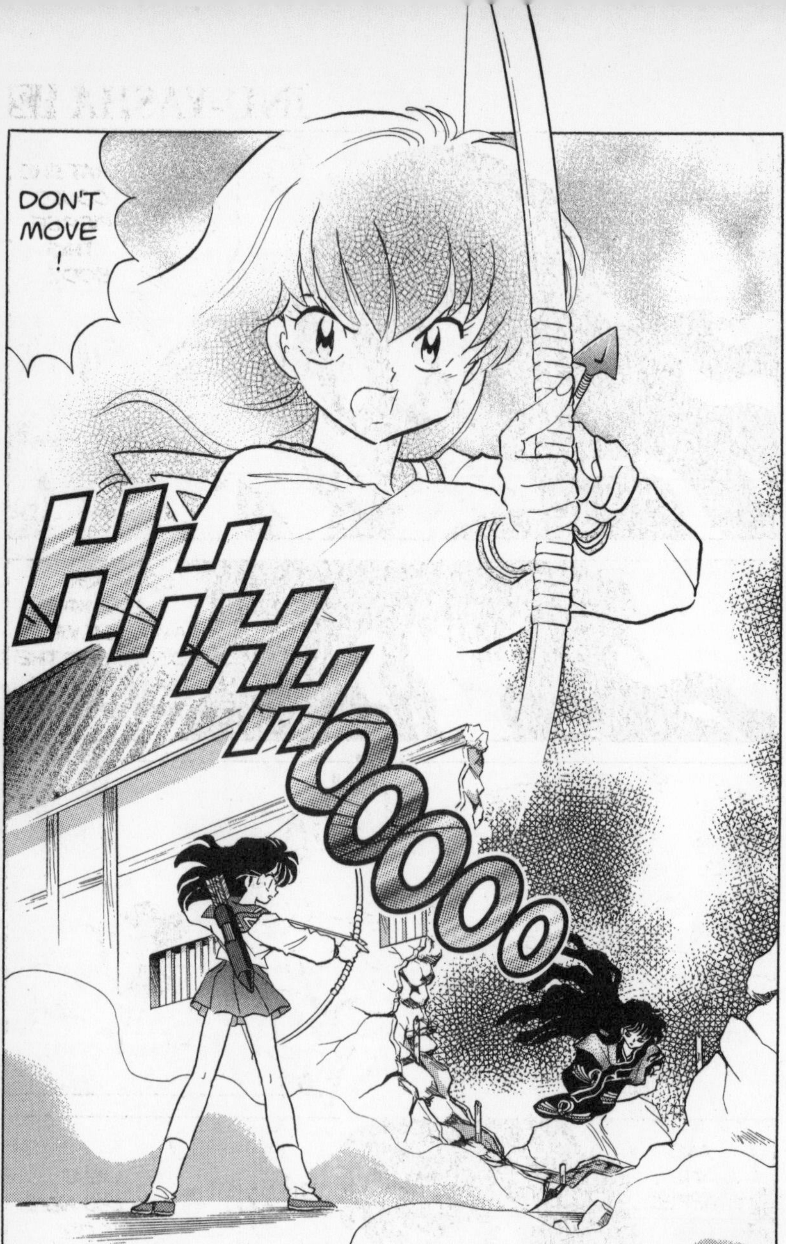
DON'T MOVE !
HHHHOOOOOO

GIRL...

WHAT **ARE** YOU...?

THAT SHE COULD PIERCE THIS BODY....

LONG AGO... THERE WAS ANOTHER WHO POSSESSED THE SAME POWER THAT YOU DO....

HE MUST MEAN KIKYO...

HHHOOOO

AND YOU TRAPPED...

KRII KRII KRII

...AND KILLED **HER** TOO!!!

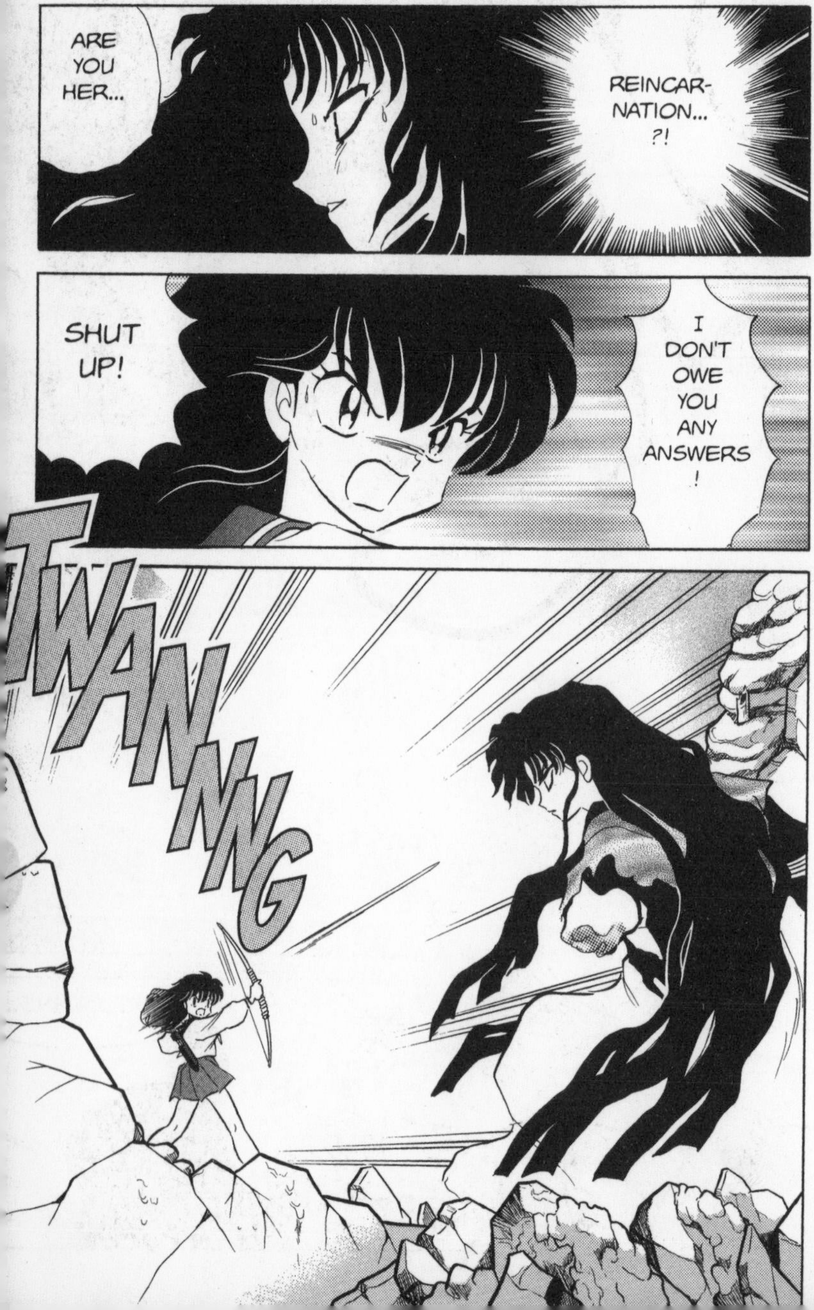
ARE YOU HER...
REINCAR-NATION... ?!
SHUT UP!
I DON'T OWE YOU ANY ANSWERS!
TWANNNG

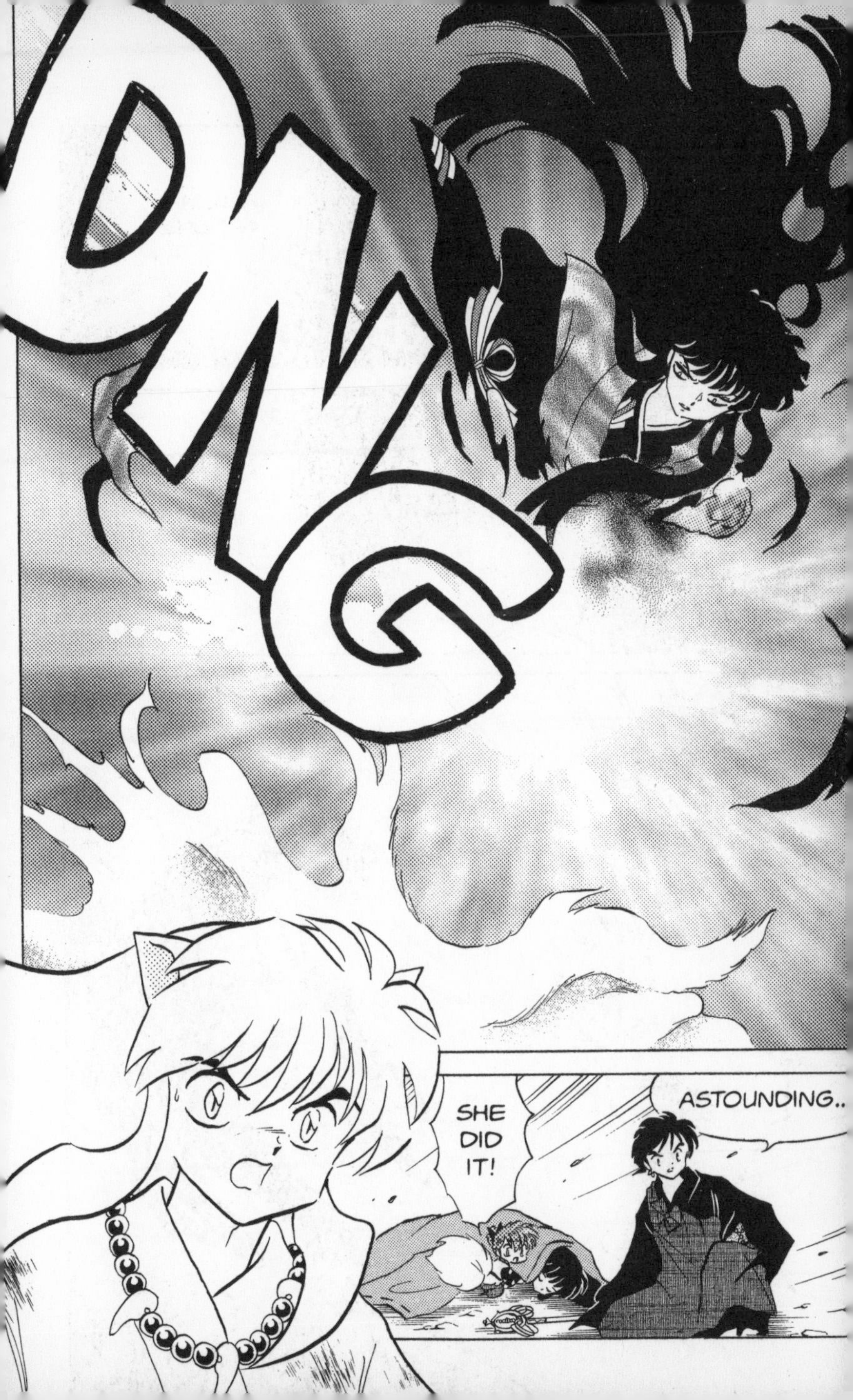
DMG
SHE DID IT!
ASTOUNDING..

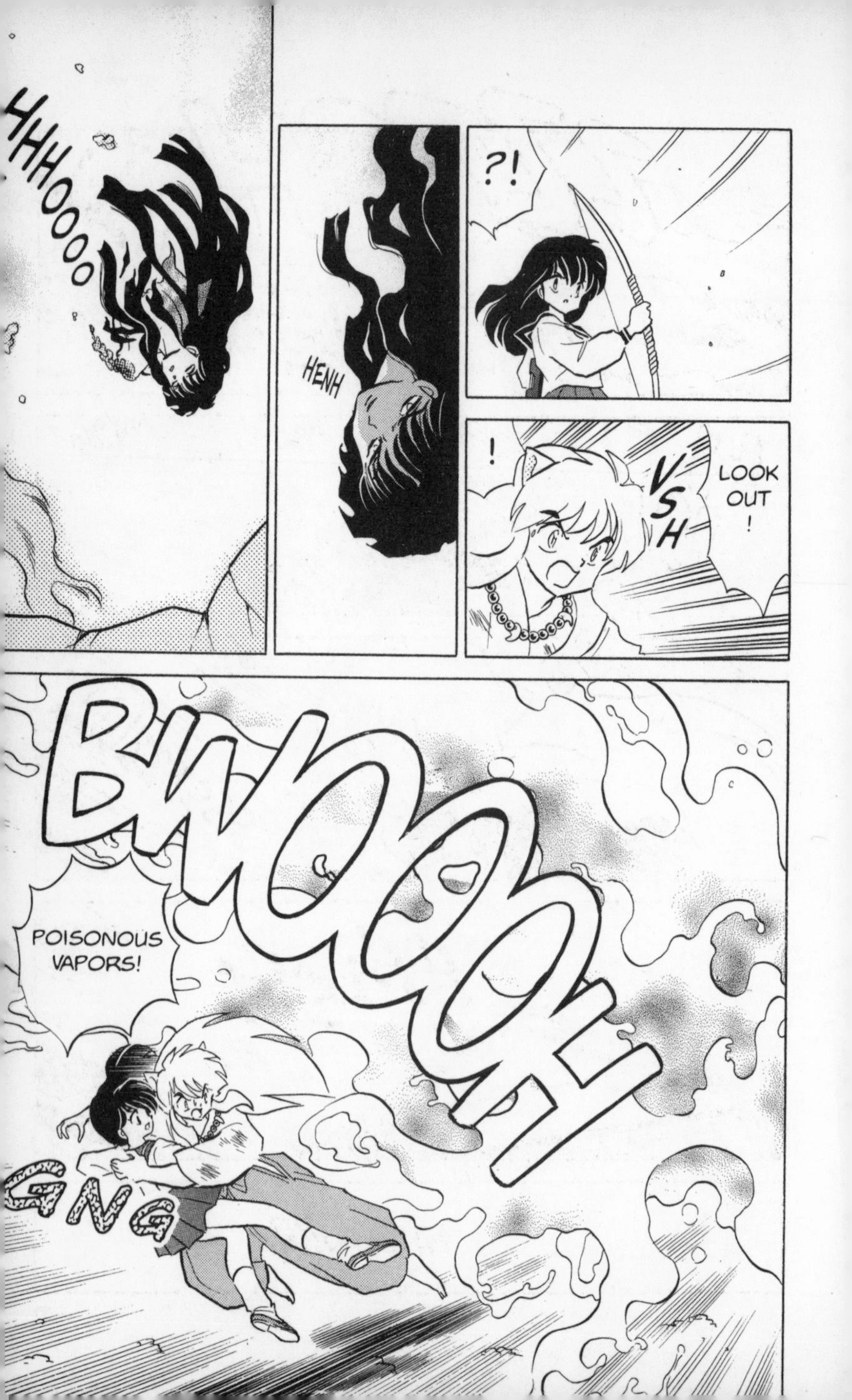
HHHOOOO
HENH
?!
!
VSH
LOOK OUT!
BWOOOOH
POISONOUS VAPORS!
GNG

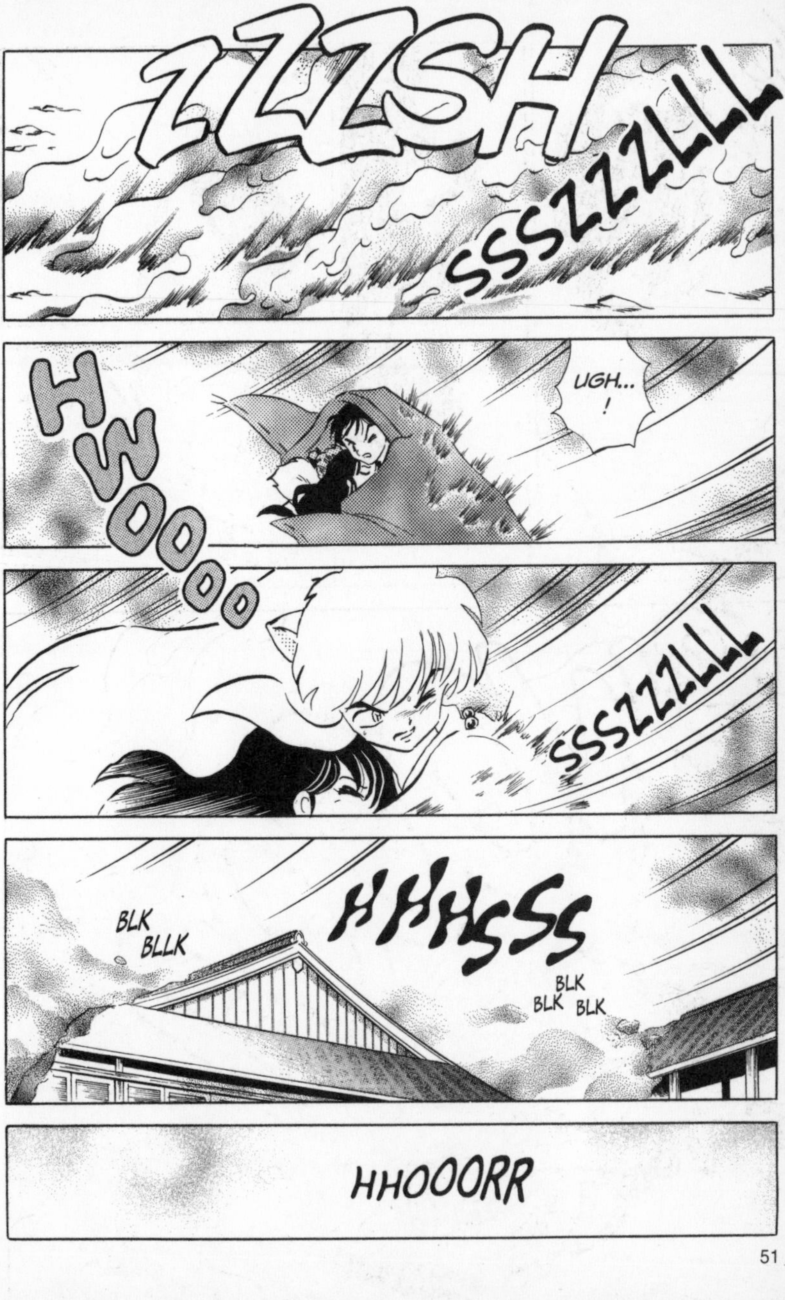
ZZZSH
SSSZZZLLL
HWOOOO
UGH... !
SSSZZZLLL
BLK
BLLK
HHHSSS
BLK
BLK BLK
HHOOORR

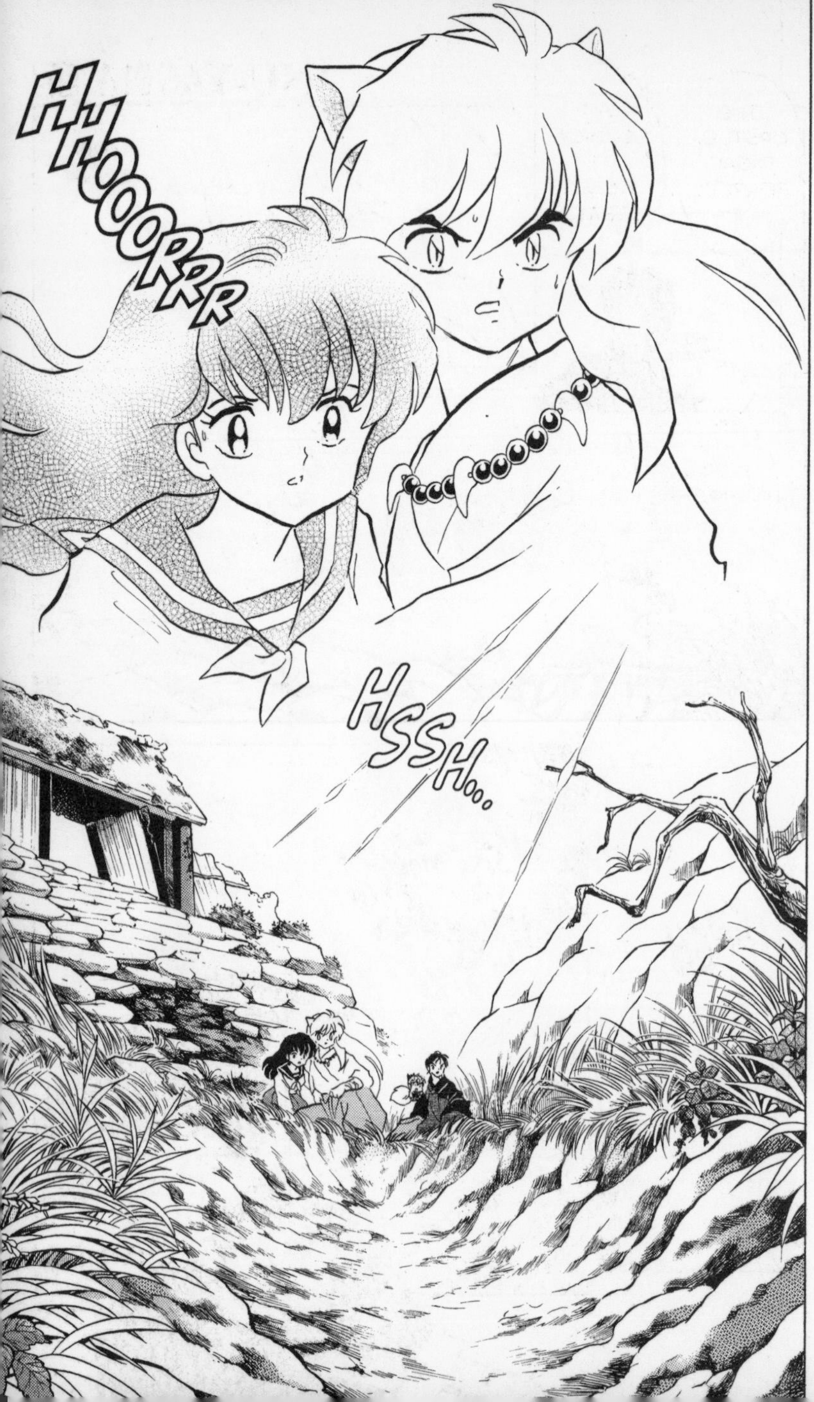
HHOOORRRR
HSSH...

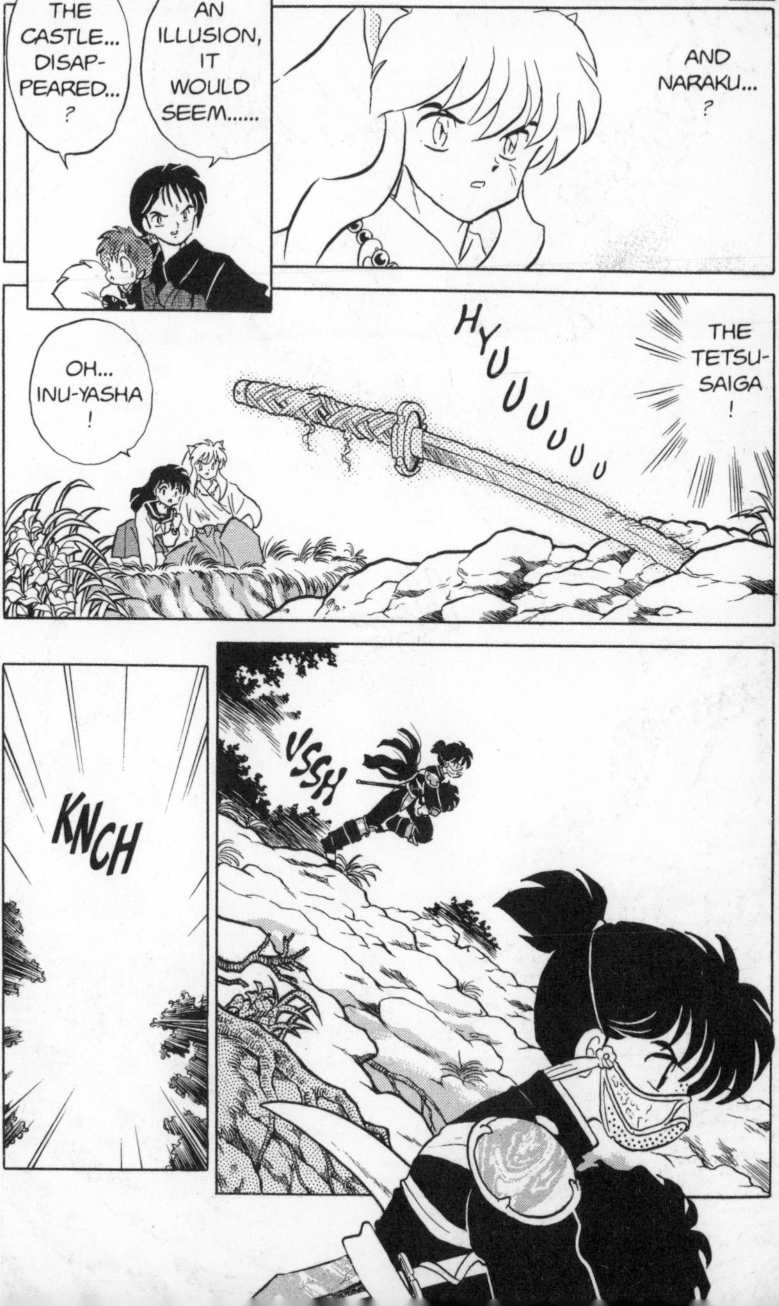
THE CASTLE... DISAPPEARED... ?
AN ILLUSION, IT WOULD SEEM......
AND NARAKU... ?
OH... INU-YASHA !
HYUUUUUUU
THE TETSU-SAIGA !
KNCH
VSSH

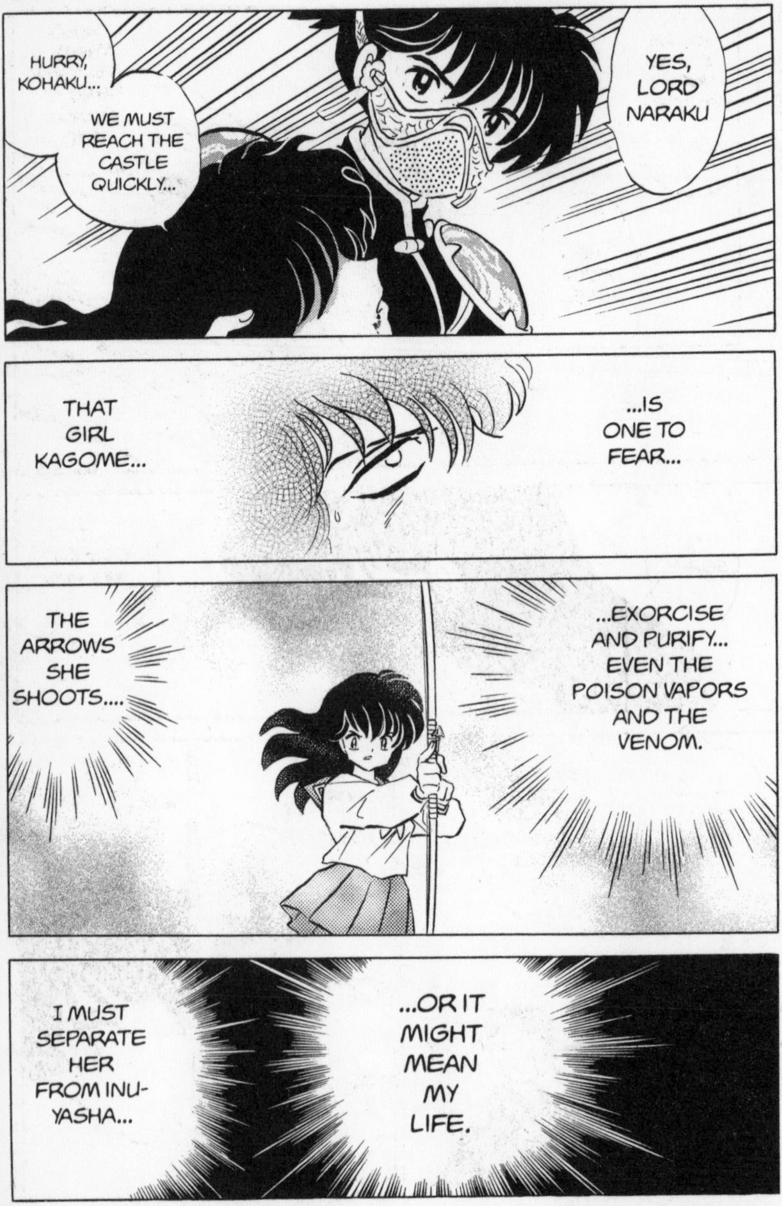
HURRY, KOHAKU...
WE MUST REACH THE CASTLE QUICKLY...
YES, LORD NARAKU
THAT GIRL KAGOME...
...IS ONE TO FEAR...
THE ARROWS SHE SHOOTS....
...EXORCISE AND PURIFY... EVEN THE POISON VAPORS AND THE VENOM.
I MUST SEPARATE HER FROM INU-YASHA...
...OR IT MIGHT MEAN MY LIFE.

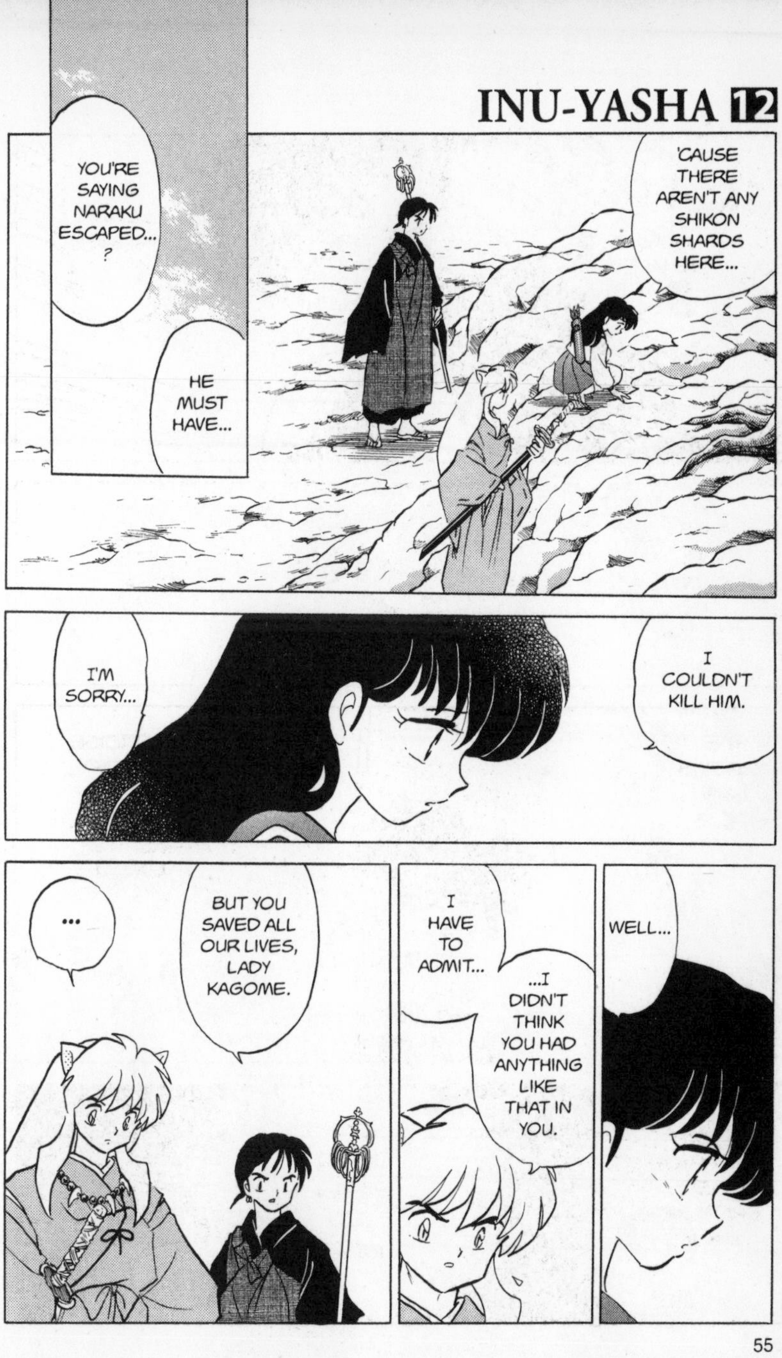
YOU'RE SAYING NARAKU ESCAPED... ?
'CAUSE THERE AREN'T ANY SHIKON SHARDS HERE...
HE MUST HAVE...
I'M SORRY...
I COULDN'T KILL HIM.
...
BUT YOU SAVED ALL OUR LIVES, LADY KAGOME.
I HAVE TO ADMIT...
...I DIDN'T THINK YOU HAD ANYTHING LIKE THAT IN YOU.
WELL...

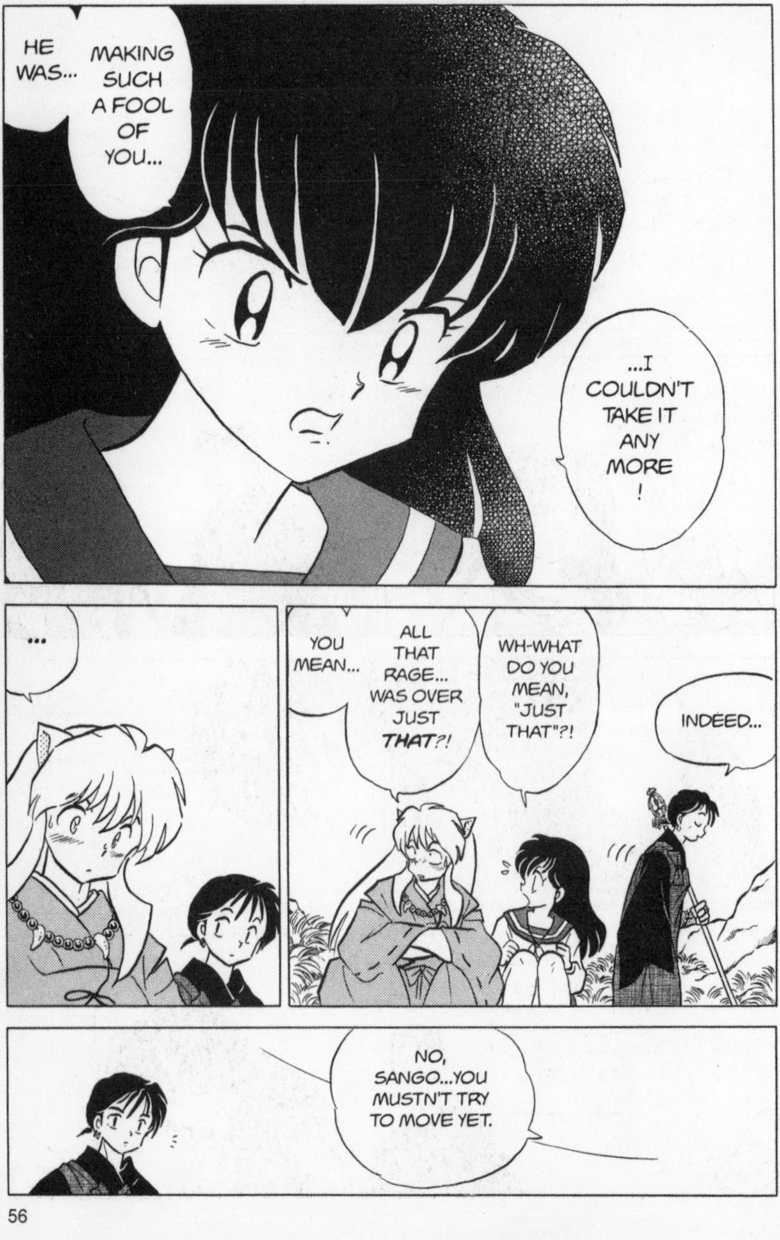
HE WAS... MAKING SUCH A FOOL OF YOU...
...I COULDN'T TAKE IT ANY MORE!
...
YOU MEAN... ALL THAT RAGE... WAS OVER JUST *THAT*?!
WH-WHAT DO YOU MEAN, "JUST THAT"?!
INDEED...
NO, SANGO...YOU MUSTN'T TRY TO MOVE YET.

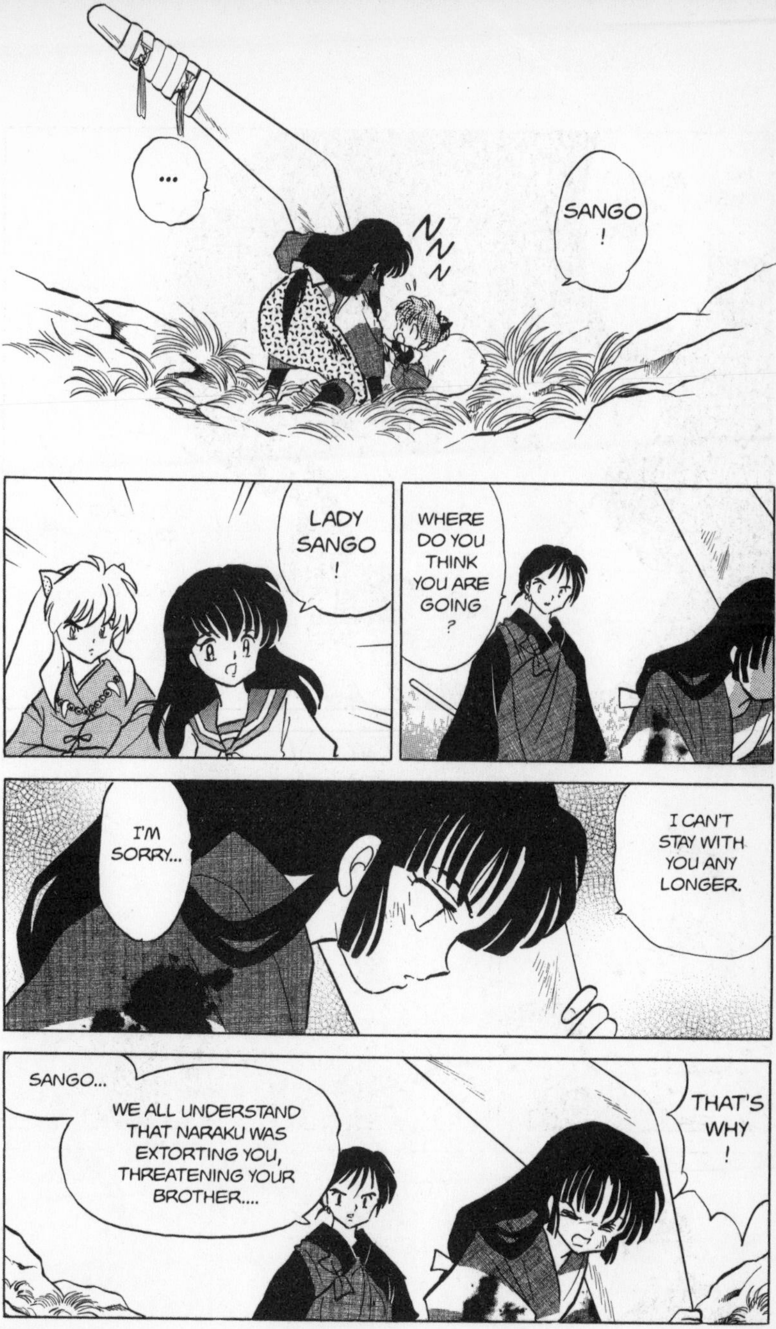
...
NNN
SANGO !
LADY SANGO !
WHERE DO YOU THINK YOU ARE GOING ?
I'M SORRY...
I CAN'T STAY WITH YOU ANY LONGER.
SANGO...
WE ALL UNDERSTAND THAT NARAKU WAS EXTORTING YOU, THREATENING YOUR BROTHER....
THAT'S WHY !

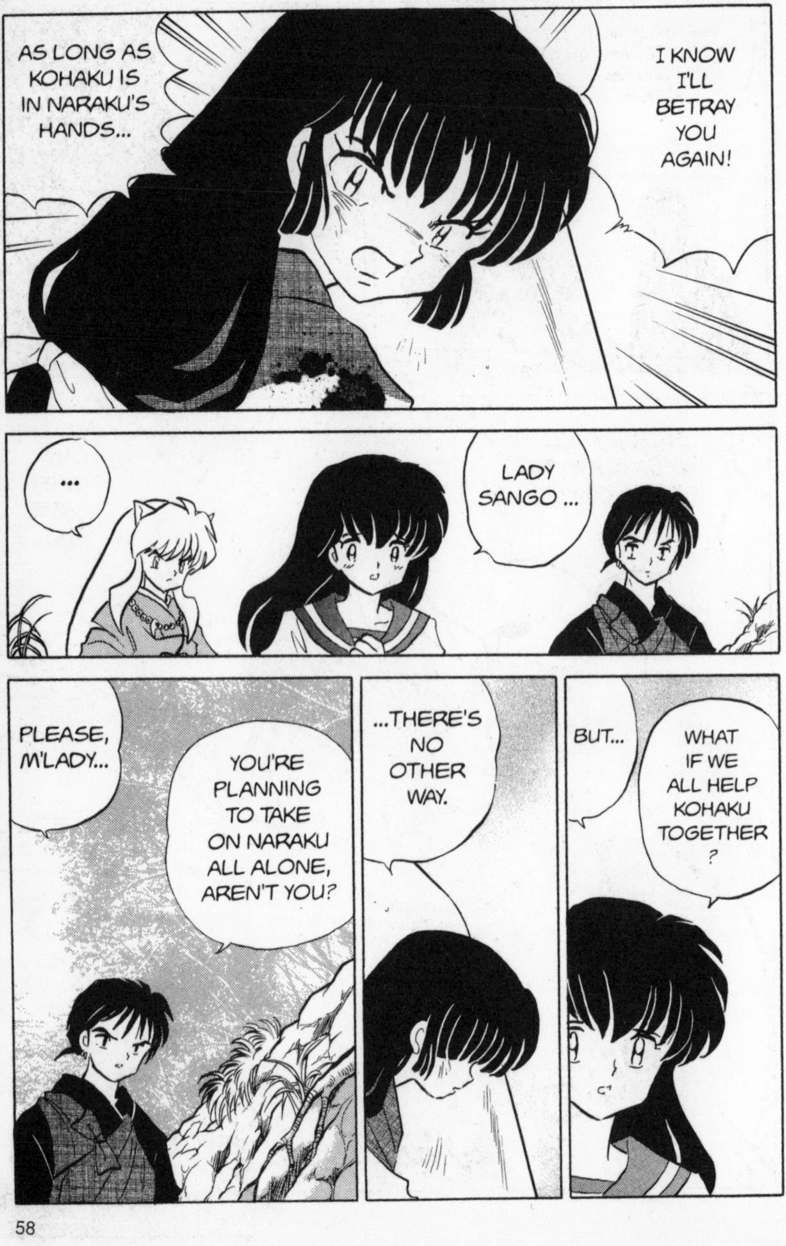
AS LONG AS KOHAKU IS IN NARAKU'S HANDS...
I KNOW I'LL BETRAY YOU AGAIN!
...
LADY SANGO ...
PLEASE, M'LADY...
YOU'RE PLANNING TO TAKE ON NARAKU ALL ALONE, AREN'T YOU?
...THERE'S NO OTHER WAY.
BUT...
WHAT IF WE ALL HELP KOHAKU TOGETHER?

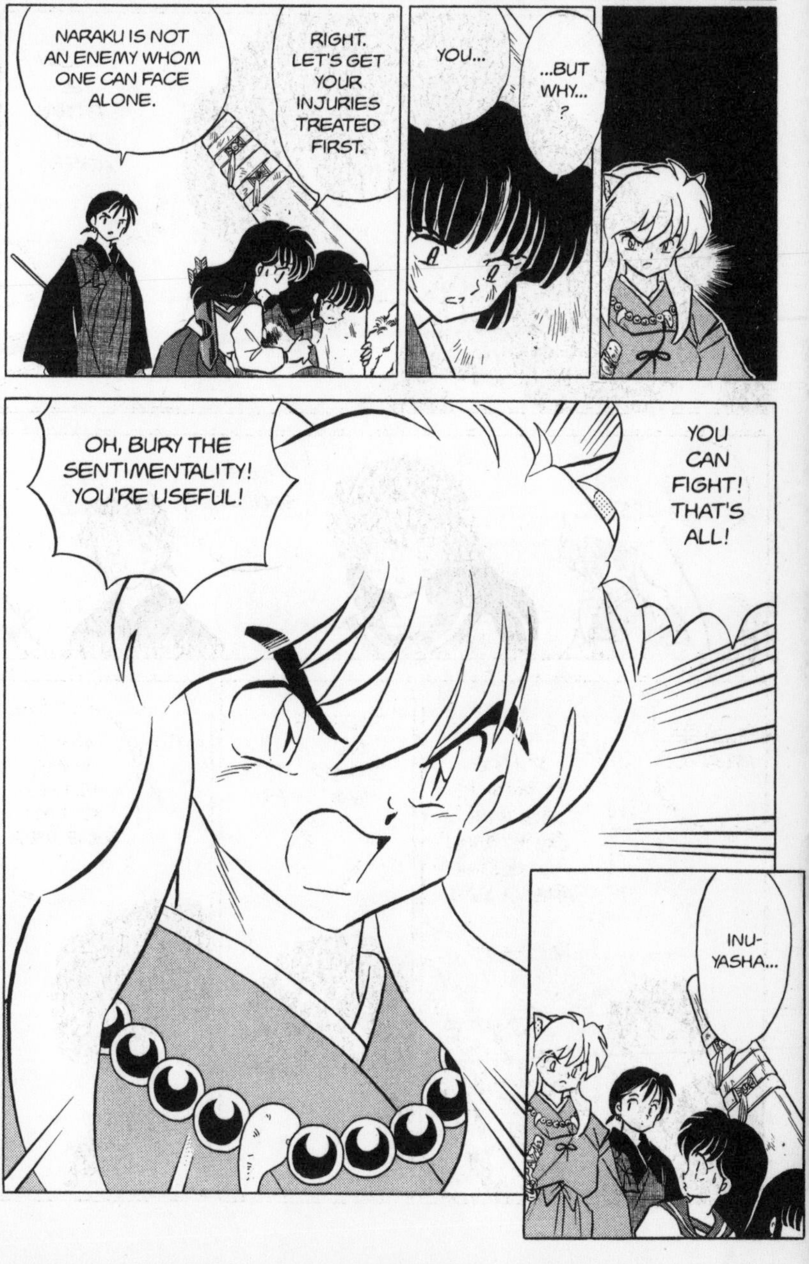
NARAKU IS NOT AN ENEMY WHOM ONE CAN FACE ALONE.
RIGHT. LET'S GET YOUR INJURIES TREATED FIRST.
YOU...
...BUT WHY... ?
OH, BURY THE SENTIMENTALITY! YOU'RE USEFUL!
YOU CAN FIGHT! THAT'S ALL!
INU-YASHA...

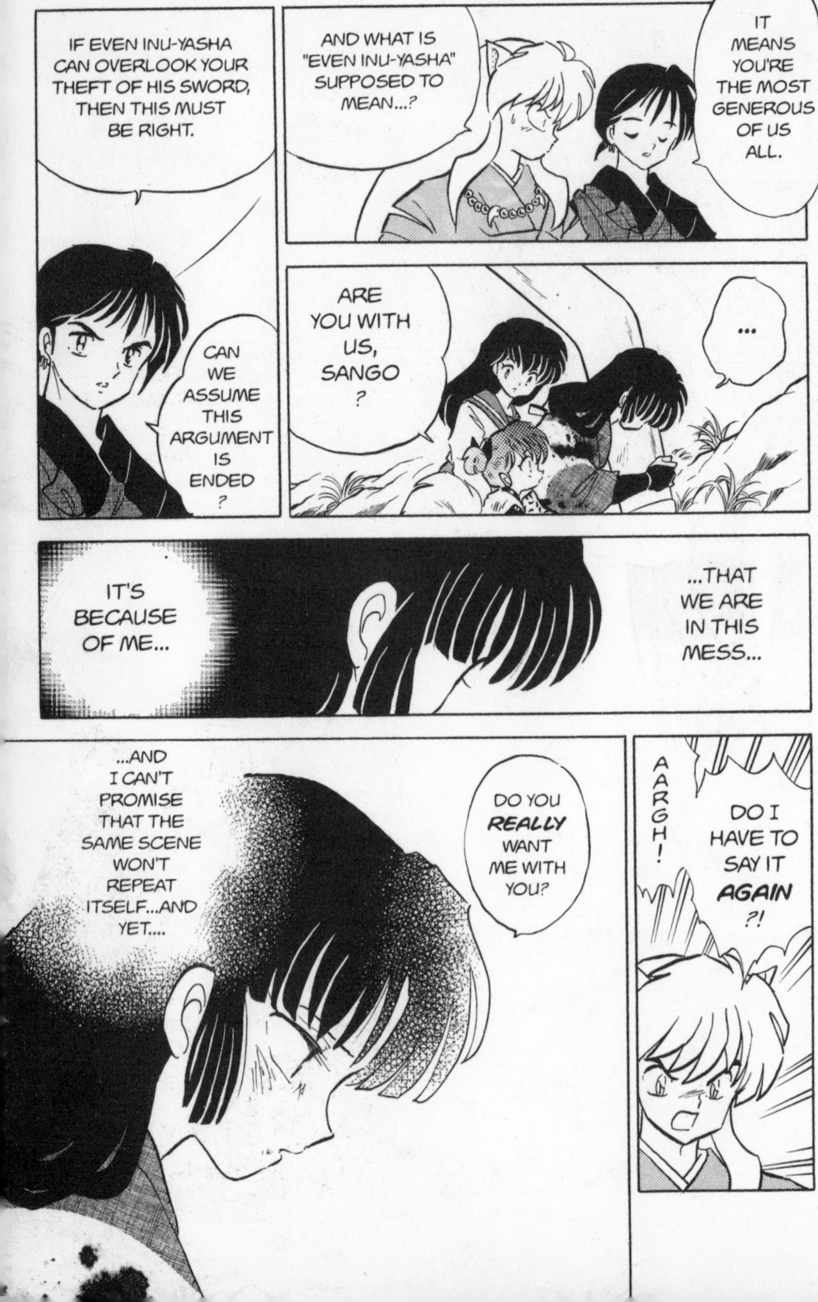
IF EVEN INU-YASHA CAN OVERLOOK YOUR THEFT OF HIS SWORD, THEN THIS MUST BE RIGHT.
CAN WE ASSUME THIS ARGUMENT IS ENDED ?
AND WHAT IS "EVEN INU-YASHA" SUPPOSED TO MEAN...?
IT MEANS YOU'RE THE MOST GENEROUS OF US ALL.
ARE YOU WITH US, SANGO ?
...
IT'S BECAUSE OF ME...
...THAT WE ARE IN THIS MESS...
...AND I CAN'T PROMISE THAT THE SAME SCENE WON'T REPEAT ITSELF...AND YET....
DO YOU **REALLY** WANT ME WITH YOU?
AARGH!
DO I HAVE TO SAY IT **AGAIN** ?!

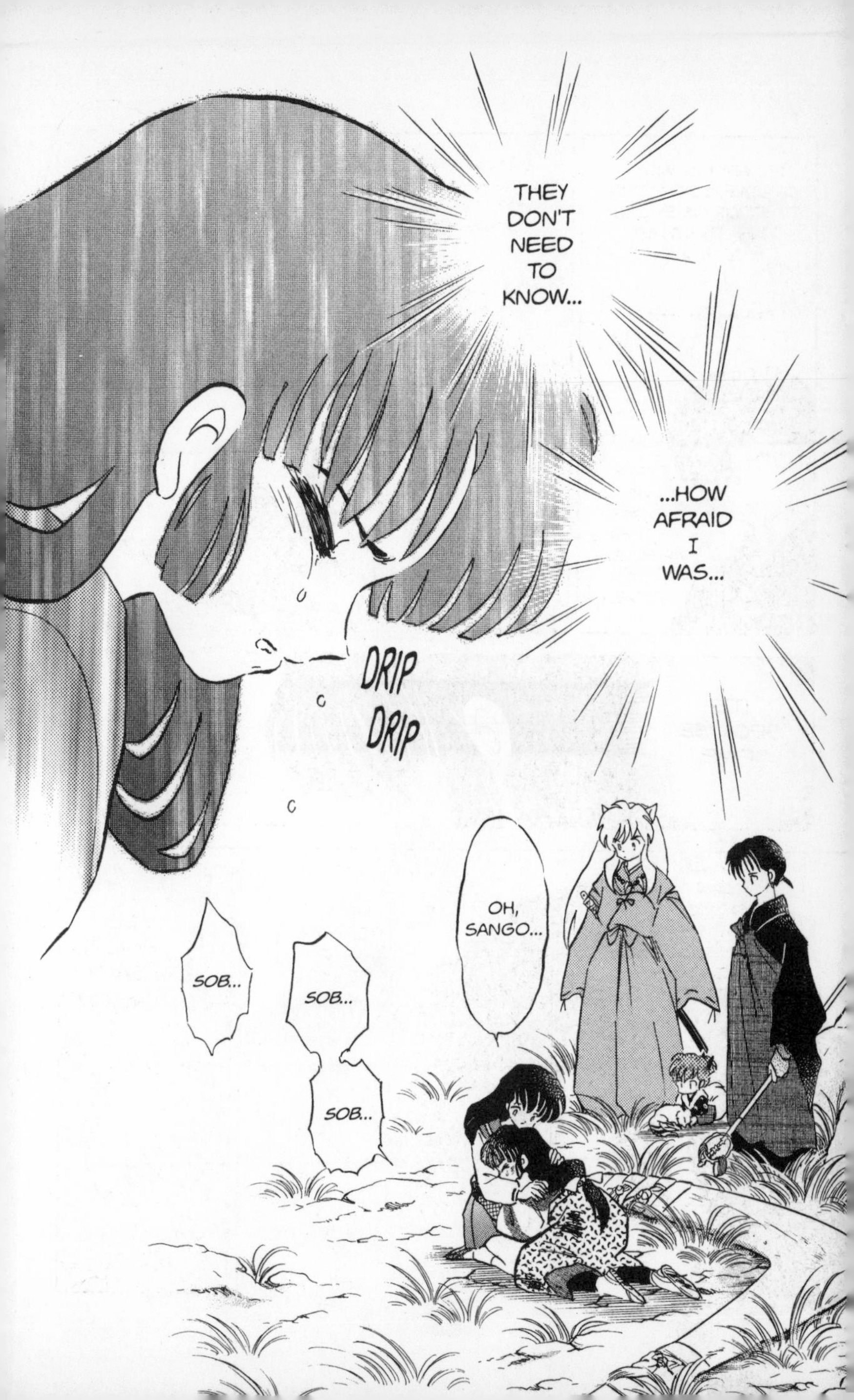
THEY DON'T NEED TO KNOW...
...HOW AFRAID I WAS...
DRIP DRIP
SOB...
SOB...
SOB...
OH, SANGO...

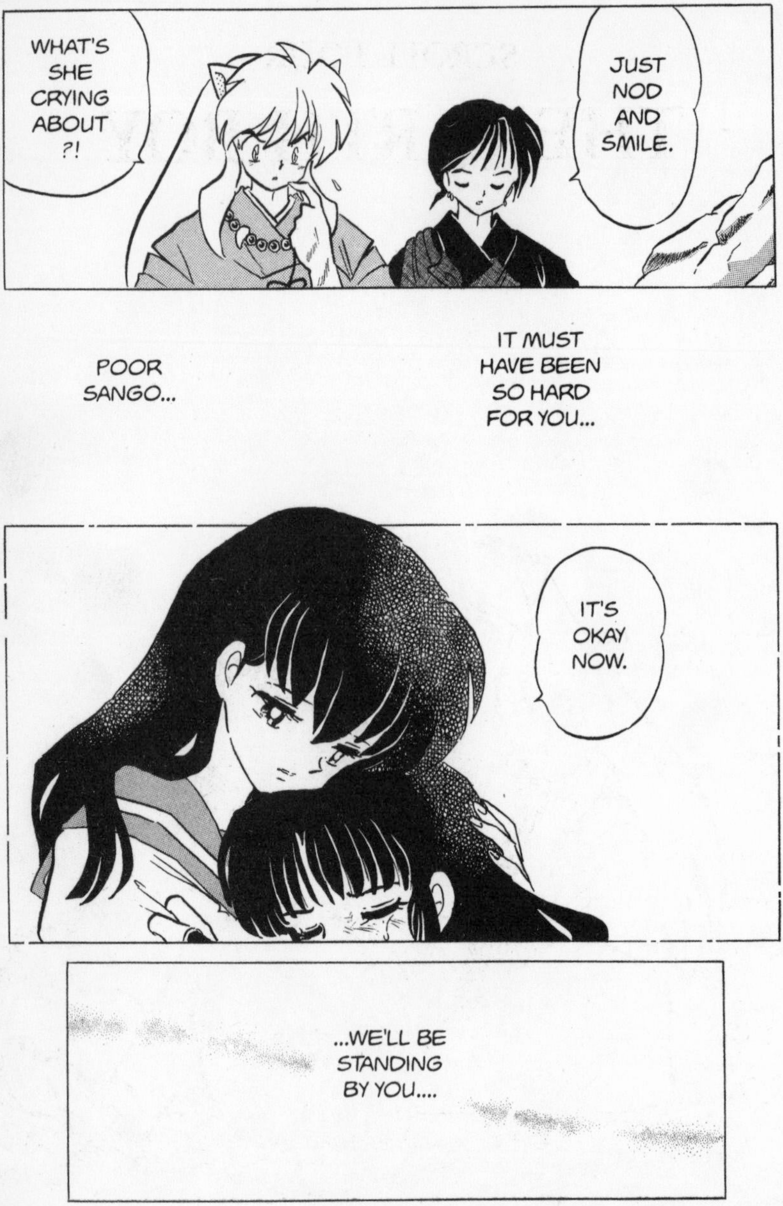
WHAT'S SHE CRYING ABOUT ?!
JUST NOD AND SMILE.
POOR SANGO...
IT MUST HAVE BEEN SO HARD FOR YOU...
IT'S OKAY NOW.
...WE'LL BE STANDING BY YOU....

SCROLL FOUR

THE EARTH BOY

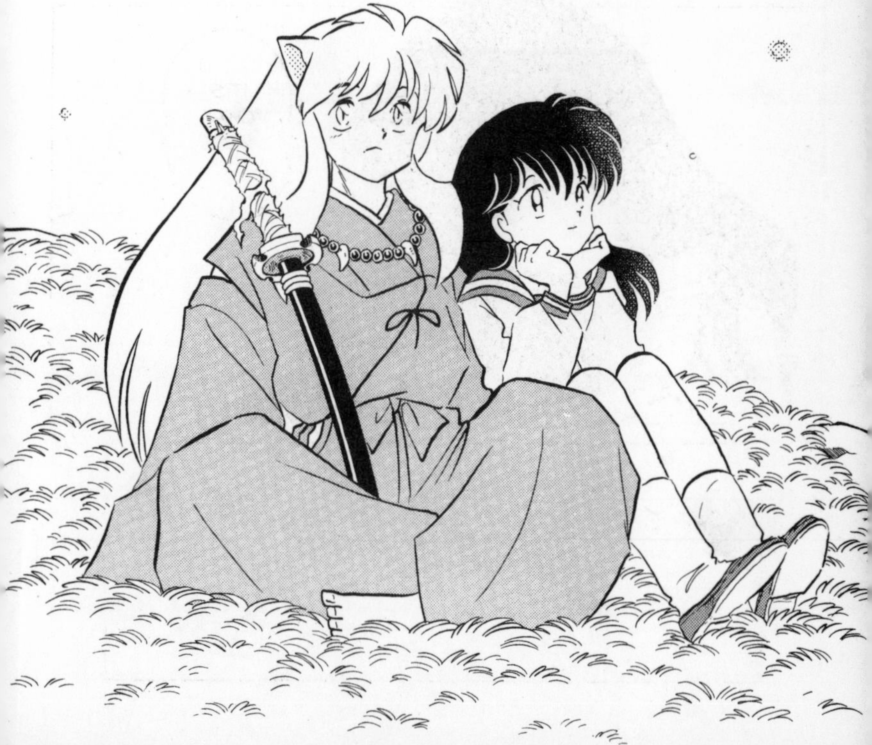

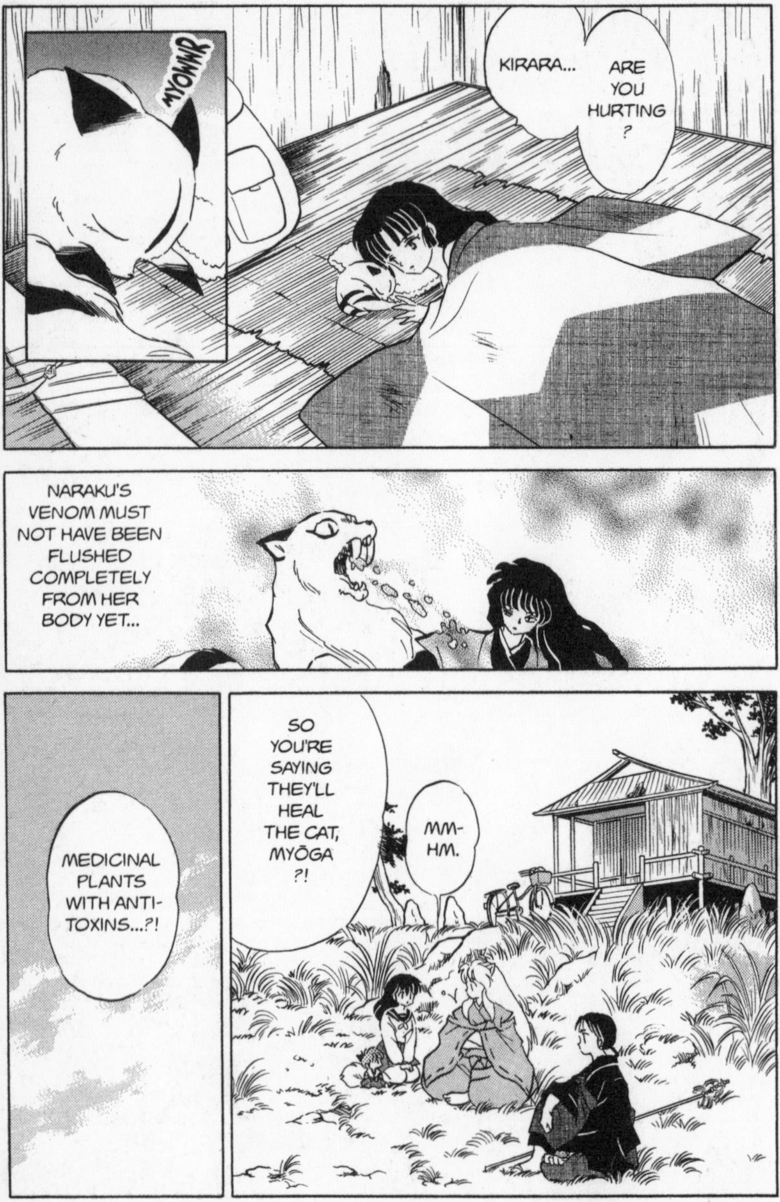
MYOWWR
KIRARA...
ARE YOU HURTING ?
NARAKU'S VENOM MUST NOT HAVE BEEN FLUSHED COMPLETELY FROM HER BODY YET...
MEDICINAL PLANTS WITH ANTI-TOXINS...?!
SO YOU'RE SAYING THEY'LL HEAL THE CAT, MYŌGA ?!
MM-HM.

IT'S NOT A MATTER OF JUST WALKING UP AND PICKING THEM.

THE CATCH IS, A DEMON SUPPOSEDLY GUARDS THE FIELD WHERE THE PLANTS ARE GROWN.

A DEMON...

SO INU-YASHA AND KAGOME WENT TO GET THE PLANTS...

RELAX AND GET SOME REST, LADY SANGO.

AND I HAVE STAYED BEHIND TO PROTECT YOU.

HMMM

...YES ?

SOMEHOW I'D FEEL SAFER IF *YOU* WEREN'T "PROTECTING" ME.

SIGH

GLARE

DON'T WORRY, SANGO.

KAGOME TOLD ME TO MAKE SURE MIROKU DOESN'T PULL ANYTHING NASTY.

SIGH

GLARE

GATATA

MAYBE IT WOULD BE QUICKER IF I WENT ALONE, EH?

JUST CAN'T WAIT TO DITCH ME, CAN YOU?

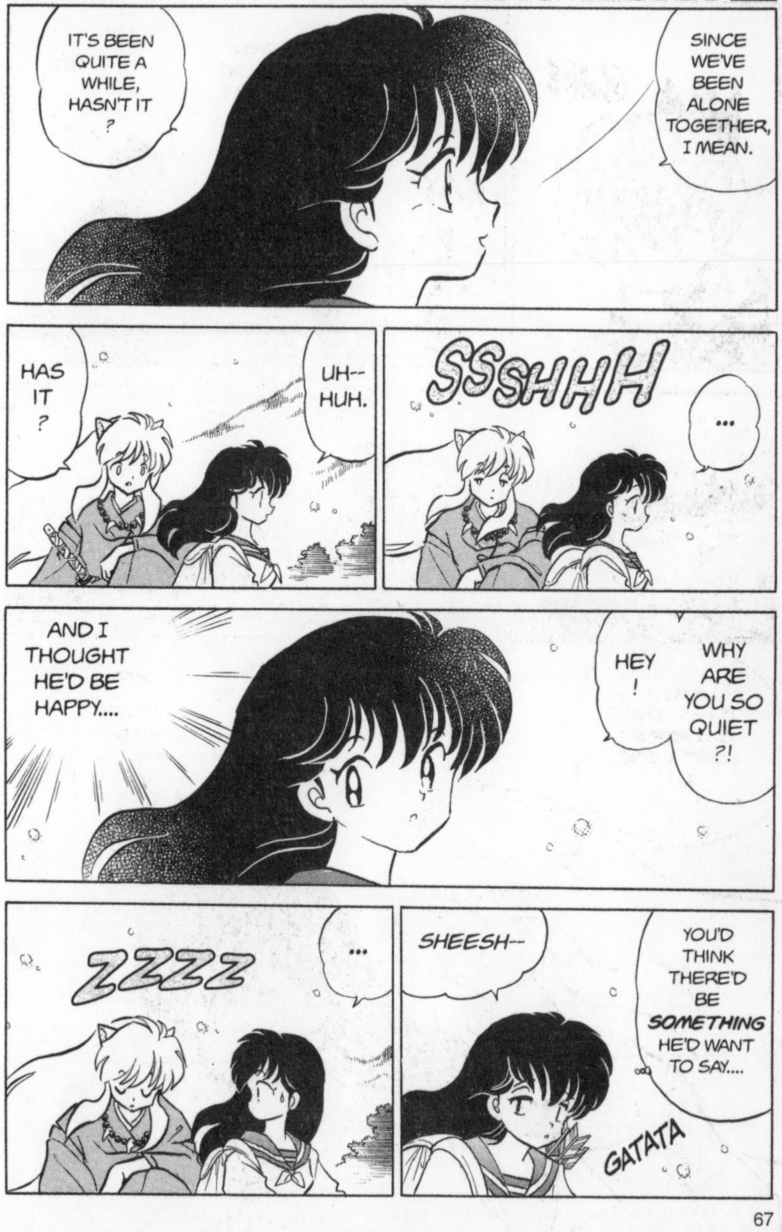
IT'S BEEN QUITE A WHILE, HASN'T IT?
SINCE WE'VE BEEN ALONE TOGETHER, I MEAN.
HAS IT?
UH--HUH.
SSSHHH
...
AND I THOUGHT HE'D BE HAPPY....
HEY! WHY ARE YOU SO QUIET?!
ZZZZ
...
SHEESH--
YOU'D THINK THERE'D BE SOMETHING HE'D WANT TO SAY....
GATATA

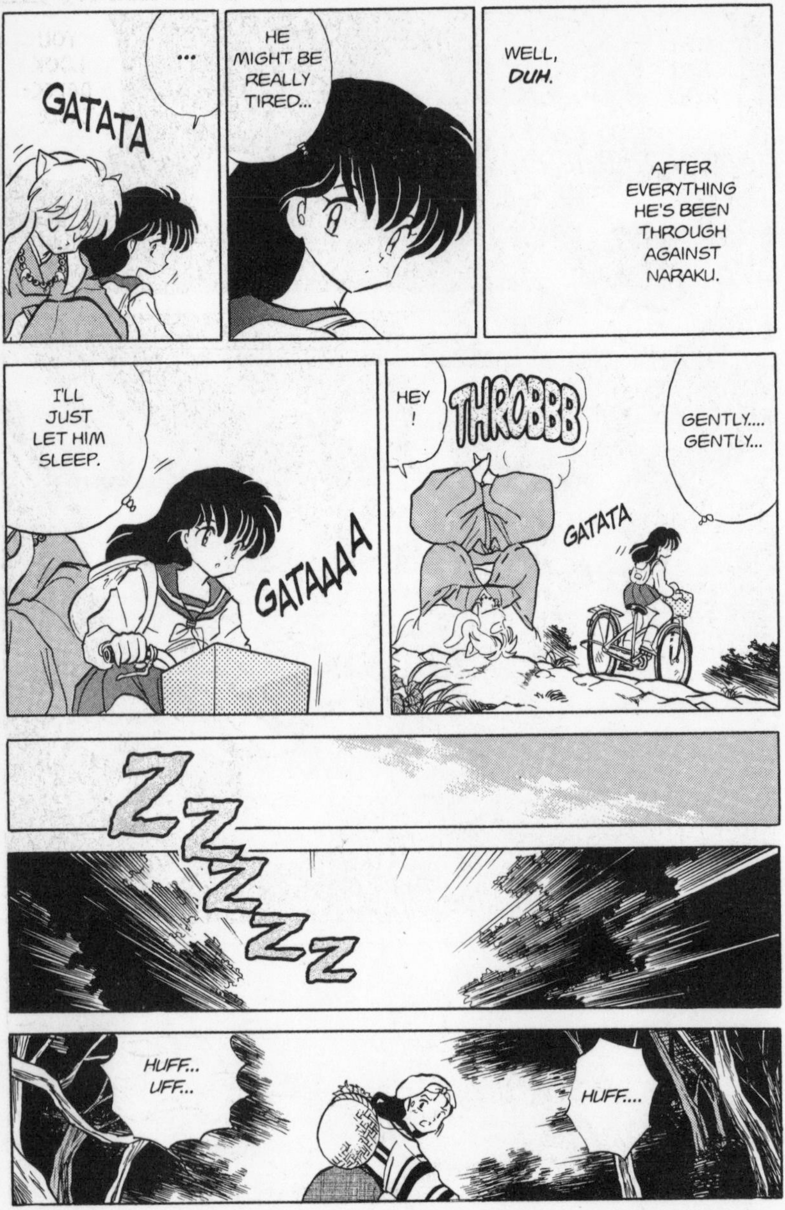
...
GATATA
HE MIGHT BE REALLY TIRED...
WELL, *DUH*.
AFTER EVERYTHING HE'S BEEN THROUGH AGAINST NARAKU.
I'LL JUST LET HIM SLEEP.
GATAAAA
HEY!
THROBBB
GENTLY.... GENTLY...
GATATA
ZZZZZZ
HUFF... UFF...
HUFF....

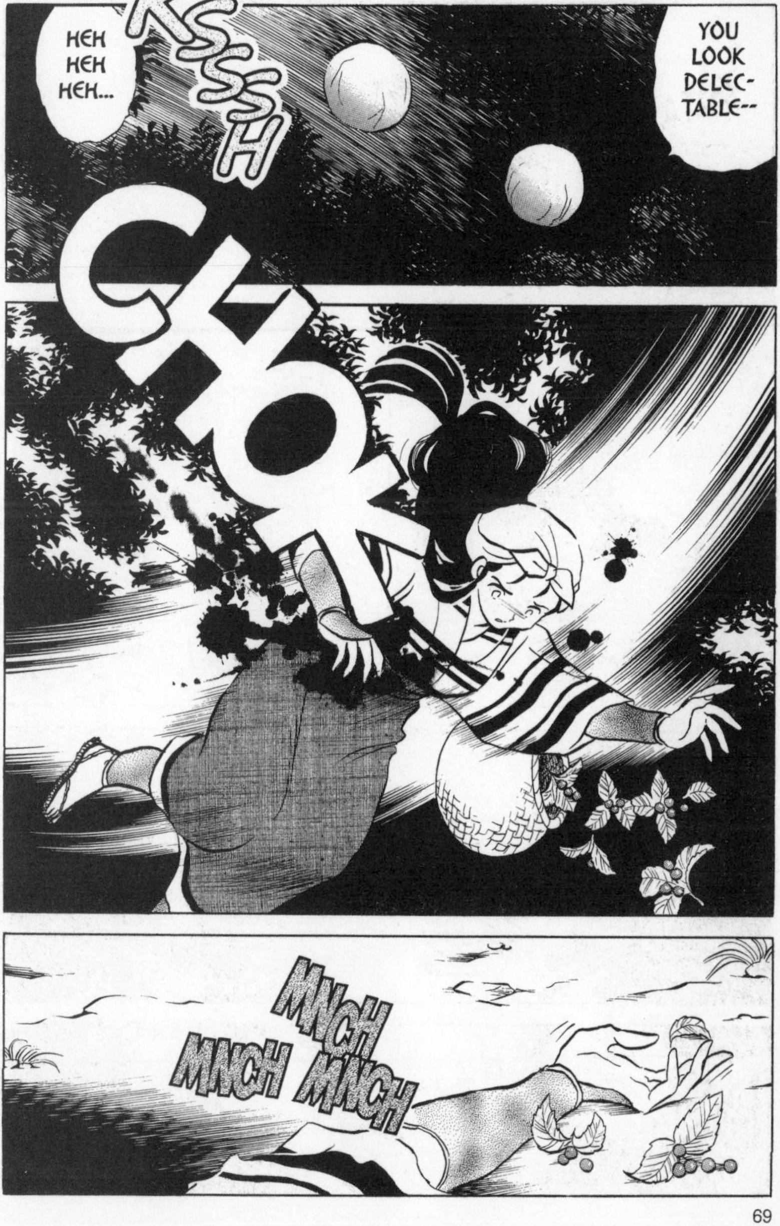
YOU LOOK DELEC-TABLE--
HEH HEH HEH...
KSSSH
CHOK
MNCH MNCH MNCH

70

HHSSSSH

THIS IS THE THIRD VICTIM.....

THE INNARDS DEVOURED ENTIRE AGAIN....

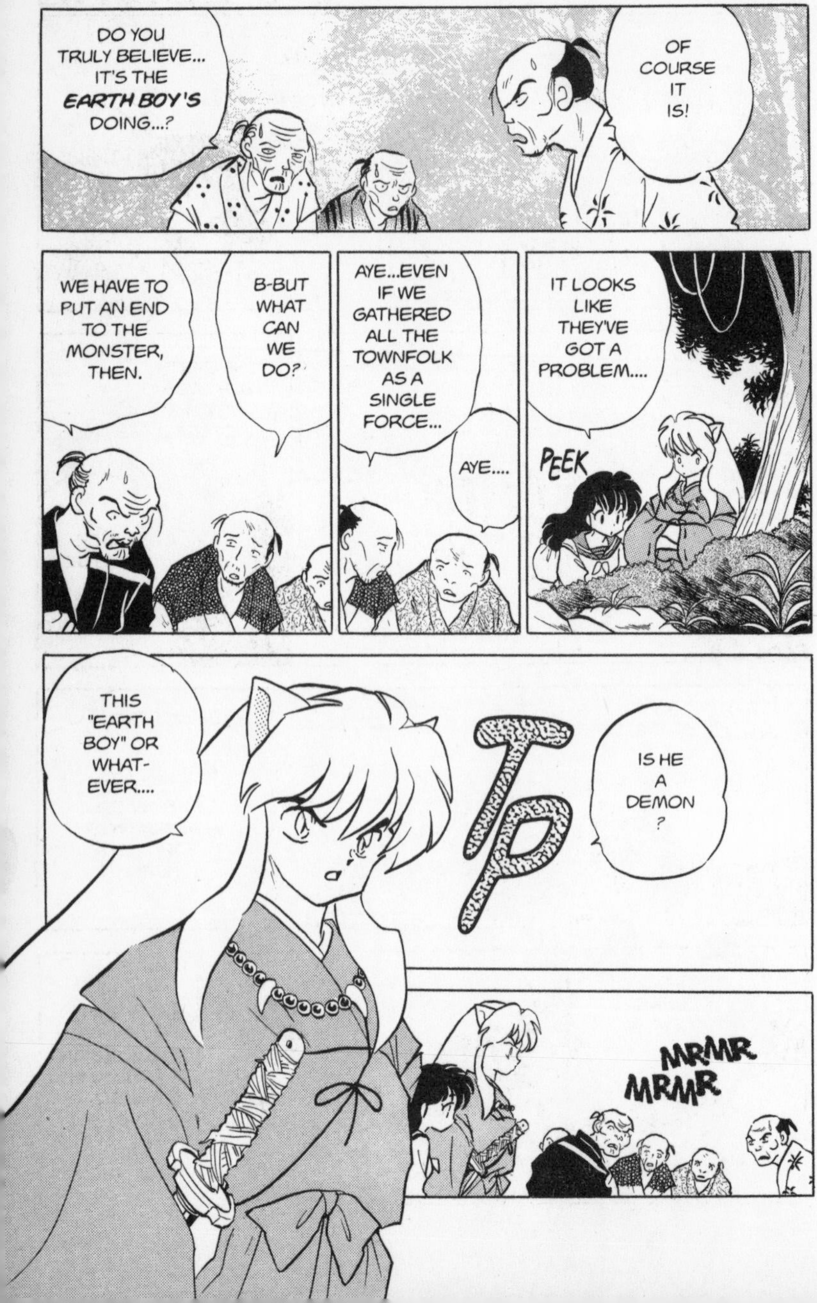
DO YOU TRULY BELIEVE... IT'S THE EARTH BOY'S DOING...?
OF COURSE IT IS!
WE HAVE TO PUT AN END TO THE MONSTER, THEN.
B-BUT WHAT CAN WE DO?
AYE...EVEN IF WE GATHERED ALL THE TOWNFOLK AS A SINGLE FORCE...
AYE....
IT LOOKS LIKE THEY'VE GOT A PROBLEM....
PEEK
THIS "EARTH BOY" OR WHAT-EVER....
TP
IS HE A DEMON ?
MRMR MRMR

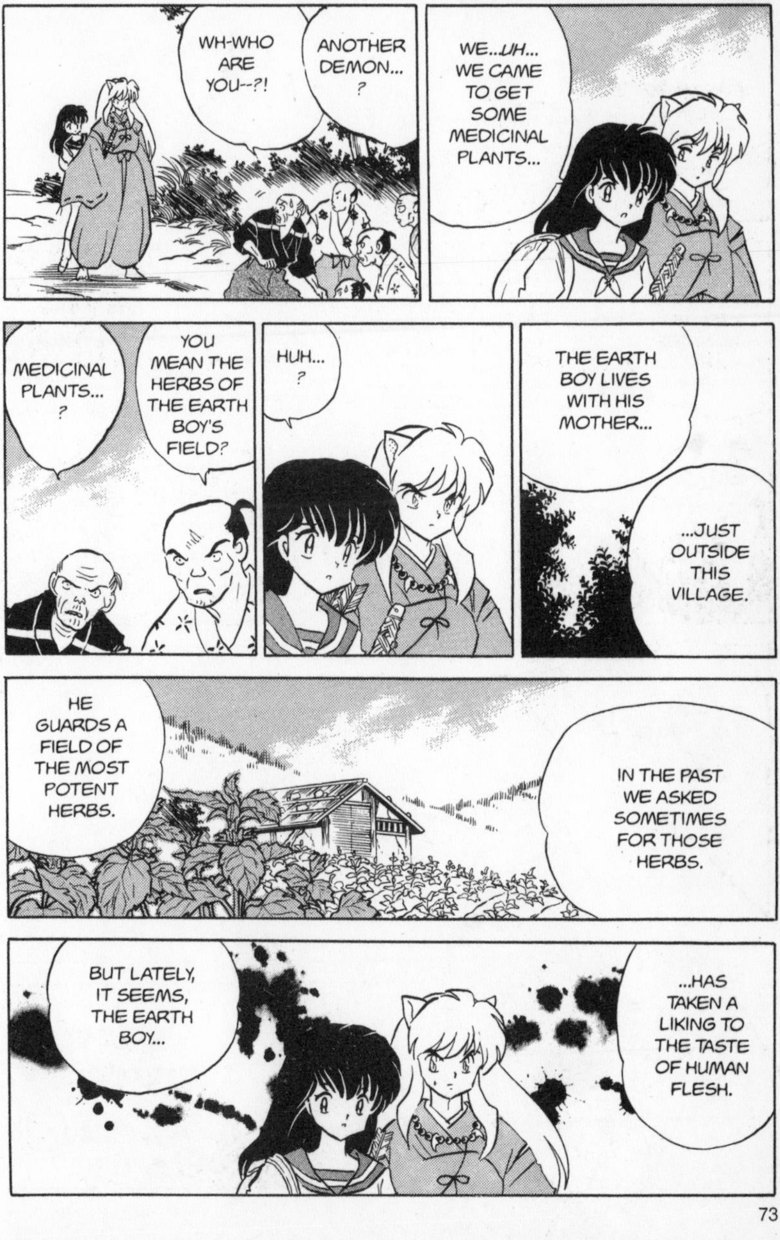
WH-WHO ARE YOU--?!
ANOTHER DEMON...?
WE...UH... WE CAME TO GET SOME MEDICINAL PLANTS...
MEDICINAL PLANTS...?
YOU MEAN THE HERBS OF THE EARTH BOY'S FIELD?
HUH...?
THE EARTH BOY LIVES WITH HIS MOTHER...
...JUST OUTSIDE THIS VILLAGE.
HE GUARDS A FIELD OF THE MOST POTENT HERBS.
IN THE PAST WE ASKED SOMETIMES FOR THOSE HERBS.
BUT LATELY, IT SEEMS, THE EARTH BOY...
...HAS TAKEN A LIKING TO THE TASTE OF HUMAN FLESH.

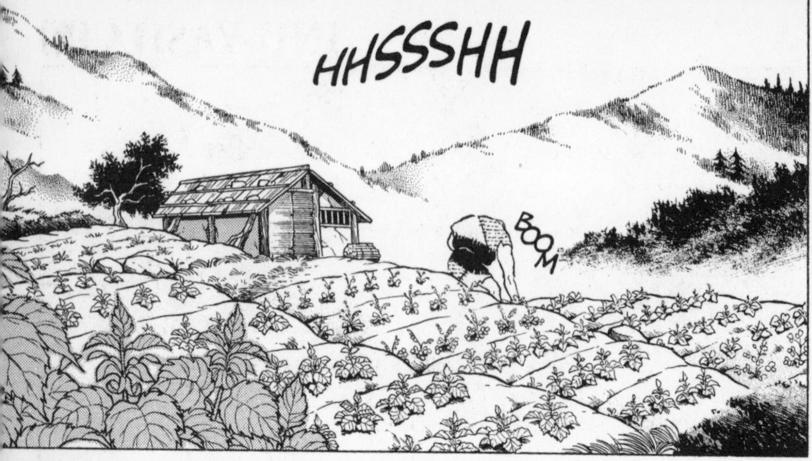
HHSSSHH
BOOM

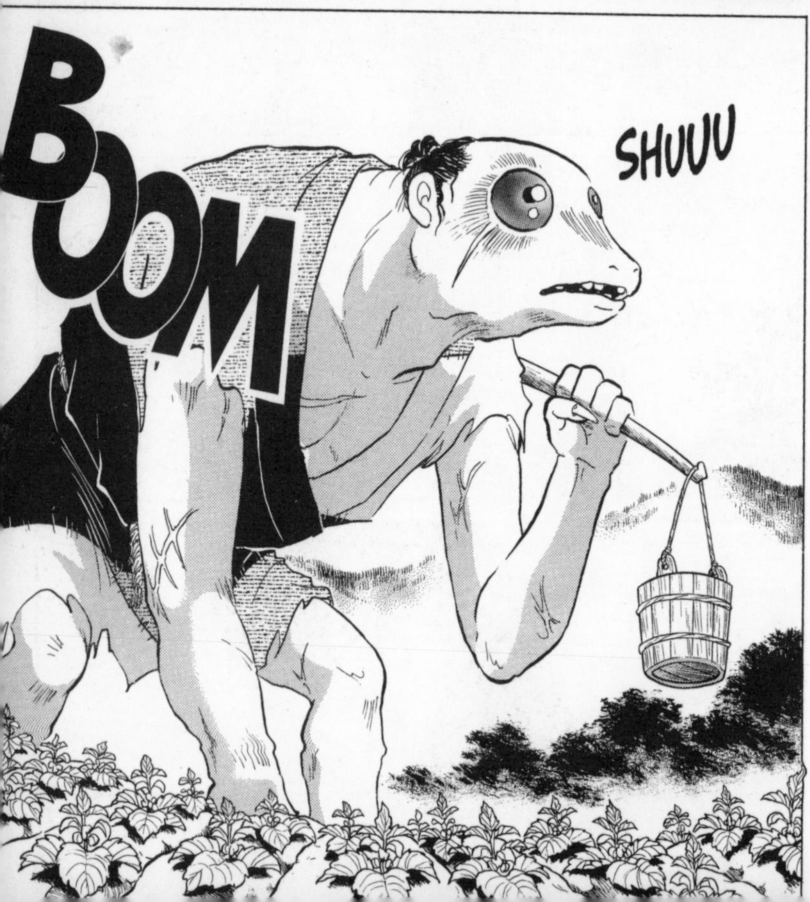
BOOM
SHUUU

76

HUH...? THIS GUY...

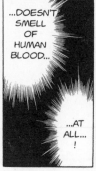

...DOESN'T SMELL OF HUMAN BLOOD...

...AT ALL...!

FSSH

KLOK

HEY, HEY! EARTH BOY, PREPARE TO DIE!

KILL HIM! HURRY!

SSSHH

BRRR BRRR BRRR

!

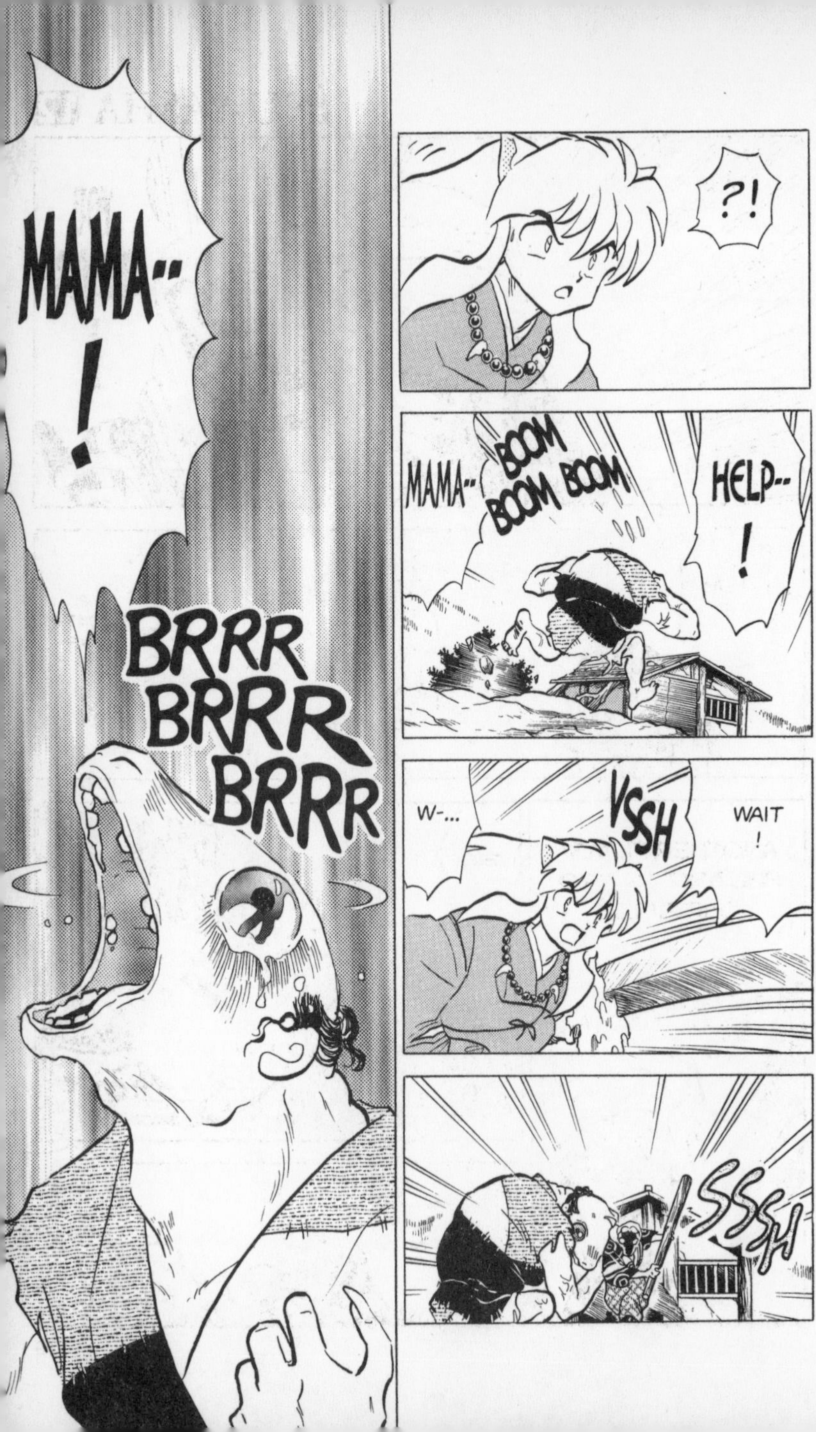
MAMA-- !
BRRR BRRR BRRR
?!
MAMA--
BOOM BOOM BOOM
HELP-- !
W-...
VSSH
WAIT !
SSSH

YOU
THIEVES
--
!

HUH
?

A
MOUNTAIN
HAG
?!

ANOTHER FLIMSY
PRETEXT TO RAID
OUR FIELD!

YEEEK
!

BWAK

WAAH!

THE LAD'S
BEEN
DONE IN!

WHAT
A
WEAKLING
!

SCROLL FIVE

THE RAID

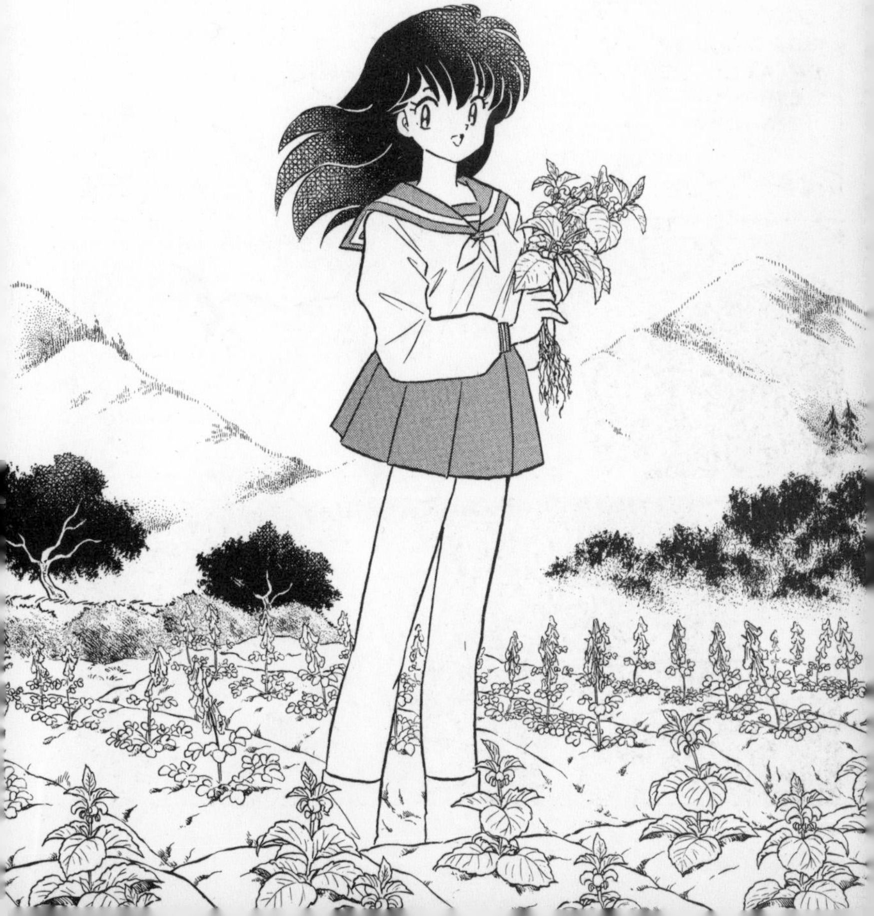

YOUR APPEARANCE WOULD SUGGEST ONLY A PARTIAL TRANSFORMATION....

PARTIAL...?

I WONDER IF SHE MEANS THESE!

FEH.

TUG TUG

YOU CAN PROBABLY IMAGINE....

JUST BECAUSE MY CHILD IS HALF-DEMON...

HSSS

...HOW WE'VE BEEN TREATED BY THESE VILLAGERS.

UM...

YOU'VE BEEN MISTREATED...?

HUH...

I CAN'T TELL YOU HOW TIMES WE'VE NEARLY BEEN KILLED.

I'M SORRY, MAMA.

YOU'VE BEEN TAUNTED BECAUSE OF ME.

H F F F

WHAT ARE YOU TALKING ABOUT, JINENJI?

YOU'VE DONE NOTHING WRONG !

YOUR DEAR FATHER...

WAS SUCH A GOOD, KIND DEMON.

AH, THAT WAS A FINE TIME...

WHEN I WAS JUST...

ABOUT *YOUR* AGE...

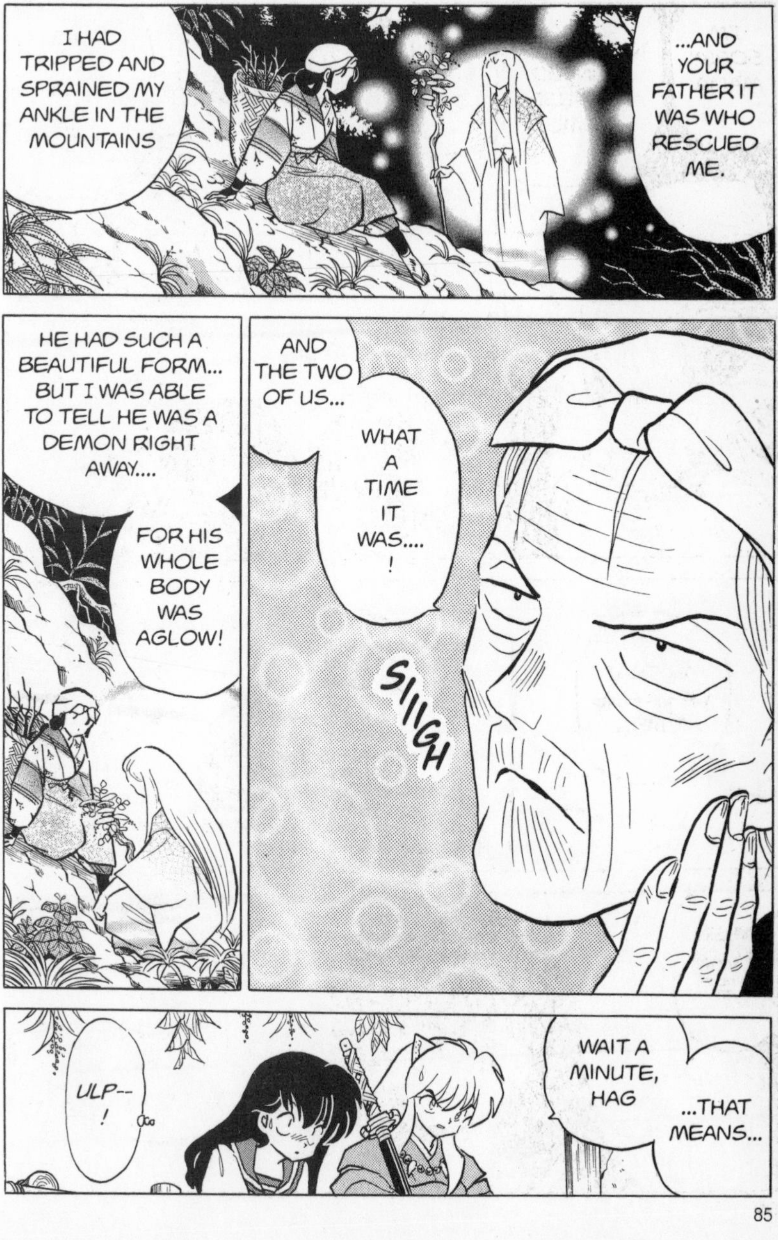
I HAD TRIPPED AND SPRAINED MY ANKLE IN THE MOUNTAINS
...AND YOUR FATHER IT WAS WHO RESCUED ME.
HE HAD SUCH A BEAUTIFUL FORM... BUT I WAS ABLE TO TELL HE WAS A DEMON RIGHT AWAY....
FOR HIS WHOLE BODY WAS AGLOW!
AND THE TWO OF US...
WHAT A TIME IT WAS.... !
SIIIGH
ULP-- !
WAIT A MINUTE, HAG
...THAT MEANS...

YOU'RE THE HUMAN?

WHAT DID YOU THINK I WAS?!

BBMP BBMP BBMP

BUT WILL HE STOP CALLING HER "HAG"....!?

HSSH...

TO OPPOSE VENOMS...

YOU SHOULD MAKE AN INFUSION WITH THESE AND HAVE HER DRINK IT.

ONCE YOU'VE GOTTEN YOUR HERBS, GET OUT OF HERE.

...THANKS.

IF YOU STICK AROUND, YOU'LL BE DRAGGED INTO THIS MESS.

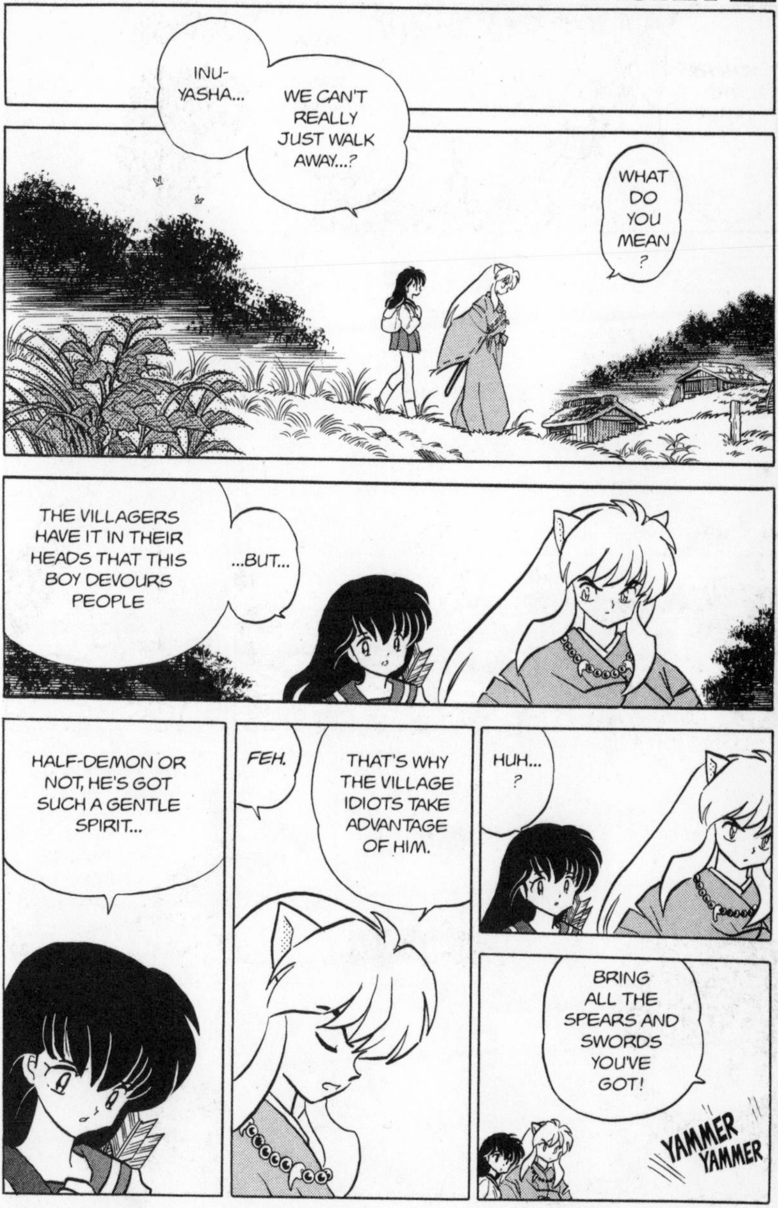
INU-YASHA... WE CAN'T REALLY JUST WALK AWAY...?
WHAT DO YOU MEAN?
THE VILLAGERS HAVE IT IN THEIR HEADS THAT THIS BOY DEVOURS PEOPLE
...BUT...
HALF-DEMON OR NOT, HE'S GOT SUCH A GENTLE SPIRIT...
FEH.
THAT'S WHY THE VILLAGE IDIOTS TAKE ADVANTAGE OF HIM.
HUH...?
BRING ALL THE SPEARS AND SWORDS YOU'VE GOT!
YAMMER YAMMER

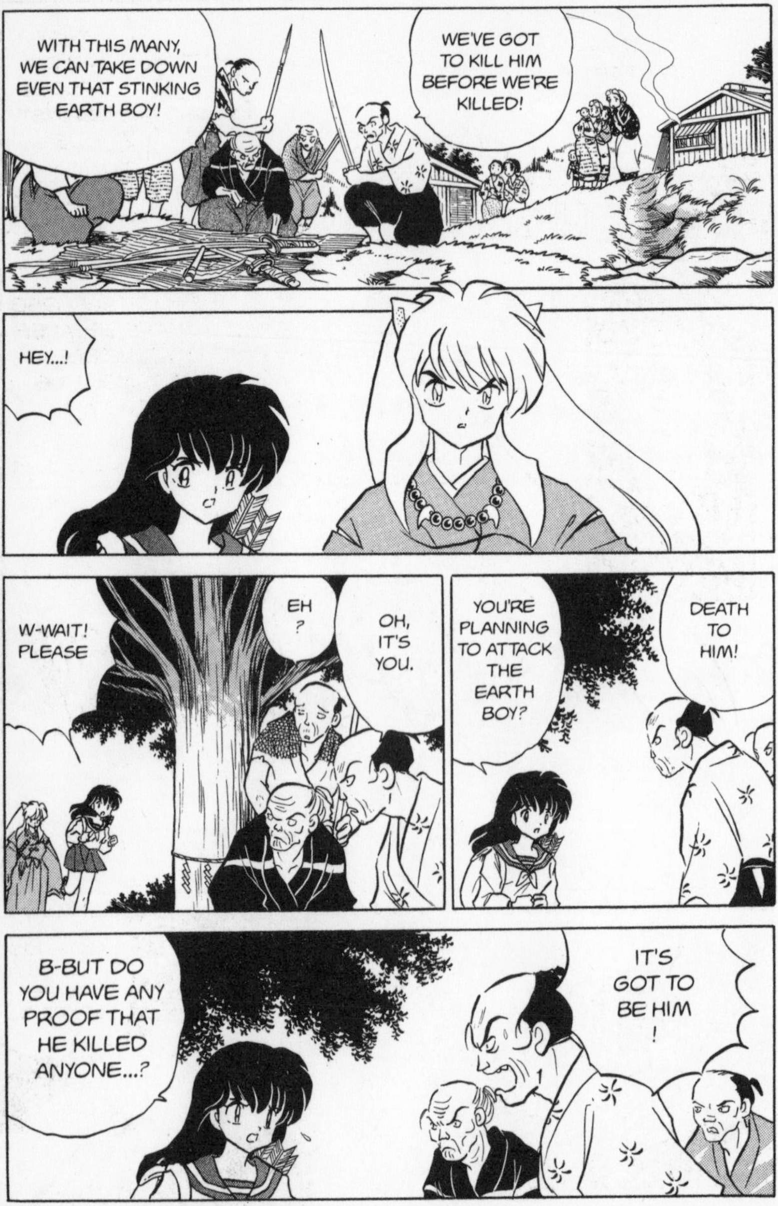
WITH THIS MANY, WE CAN TAKE DOWN EVEN THAT STINKING EARTH BOY!
WE'VE GOT TO KILL HIM BEFORE WE'RE KILLED!
HEY...!
W-WAIT! PLEASE
EH ?
OH, IT'S YOU.
YOU'RE PLANNING TO ATTACK THE EARTH BOY?
DEATH TO HIM!
B-BUT DO YOU HAVE ANY PROOF THAT HE KILLED ANYONE...?
IT'S GOT TO BE HIM !

THAT'S AN EVIL FAMILY!

THEY HOLD A GRUDGE AGAINST US!

THEY DO, EH?

DO YOU SUPPOSE THAT'S BECAUSE YOU'VE BEEN TORMENTING THEM!?

KNCH

WHAT...?

WHAT ARE YOU TALKING ABOUT!?

FLINCH

INU-YASHA...

NOTHING'S GOING TO BE SETTLED....

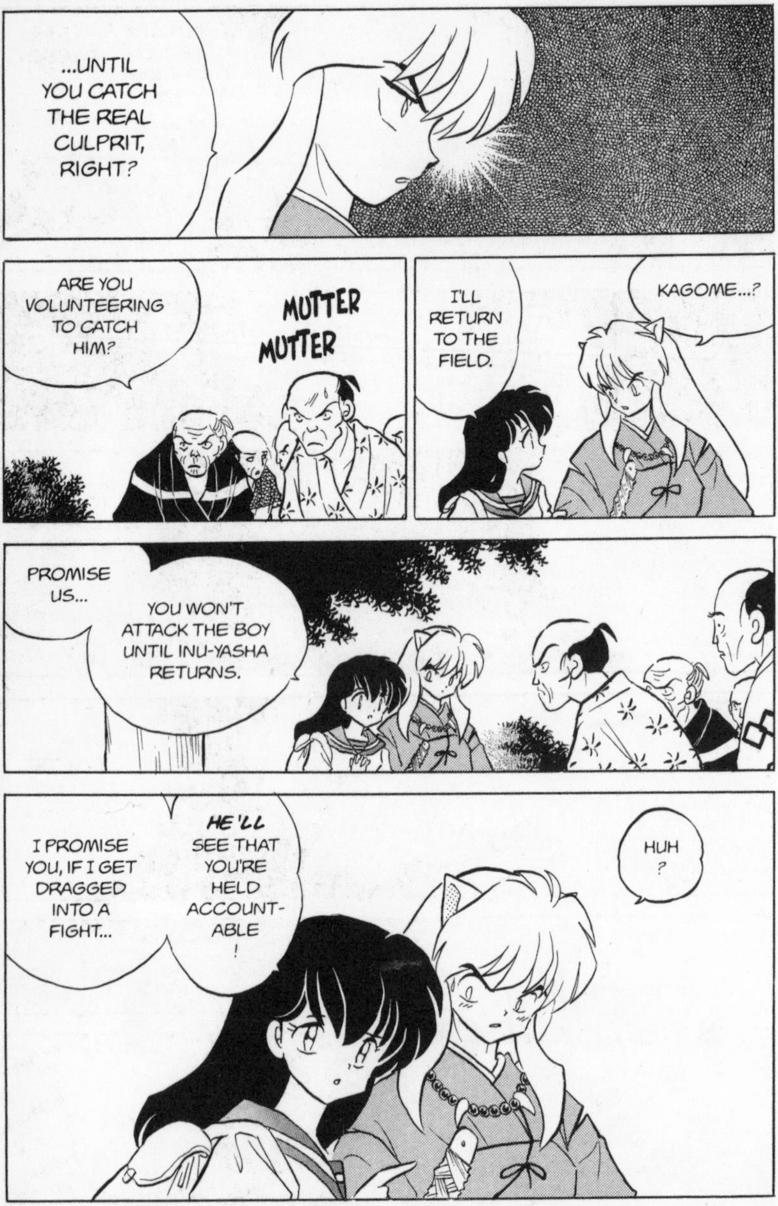
...UNTIL YOU CATCH THE REAL CULPRIT, RIGHT?
ARE YOU VOLUNTEERING TO CATCH HIM?
MUTTER MUTTER
I'LL RETURN TO THE FIELD.
KAGOME...?
PROMISE US...
YOU WON'T ATTACK THE BOY UNTIL INU-YASHA RETURNS.
I PROMISE YOU, IF I GET DRAGGED INTO A FIGHT...
HE'LL SEE THAT YOU'RE HELD ACCOUNTABLE!
HUH?

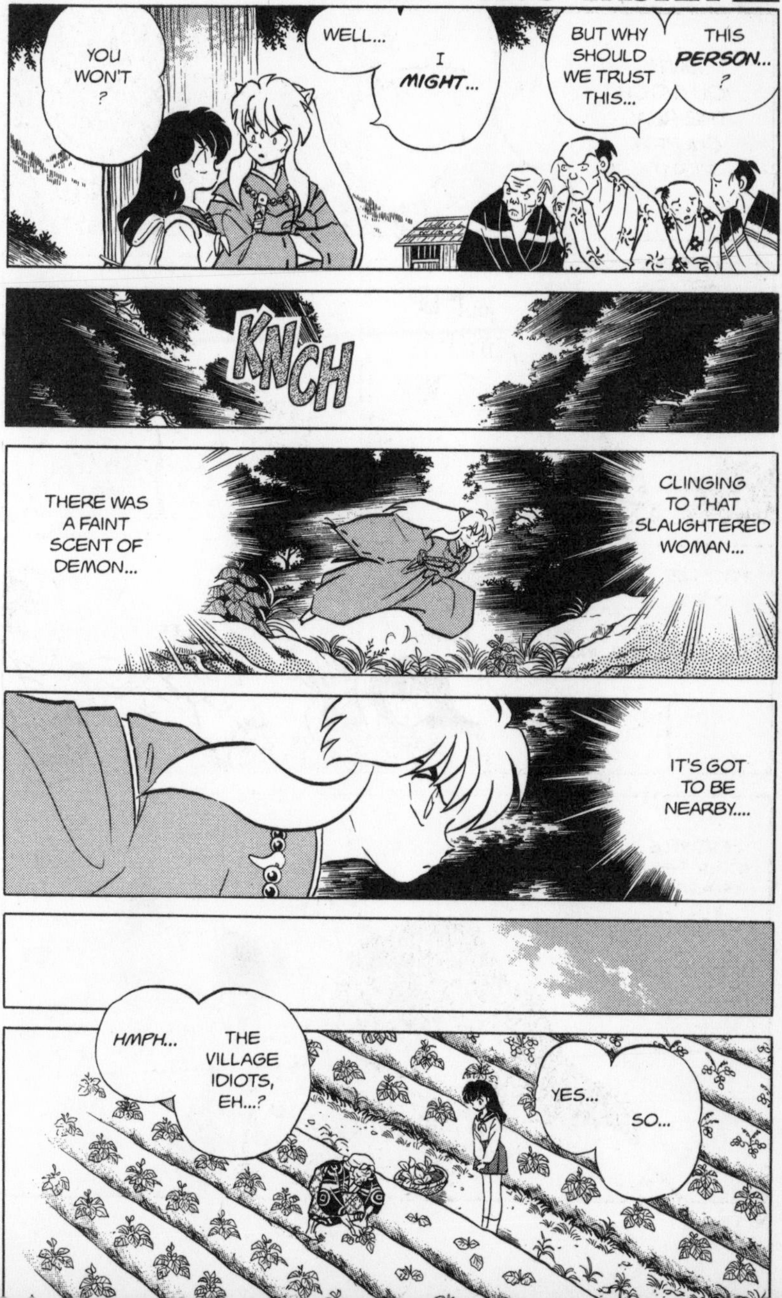
YOU WON'T ?
WELL...
I *MIGHT*...
BUT WHY SHOULD WE TRUST THIS...
THIS *PERSON*... ?
KNCH
THERE WAS A FAINT SCENT OF DEMON...
CLINGING TO THAT SLAUGHTERED WOMAN...
IT'S GOT TO BE NEARBY....
HMPH...
THE VILLAGE IDIOTS, EH...?
YES...
SO...

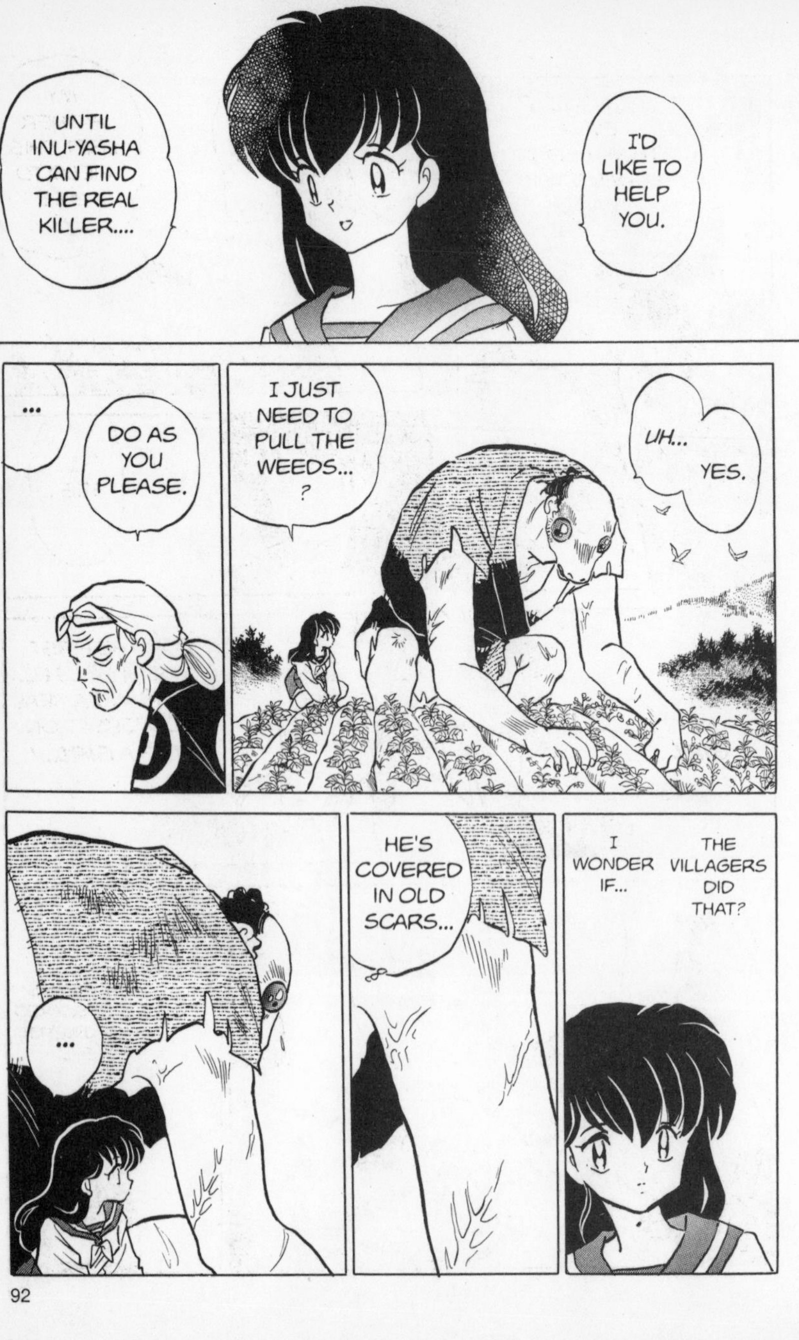
UNTIL INU-YASHA CAN FIND THE REAL KILLER....
I'D LIKE TO HELP YOU.
...
DO AS YOU PLEASE.
I JUST NEED TO PULL THE WEEDS... ?
UH...
YES.
...
HE'S COVERED IN OLD SCARS...
I WONDER IF...
THE VILLAGERS DID THAT?

HEY... DIDN'T YOU EVER THINK ABOUT LEAVING THIS PLACE?

I LIKE IT HERE.

MY FATHER LEFT THIS FIELD TO ME...

HHSSS

I SEE...

I-I'M TALKING... TO A *GIRL*...

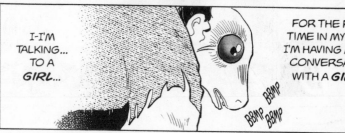

FOR THE FIRST TIME IN MY LIFE... I'M HAVING A REAL CONVERSATION WITH A *GIRL*...!

BBMP BBMP BBMP

YAAAA...!

FLINCH

IT'S A W-WORM--!

OH!

SHE'S SCARED OF *WORMS*... BUT SHE'S NOT SCARED OF JINENJI, EH...?

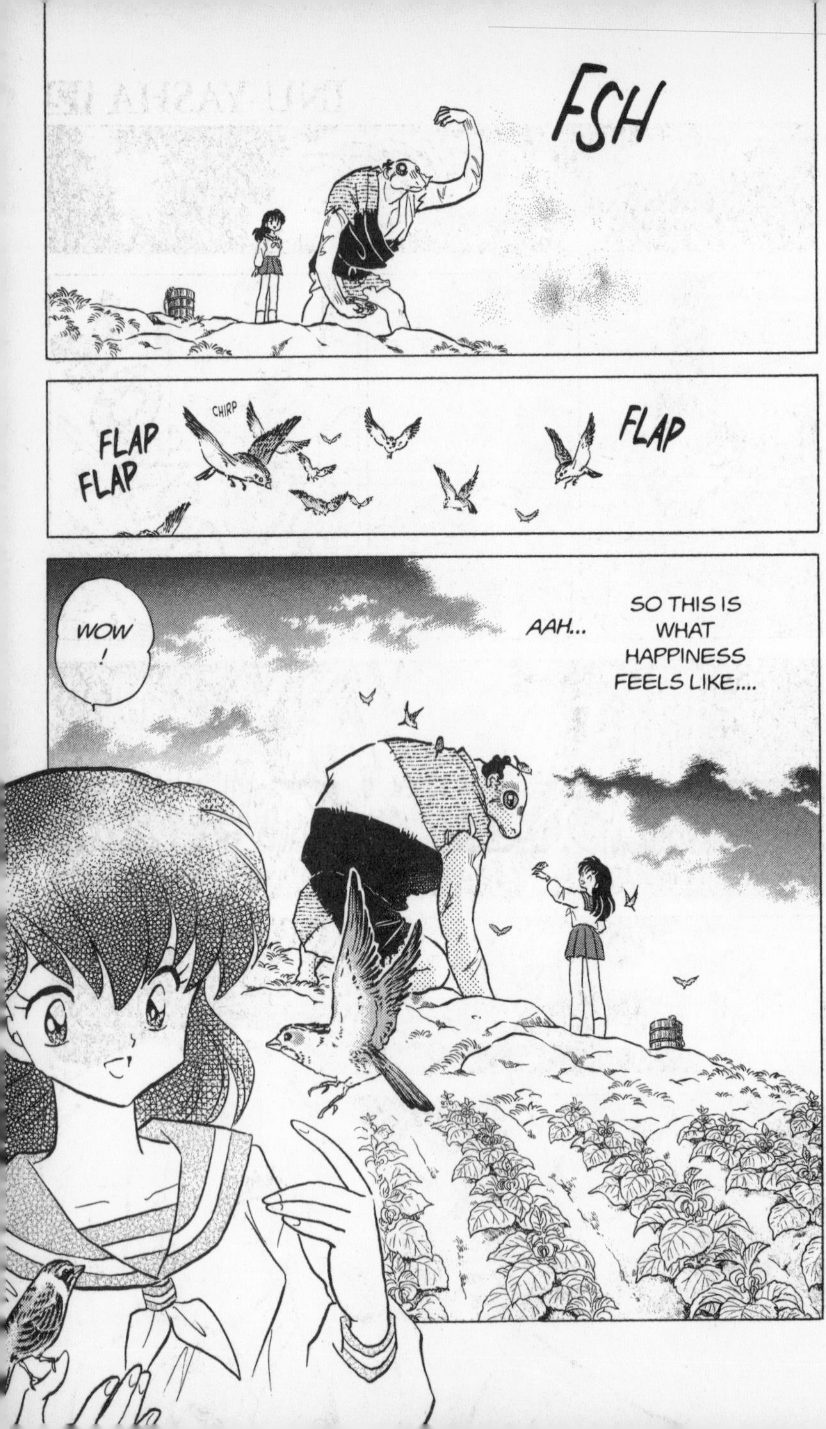
FSH
FLAP
FLAP
CHIRP
FLAP
WOW!
AAH...
SO THIS IS WHAT HAPPINESS FEELS LIKE....

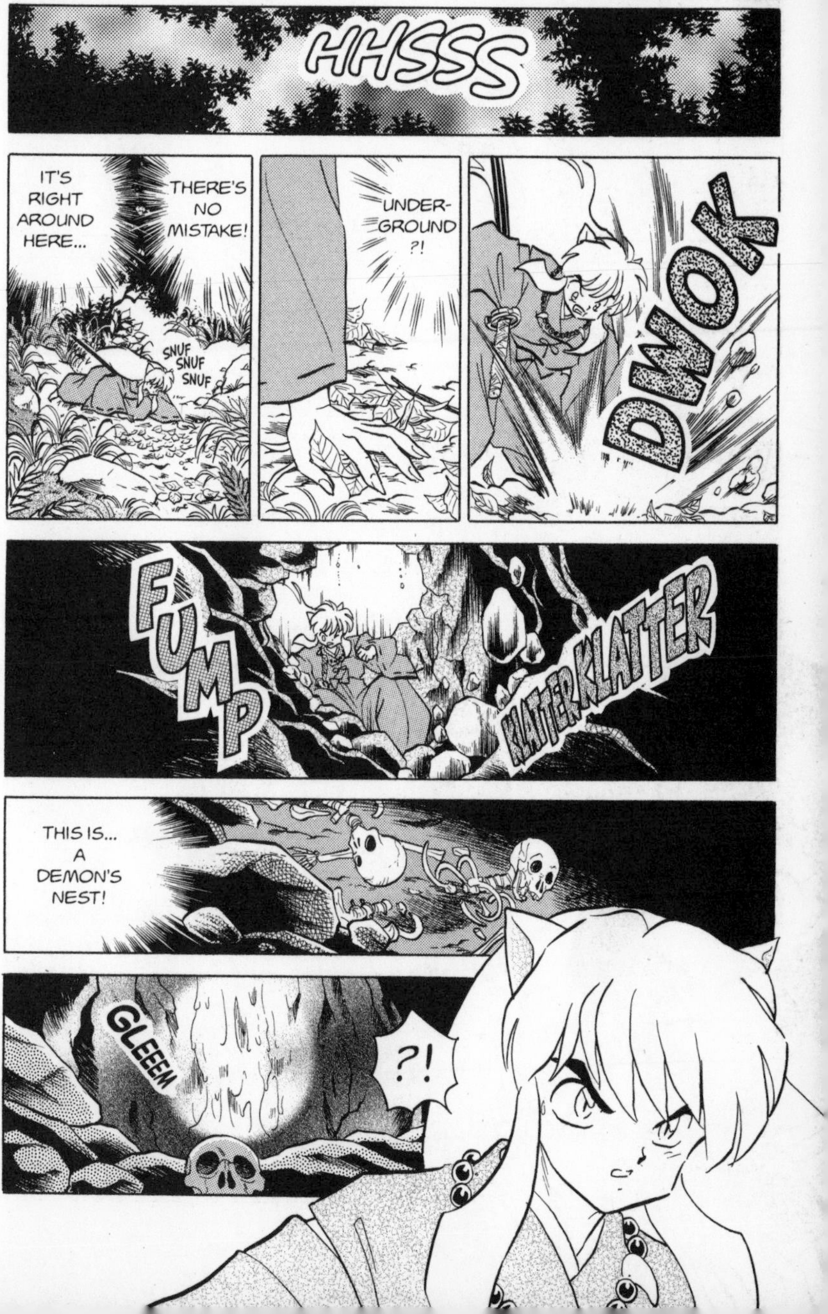
HHSSS
IT'S RIGHT AROUND HERE...
THERE'S NO MISTAKE!
SNUF SNUF SNUF
UNDER-GROUND ?!
DWOK
FUMP
KLATTER KLATTER
THIS IS... A DEMON'S NEST!
GLEEEM
?!

AND THOSE...

GLEEEM

DLLLRB

NEWLY HATCHED, TOO...

...ARE EGGS !?

...THERE'S NOT A SINGLE ONE HERE...

DID THEY ABANDON THEIR NEST ?

NO, THAT'S NOT IT!

THE MOTHER DEMON TOOK HER HATCHLINGS OUT OF THE NEST...

...WHICH MAKES HER MOTIVE CLEAR...

SHE'S TEACHING THEM TO HUNT!

TO HUNT HUMAN ENTRAILS !

THE HUNTING GROUND IS THE VILLAGE...

KAGOME'S IN DANGER!

WE'LL DO HIM IN, EH?

MUMBLE MUMBLE

DON'T TROUBLE YOUR MIND ABOUT IT...

THE EARTH BOY IS THE ONLY POSSIBLE CULPRIT....

WE CAN'T TRUST THAT OTHER DEMON'S LIES....

HHSSSH

THESE FEELINGS... WHAT ARE THEY...?

WHEN I'M WITH THIS GIRL...

MY HEART FEELS SO WARM...

THE HALF-BREED'S HEART

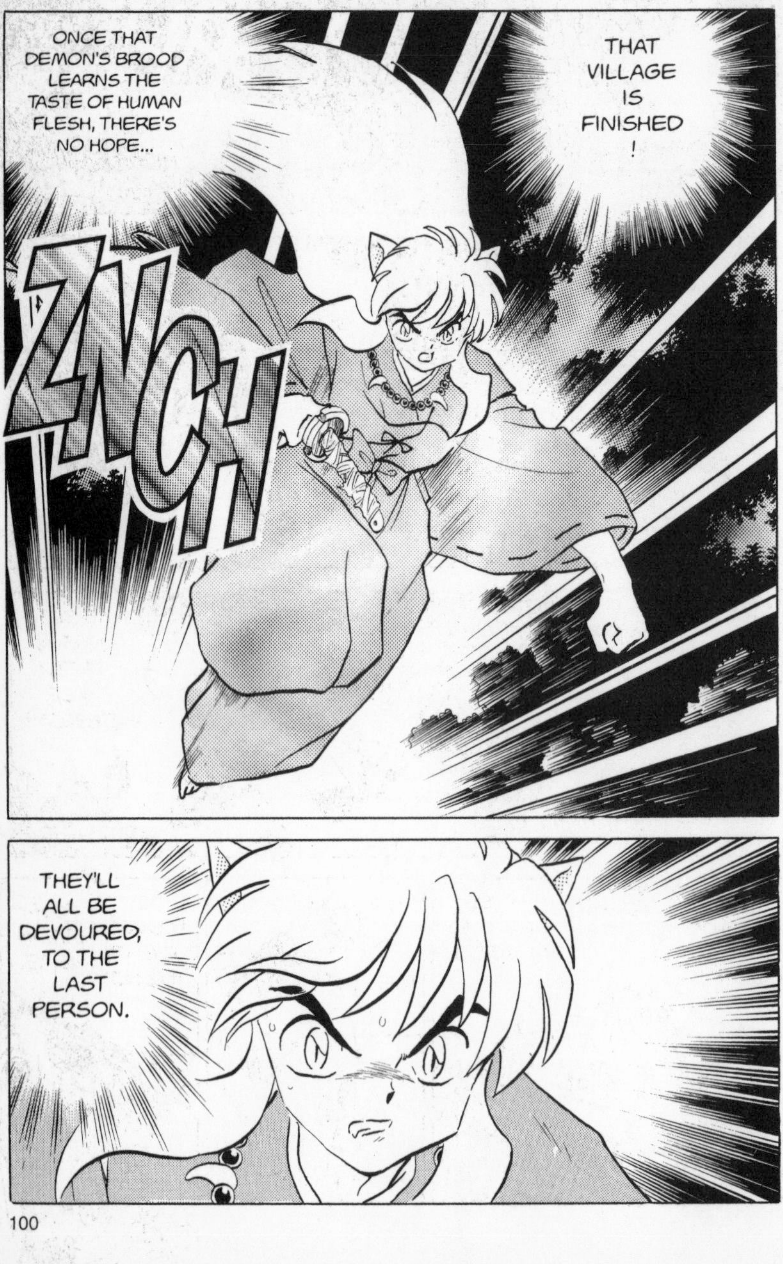
ONCE THAT DEMON'S BROOD LEARNS THE TASTE OF HUMAN FLESH, THERE'S NO HOPE...
THAT VILLAGE IS FINISHED !
ZNCH
THEY'LL ALL BE DEVOURED, TO THE LAST PERSON.

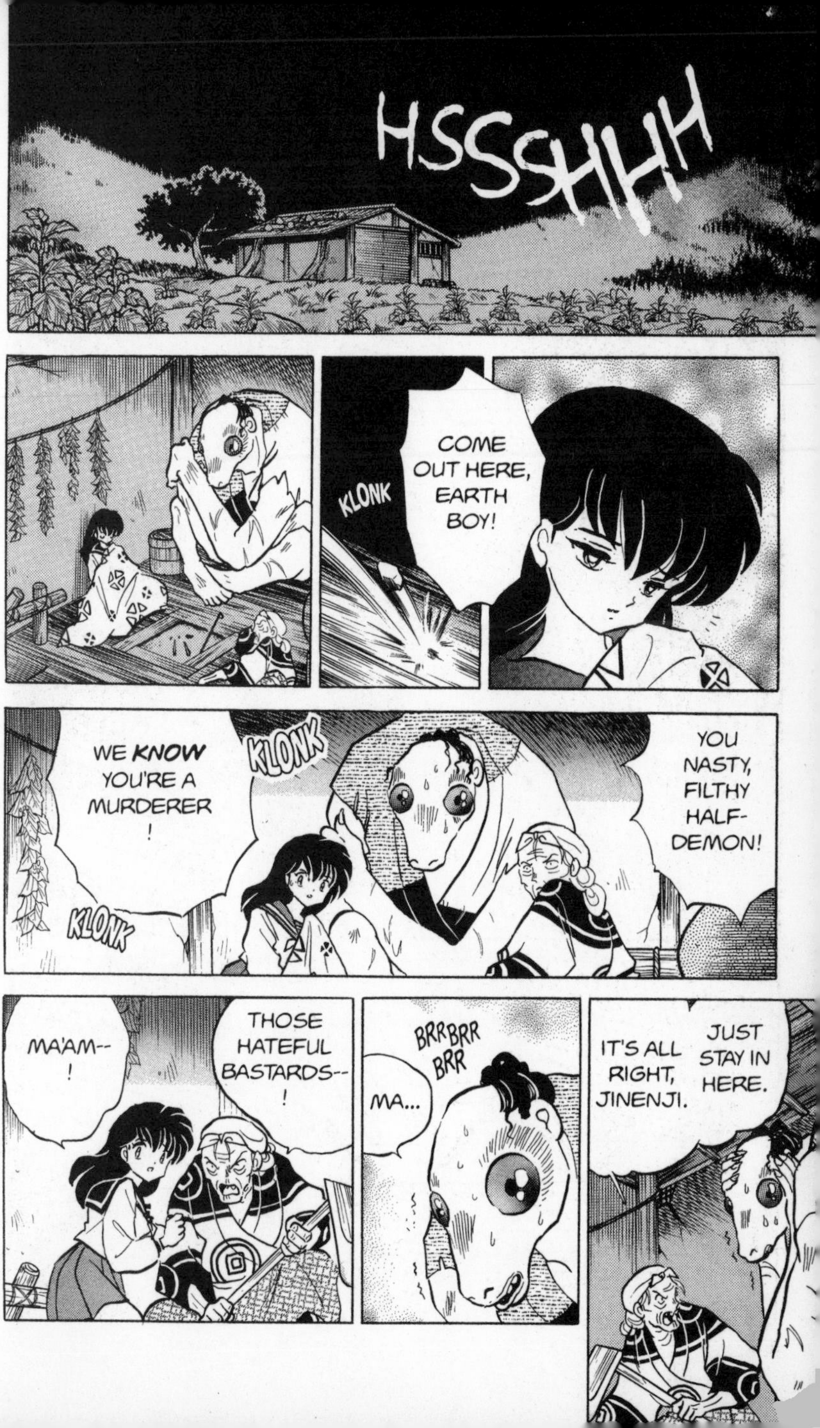
HSSSHHH
KLONK
COME OUT HERE, EARTH BOY!
WE KNOW YOU'RE A MURDERER!
KLONK
KLONK
YOU NASTY, FILTHY HALF-DEMON!
MA'AM--!
THOSE HATEFUL BASTARDS--!
BRRBRR BRR
MA...
IT'S ALL RIGHT, JINENJI.
JUST STAY IN HERE.

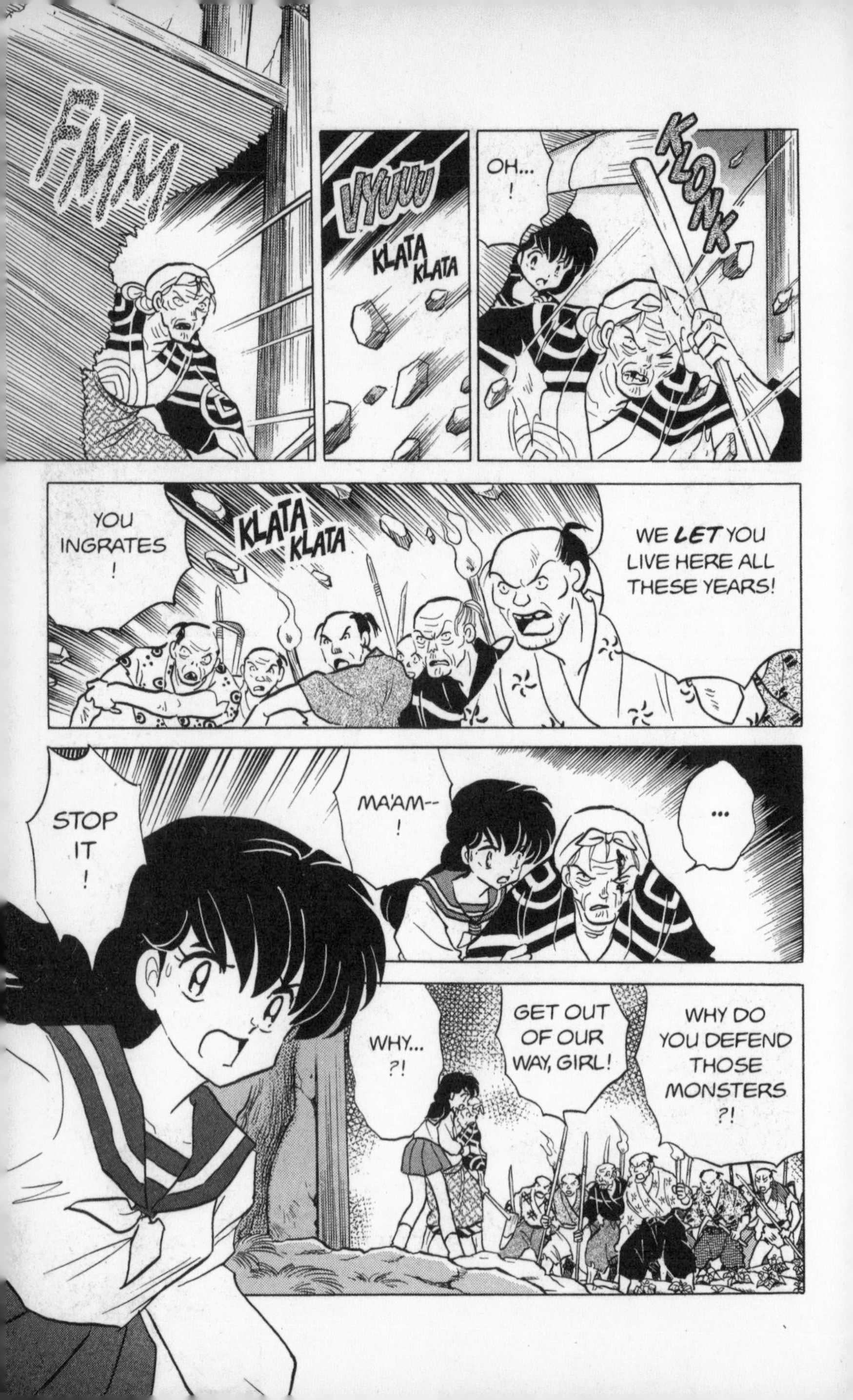
FMM
VYUUU
KLATA KLATA
OH... !
KLONK
YOU INGRATES !
KLATA KLATA
WE LET YOU LIVE HERE ALL THESE YEARS!
STOP IT !
MA'AM-- !
...
WHY... ?!
GET OUT OF OUR WAY, GIRL!
WHY DO YOU DEFEND THOSE MONSTERS ?!

BECAUSE...

JINENJI WOULD NEVER KILL ANYONE!

IF YOU SPENT ANY TIME WITH HIM AT ALL, YOU'D KNOW THAT!

HE'S A KIND AND GENTLE PERSON!

THE GIRL'S DOOMED HERSELF ALONG WITH THE OTHERS!

SHE LOVES THAT DEMON LAD!

SHE'S GOT A DEMON'S SOUL!

V-OOOO!

BWAK BWAK

THE SHED...!

NGGH...!

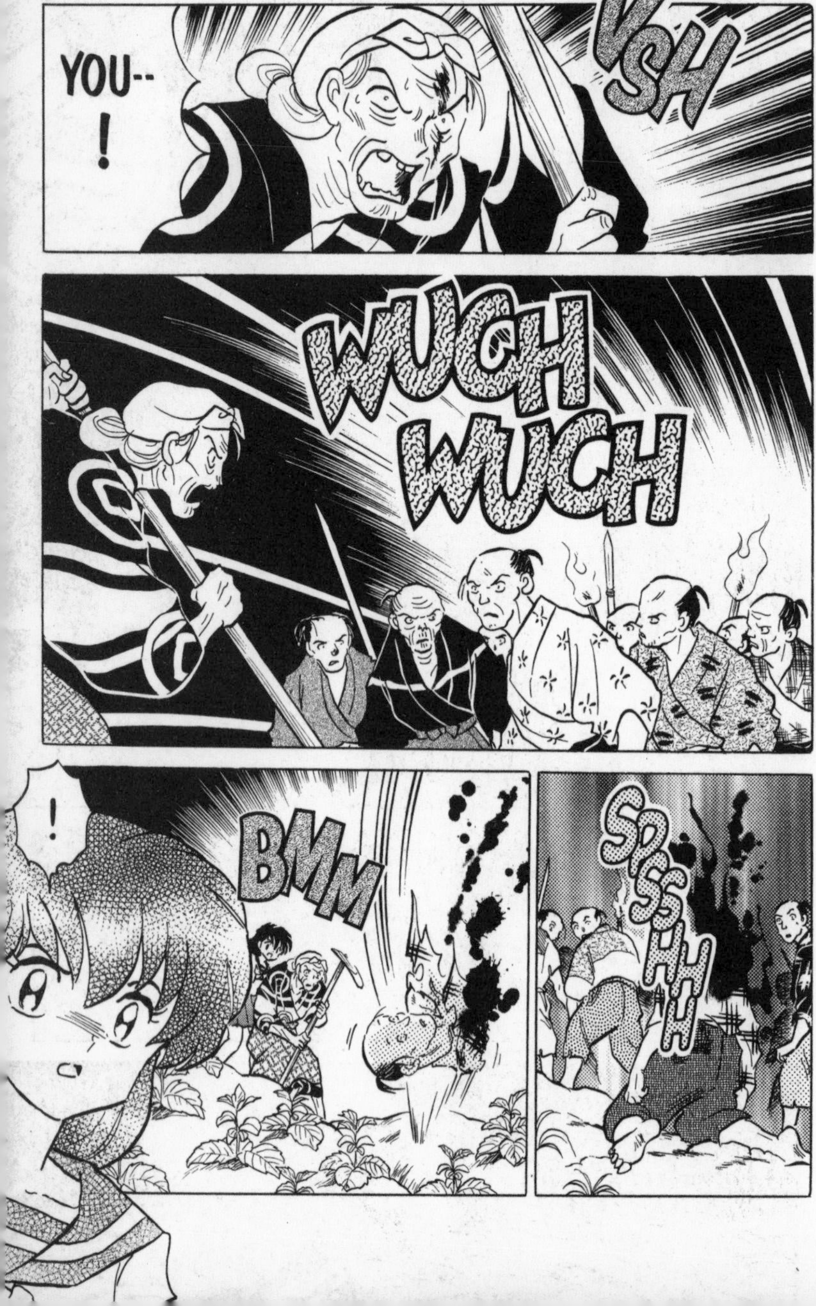
YOU--
!
VSH
WUGH WUGH
!
BMM
SPSSSHHH

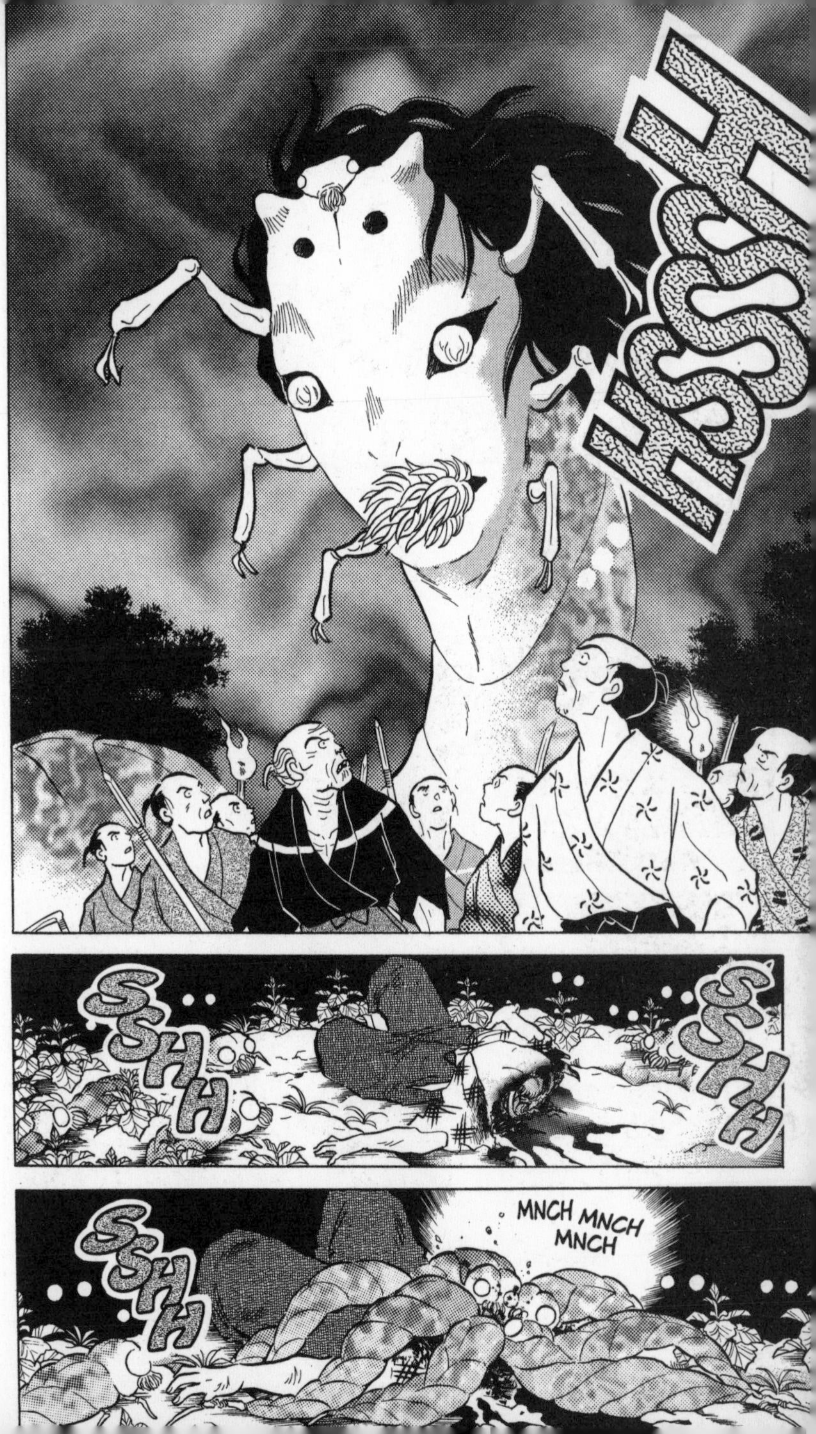
HISSSH!
SSHH
SSHH
SSHH
MNCH MNCH
MNCH

... MNCH MNCH MNCH

LOOK, YOU....

THEY WERE THE ONES... WHO WERE DEVOURING THE INNOCENT...!

HOOSH

UGH...

THUG

WAAH!

?!

BWACH BWACH

NOW, MY SWEETS... **YOU** HUNT THEM...!

HHSSS

CHITTER CHITTER CHITTER

HSSSHHH

NO...

NOO OO--!

I'VE **GOT** TO DO SOME- THING...!

SOME- HOW...

DGGG

OH...!

JINENJI, STAY AND PROTECT YOUR MOM!

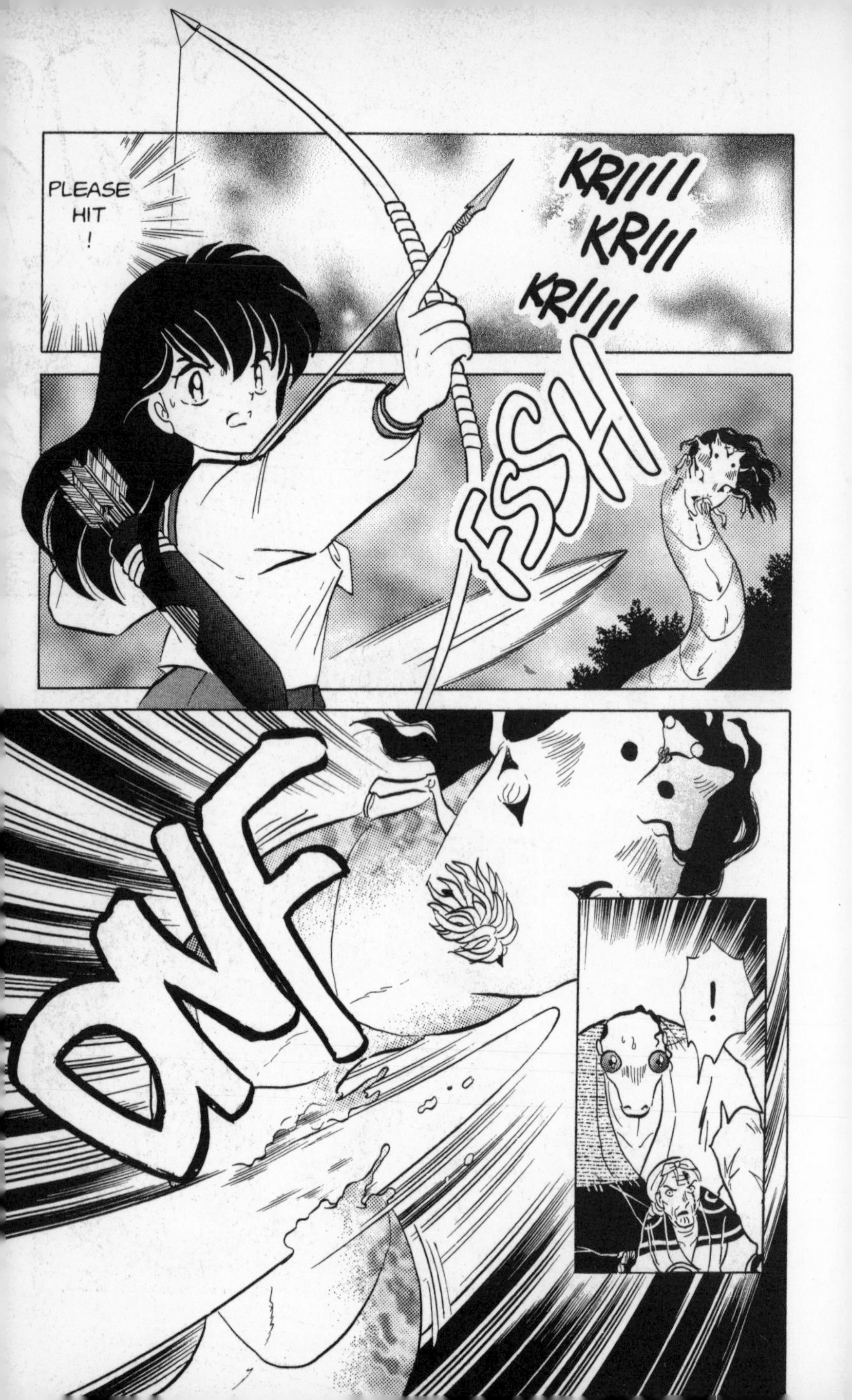
PLEASE HIT !
KRIIII KRIII KRIIII
FSSH
!

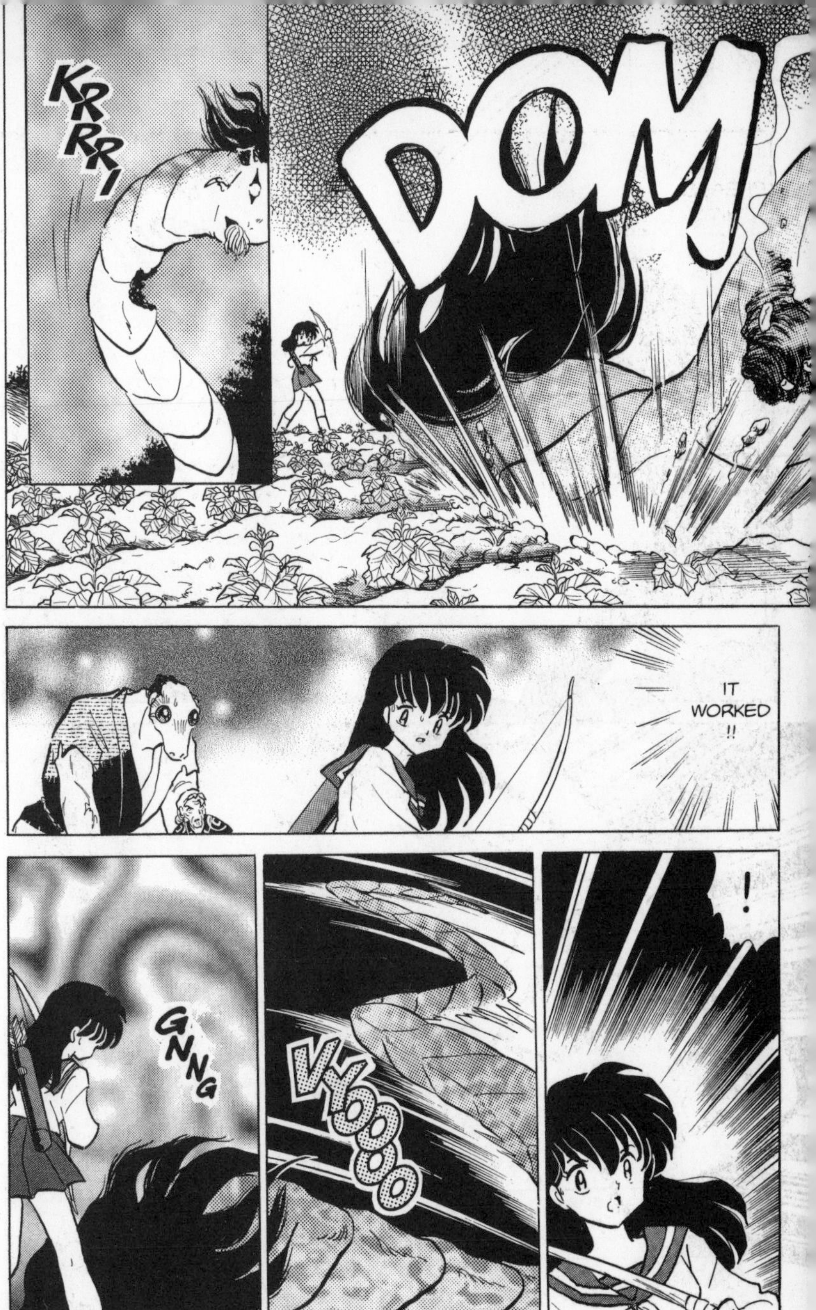
KRRRI
DOM
IT WORKED !!
GNNG
VYOOOO
!

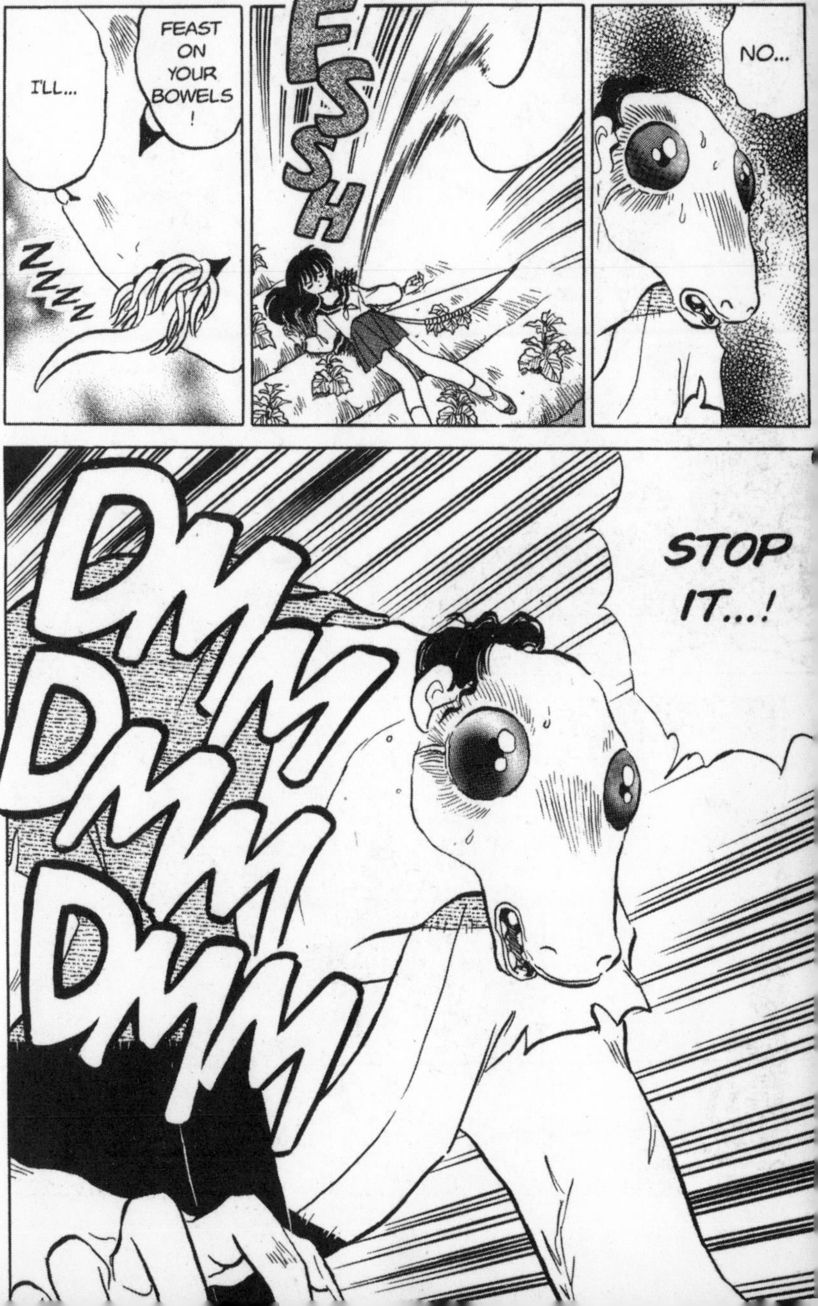
FEAST ON YOUR BOWELS !
I'LL...
ZZZZZ
FSSH
NO...
DMM DMM DMM
STOP IT...!

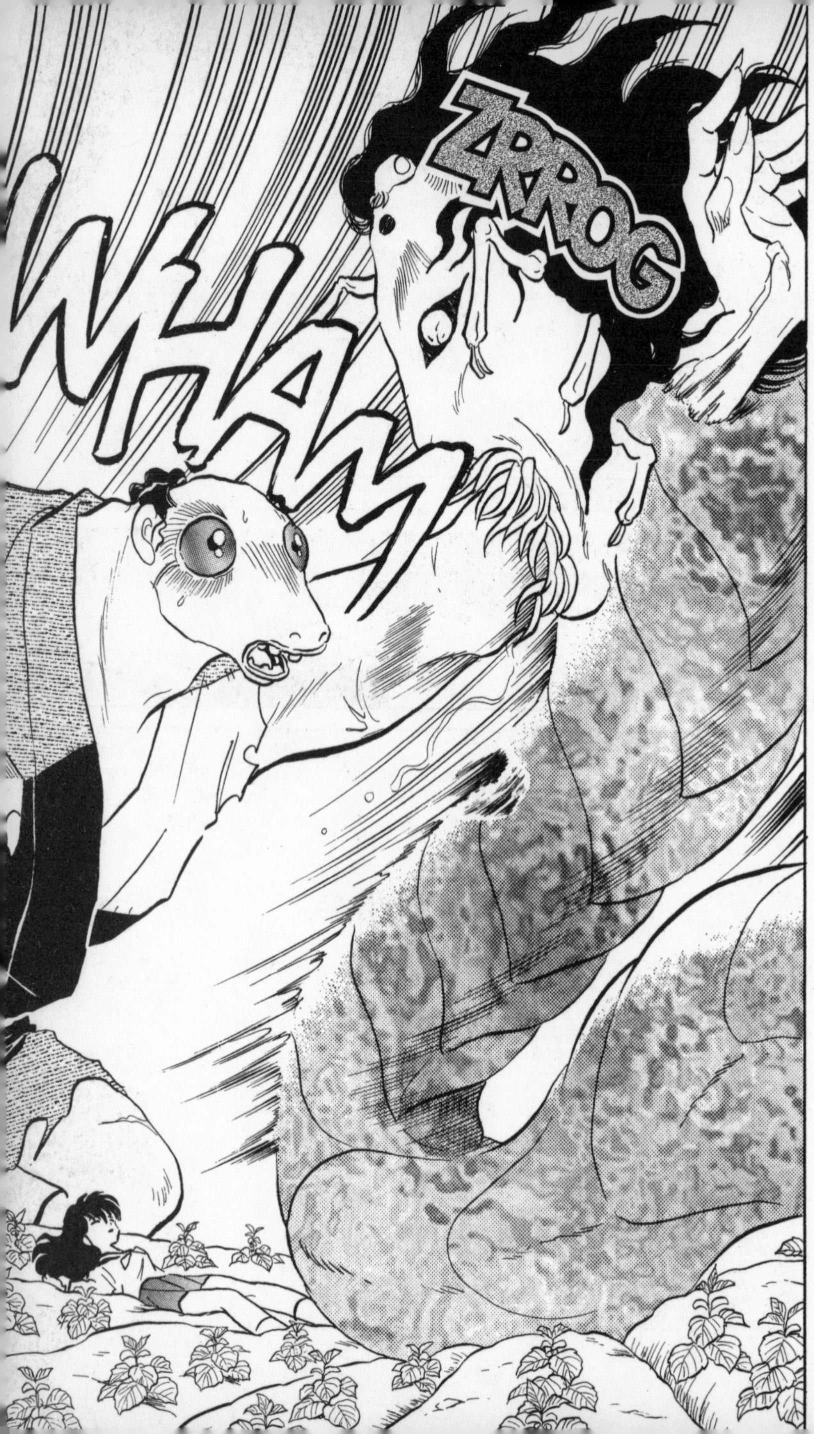
WHAM
ZRROG

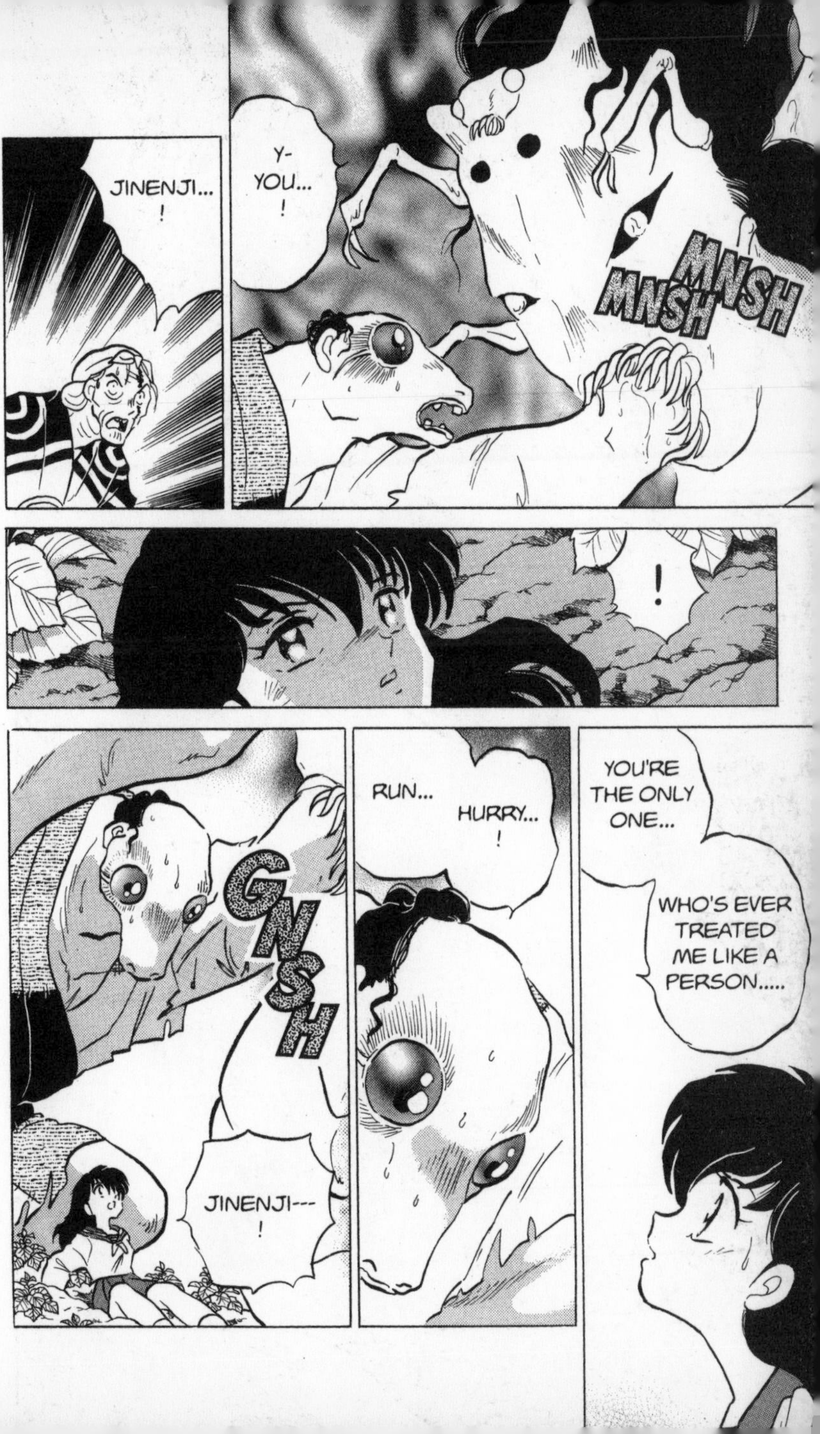
JINENJI... !
Y- YOU... !
MNSH MNSH
!
GNSH
JINENJI--- !
RUN... HURRY... !
YOU'RE THE ONLY ONE...
WHO'S EVER TREATED ME LIKE A PERSON.....

SCROLL SEVEN

THE BELONGING PLACE

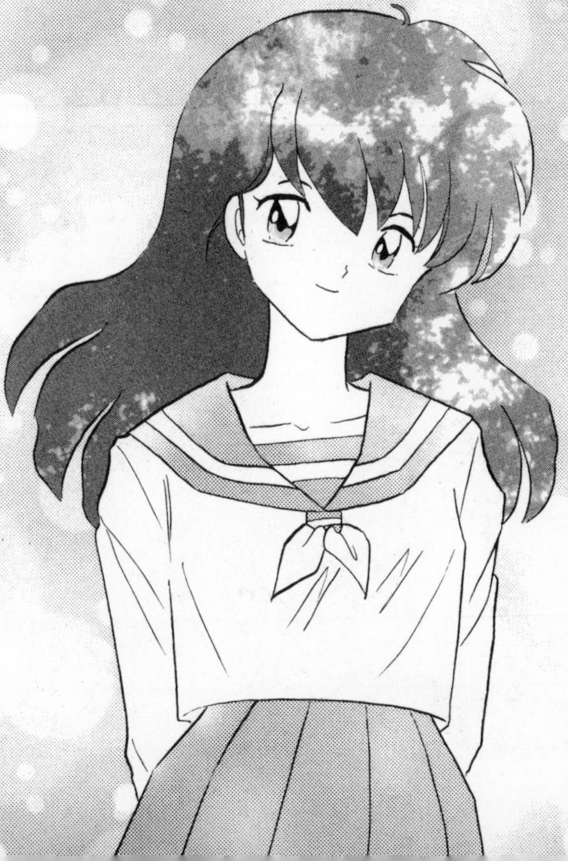

118

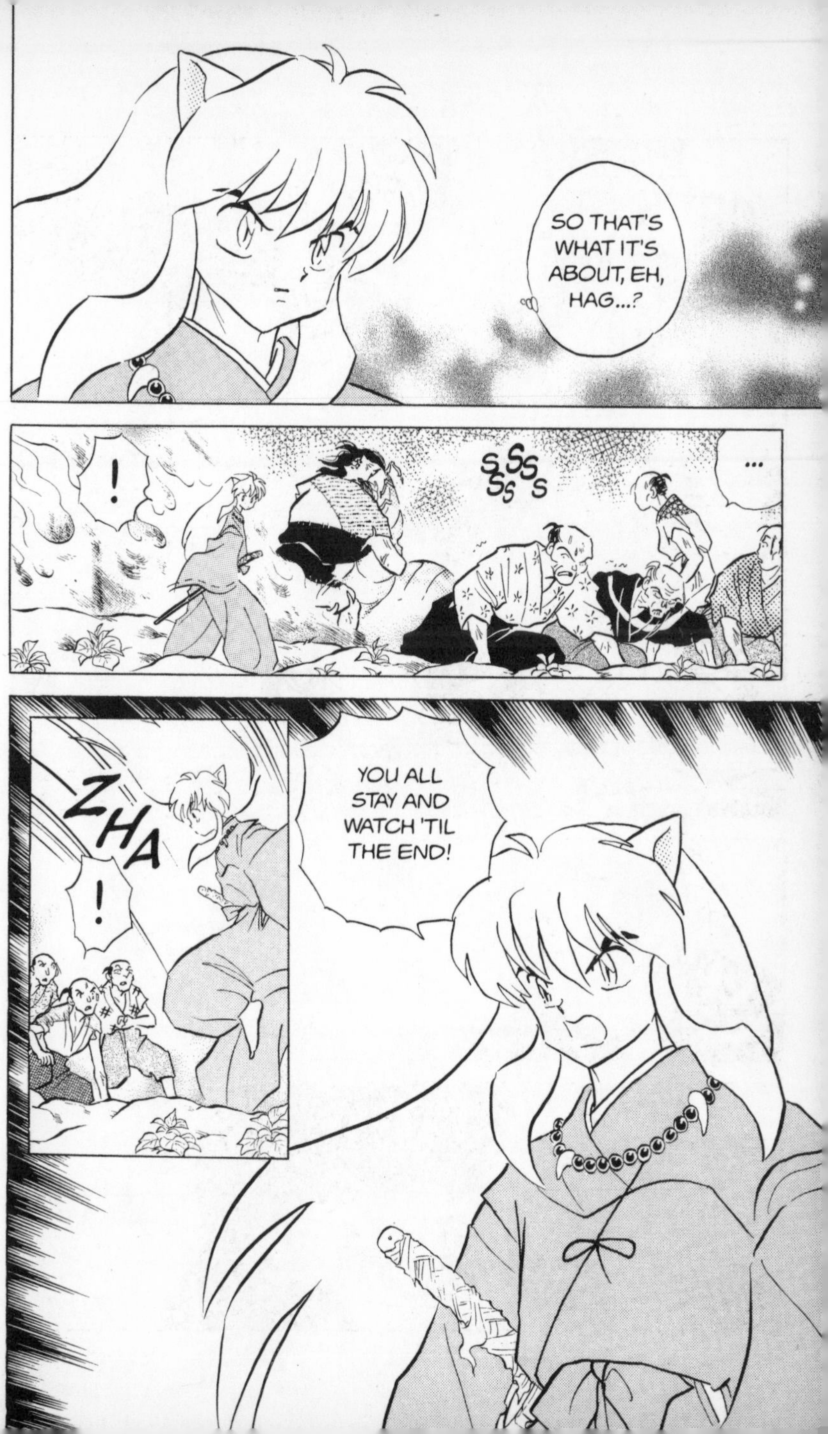
SO THAT'S WHAT IT'S ABOUT, EH, HAG...?
!
SSSSSS
...
ZHA
!
YOU ALL STAY AND WATCH 'TIL THE END!

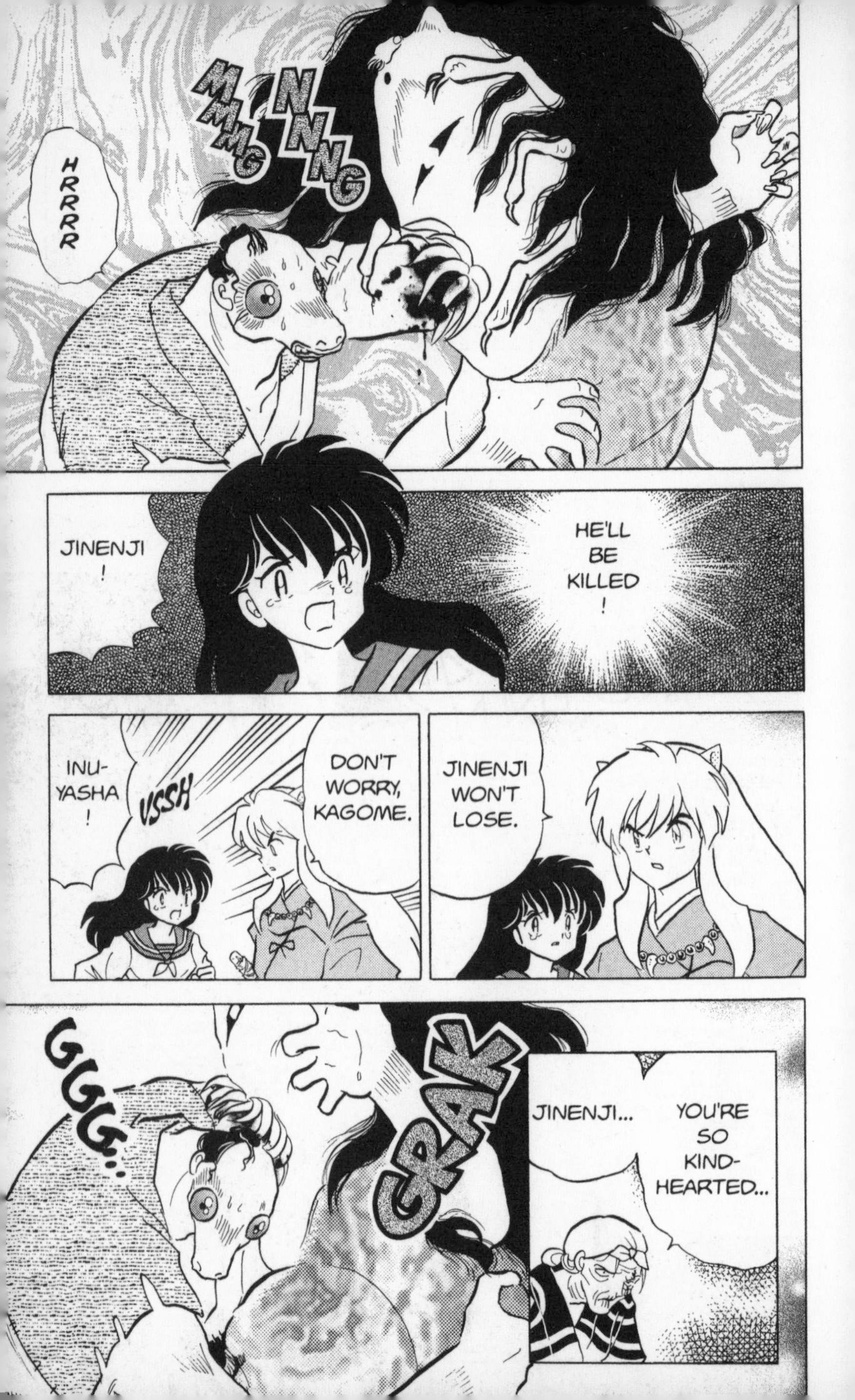
HRRRR
MMMG
NNNG
JINENJI!
HE'LL BE KILLED!
INU-YASHA!
VSSH
DON'T WORRY, KAGOME.
JINENJI WON'T LOSE.
GGG...
GRAK
JINENJI...
YOU'RE SO KIND-HEARTED...

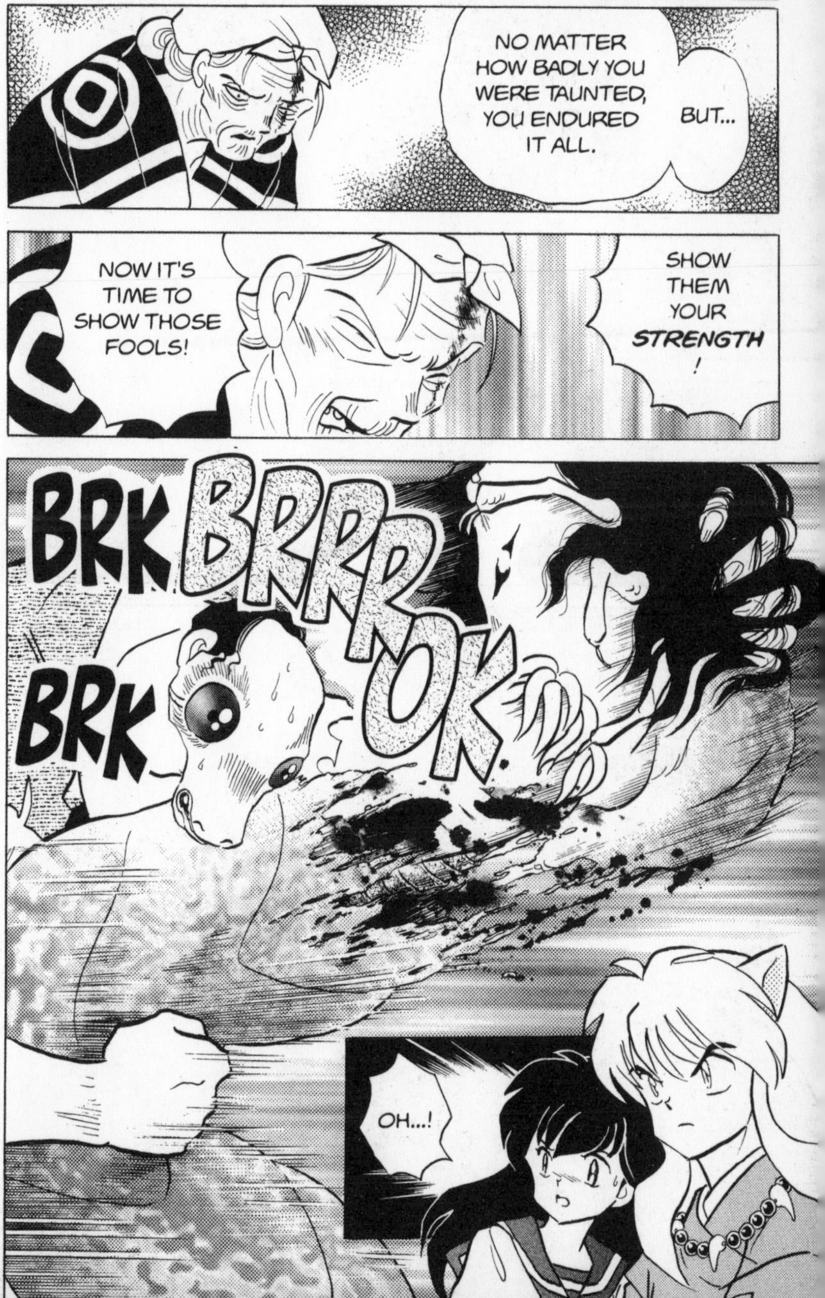
NO MATTER HOW BADLY YOU WERE TAUNTED, YOU ENDURED IT ALL.
BUT...
NOW IT'S TIME TO SHOW THOSE FOOLS!
SHOW THEM YOUR STRENGTH!
BRK
BRRRROK.
BRK
OH...!

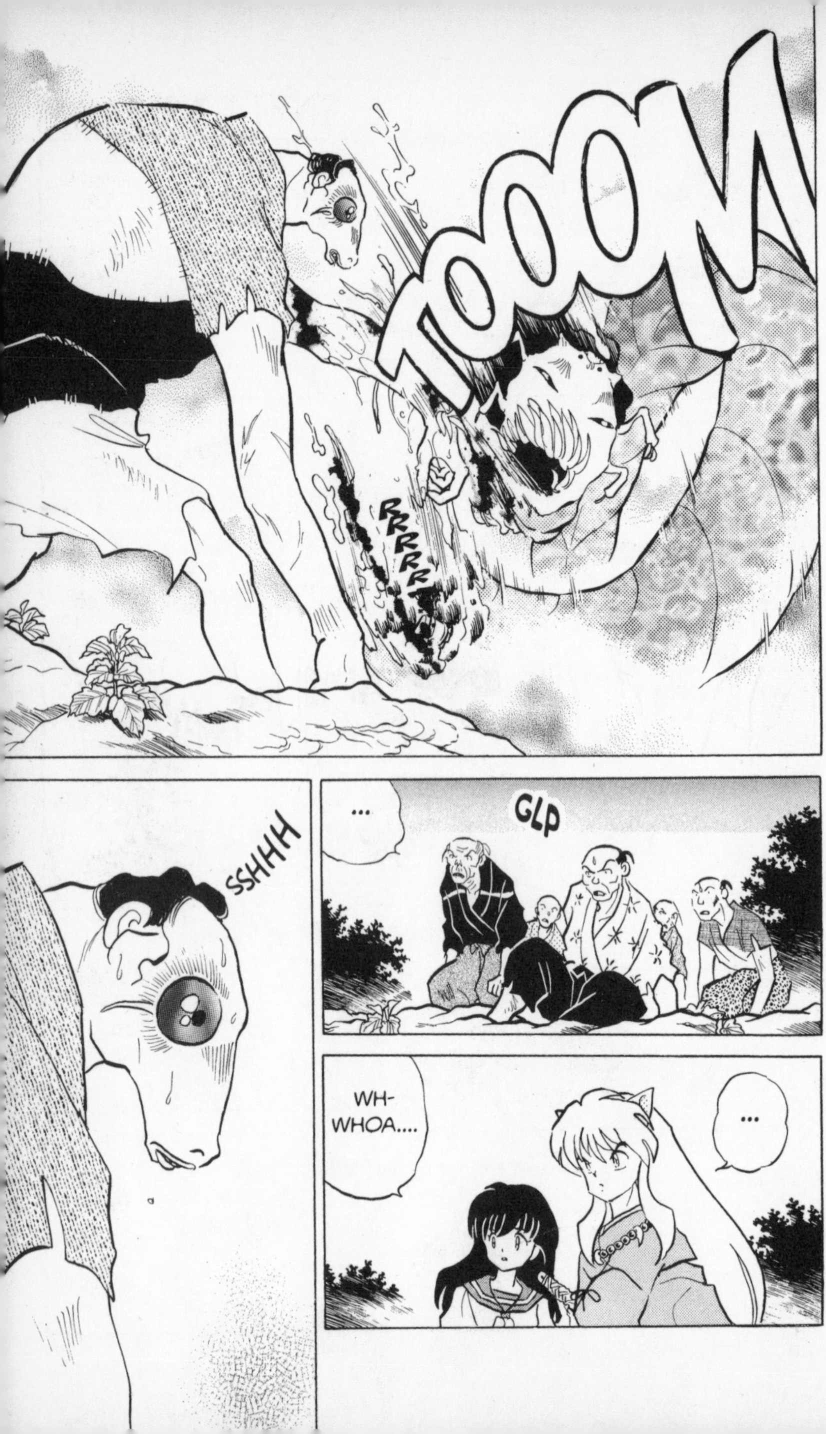
TOOOM
RRRRRT
SSHHH
...
GLP
WH-
WHOA....
...

HEH. MAYBE NOW THOSE VILLAGERS...

...WILL LAY OFF A BIT, EH?

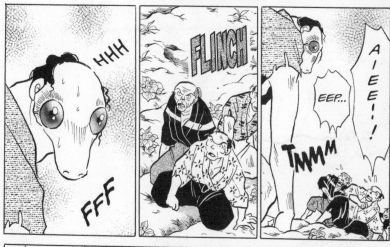

HHH

FFF

FLINCH

EEP...

A I E E !!!

TMMMM

WE'RE SORRY WE DISTRUSTED YOU!

P- PLEASE DON'T KILL US--!

THEY'RE TERRIFIED OF HIM!

SO ?

HOW ELSE DO YOU WANT IT?

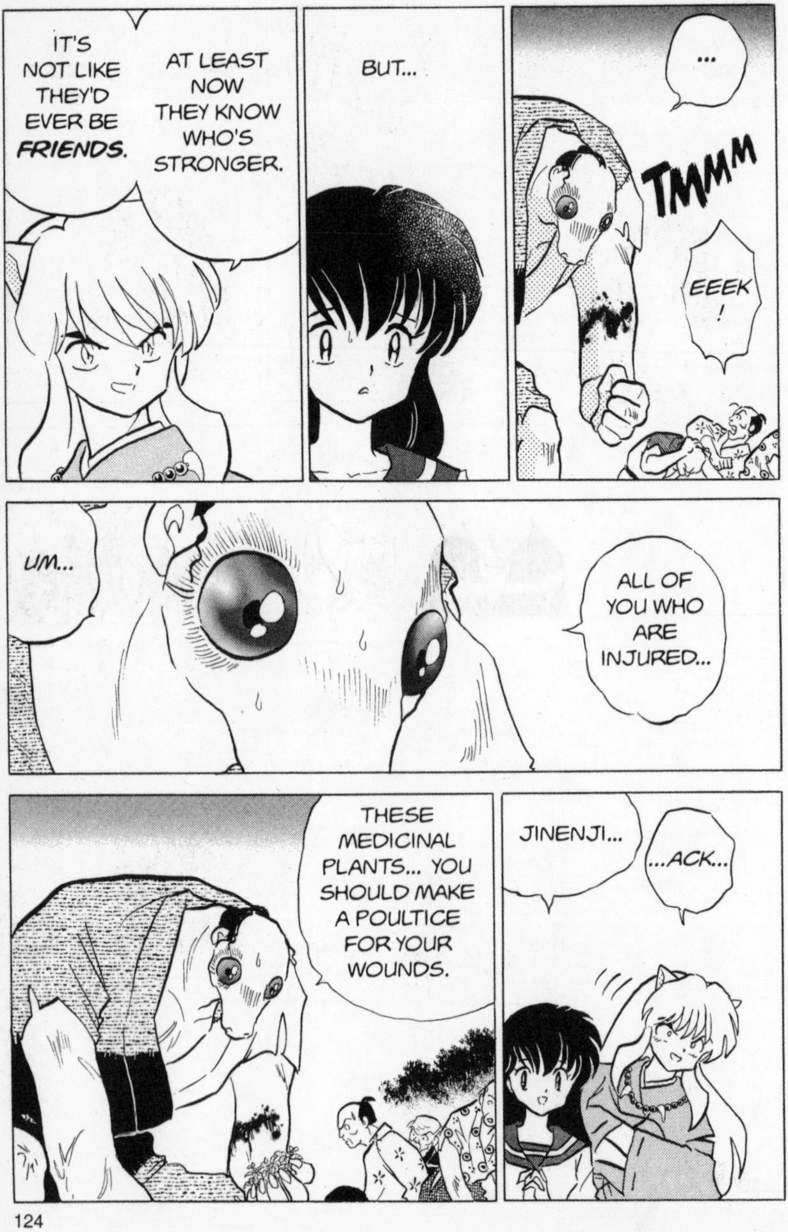
IT'S NOT LIKE THEY'D EVER BE *FRIENDS*.
AT LEAST NOW THEY KNOW WHO'S STRONGER.
BUT...
...
TMMM
EEEK!
UM...
ALL OF YOU WHO ARE INJURED...
THESE MEDICINAL PLANTS... YOU SHOULD MAKE A POULTICE FOR YOUR WOUNDS.
JINENJI...
...ACK...

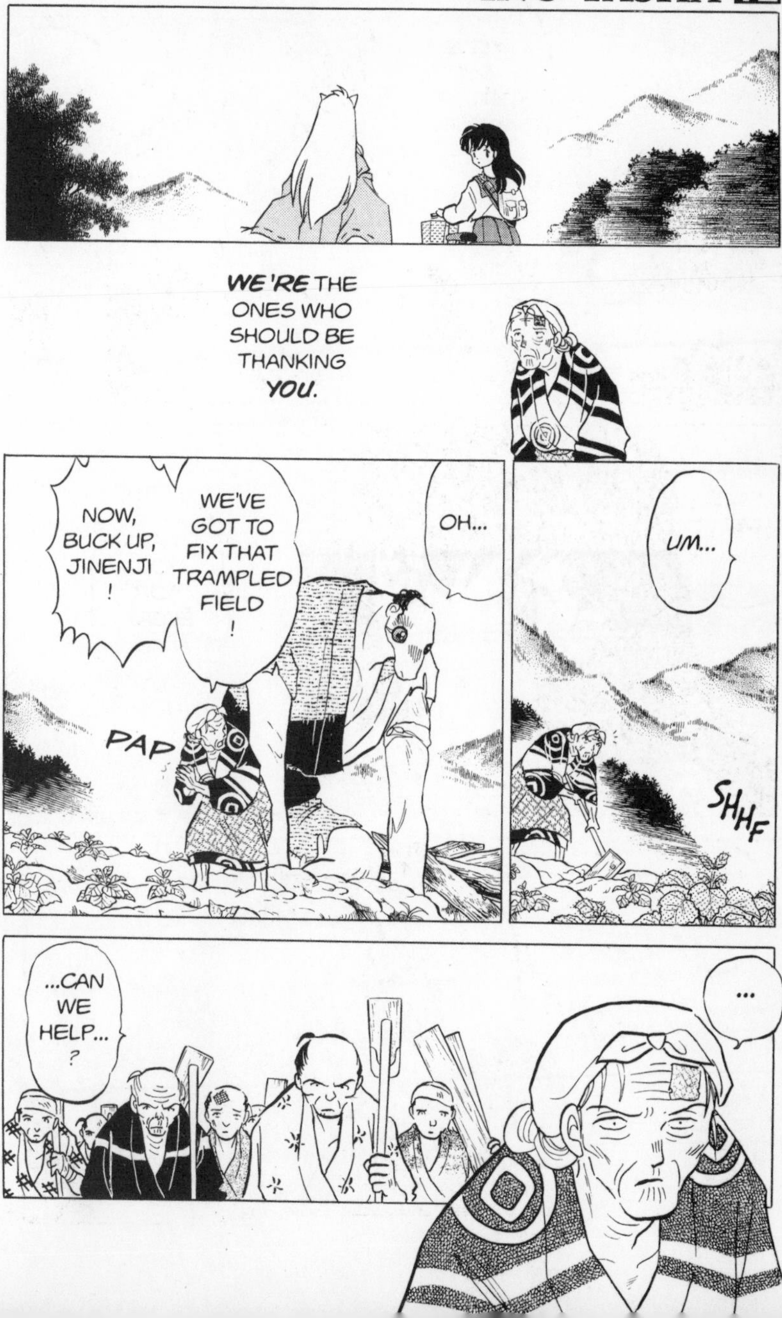
WE'RE THE ONES WHO SHOULD BE THANKING YOU.
NOW, BUCK UP, JINENJI!
WE'VE GOT TO FIX THAT TRAMPLED FIELD!
OH...
PAP
UM...
SHHF
...CAN WE HELP...?
...

DO AS YOU PLEASE.

KONG KONG

HEY...

YEAH--?

DID ANY-THING LIKE THAT...

EVER HAPPEN TO YOU TOO, INU-YASHA?

WHAT?

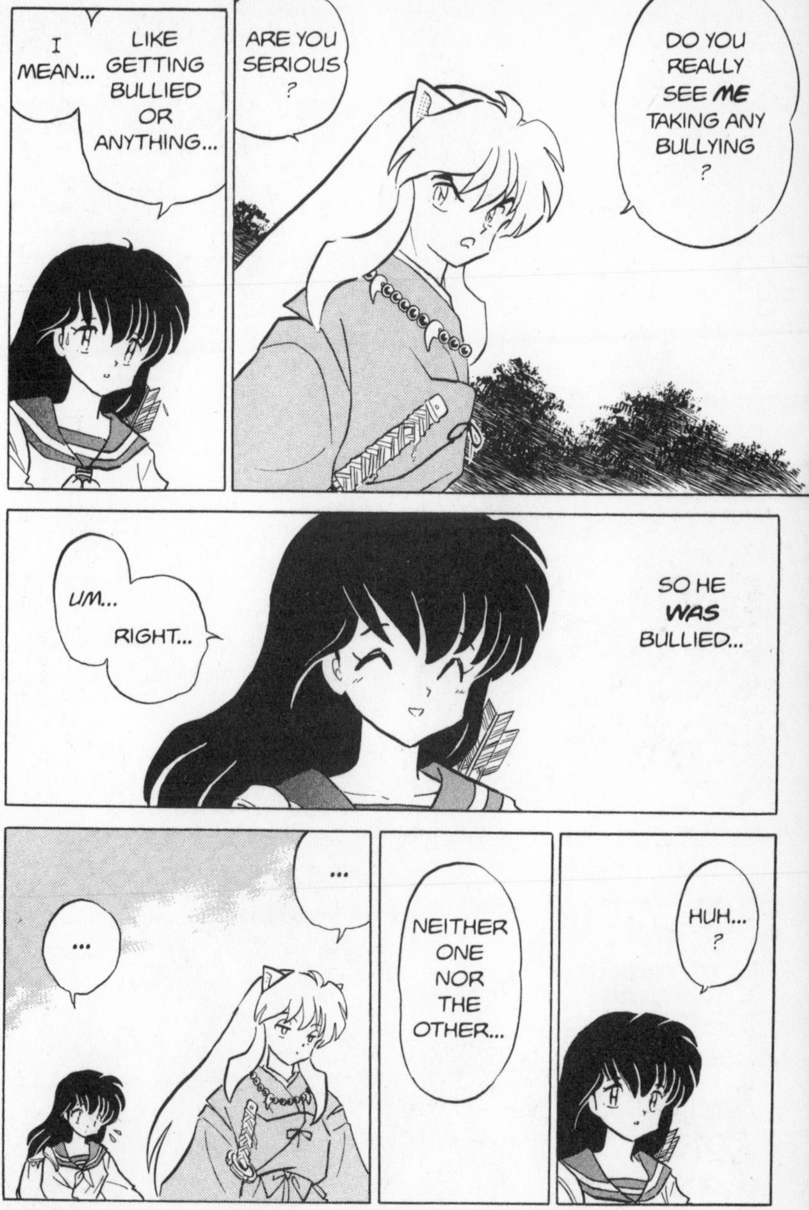

I MEAN... LIKE GETTING BULLIED OR ANYTHING...
ARE YOU SERIOUS?
DO YOU REALLY SEE *ME* TAKING ANY BULLYING?
UM... RIGHT...
SO HE *WAS* BULLIED...
...
...
NEITHER ONE NOR THE OTHER...
HUH...?

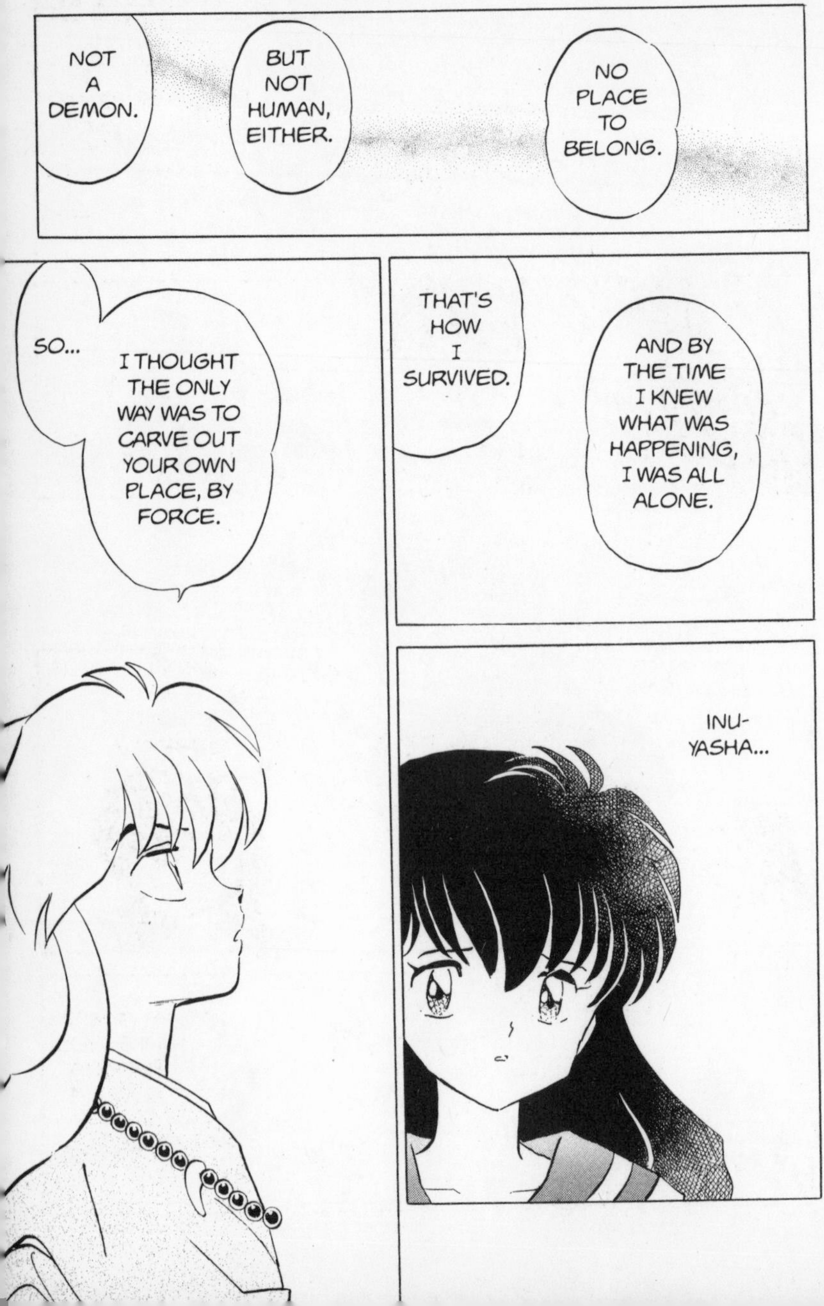
NOT A DEMON.
BUT NOT HUMAN, EITHER.
NO PLACE TO BELONG.
SO...
I THOUGHT THE ONLY WAY WAS TO CARVE OUT YOUR OWN PLACE, BY FORCE.
THAT'S HOW I SURVIVED.
AND BY THE TIME I KNEW WHAT WAS HAPPENING, I WAS ALL ALONE.
INU-YASHA...

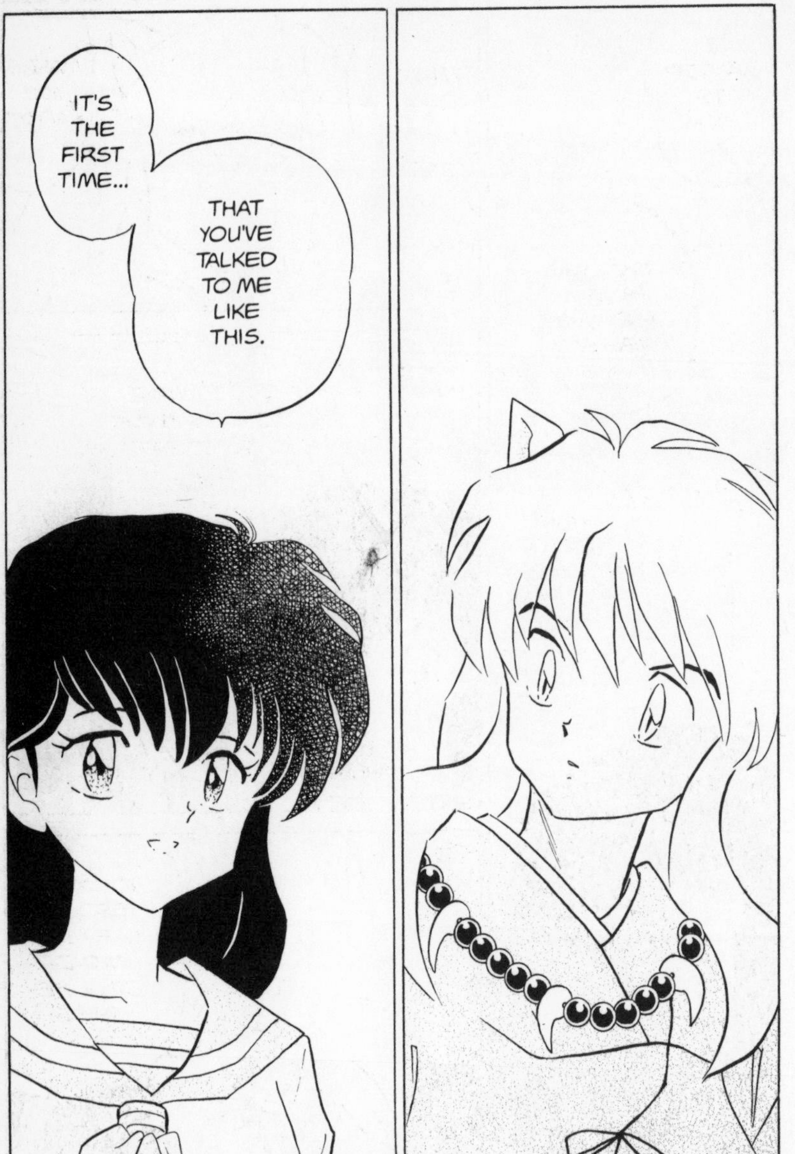
IT'S THE FIRST TIME...
THAT YOU'VE TALKED TO ME LIKE THIS.

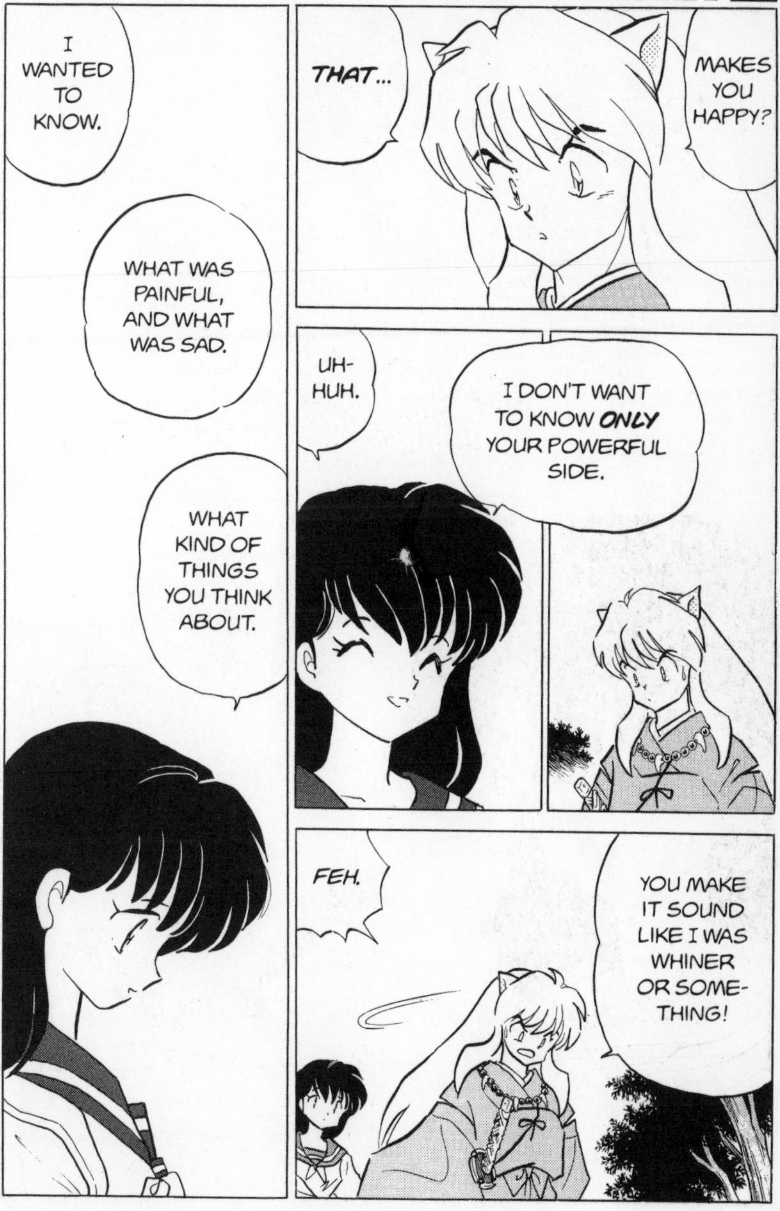
I WANTED TO KNOW.
WHAT WAS PAINFUL, AND WHAT WAS SAD.
WHAT KIND OF THINGS YOU THINK ABOUT.
THAT...
MAKES YOU HAPPY?
UH-HUH.
I DON'T WANT TO KNOW ONLY YOUR POWERFUL SIDE.
FEH.
YOU MAKE IT SOUND LIKE I WAS WHINER OR SOME-THING!

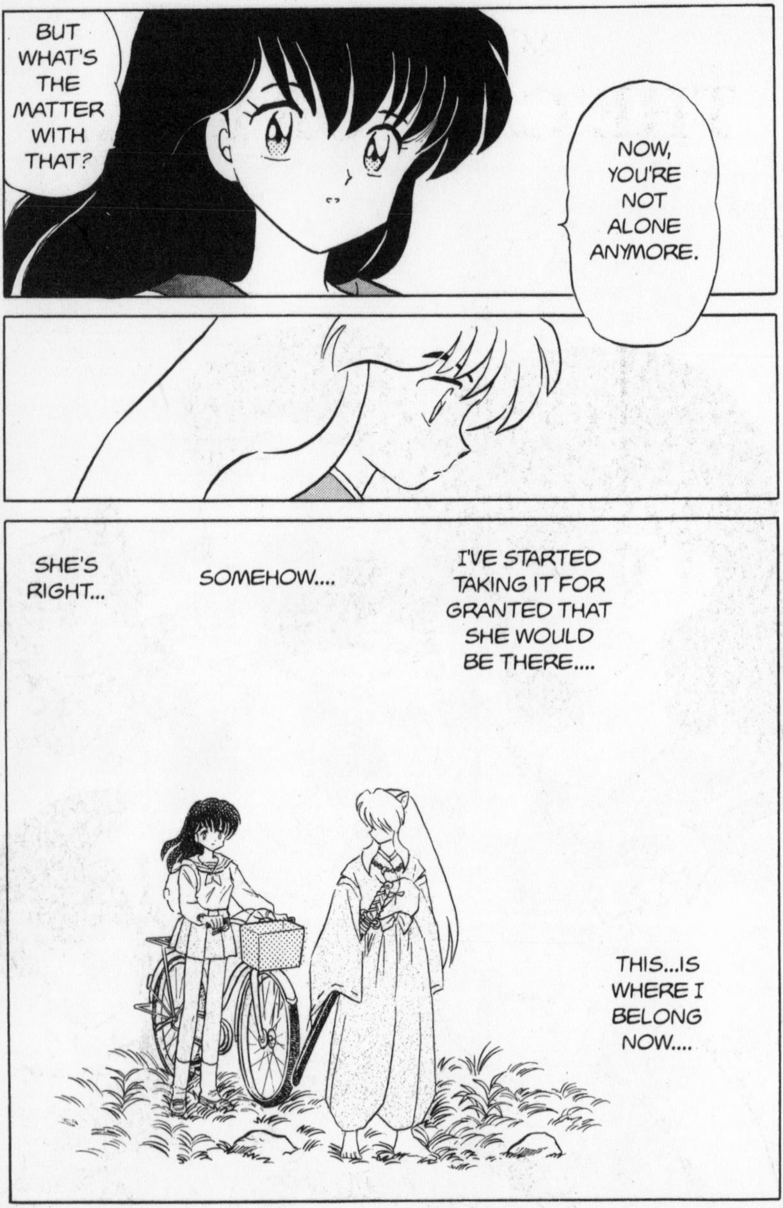
BUT WHAT'S THE MATTER WITH THAT?
NOW, YOU'RE NOT ALONE ANYMORE.
SHE'S RIGHT...
SOMEHOW....
I'VE STARTED TAKING IT FOR GRANTED THAT SHE WOULD BE THERE....
THIS...IS WHERE I BELONG NOW....

SCROLL EIGHT

THE CAVE OF EVIL

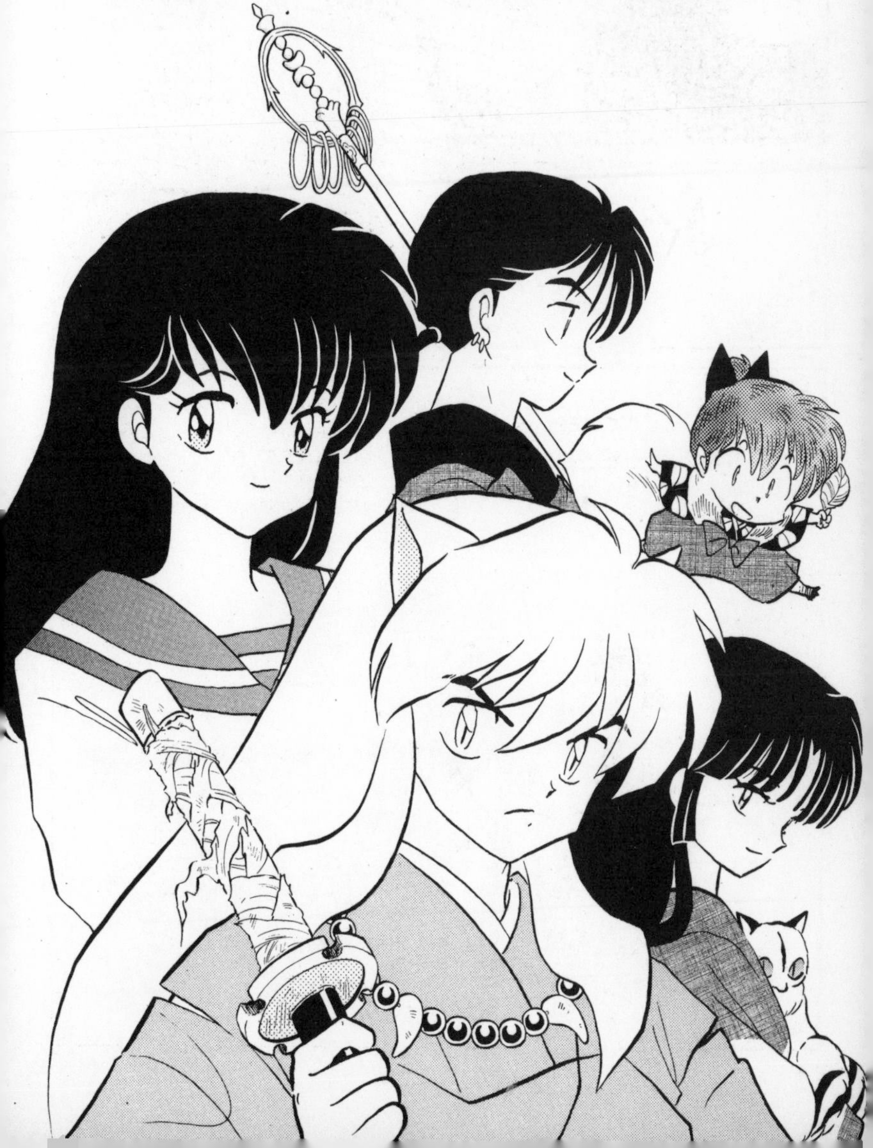

IS THIS THE TEMPLE WHERE THE PRIESTESS KNOWN AS KIKYO LIVES?!

ARE YOU HER...?

B-BMP

THE ONE WHO TREATS THOSE WHO HAVE BEEN INJURED IN BATTLE, BE THEY FRIEND OR FOE...?

I HEAR THAT YOUR WONDROUS SPELLS HAVE PLUCKED COUNTLESS SOULS FROM DEATH'S DOORWAY.

...

THERE ARE NO WONDROUS SPELLS.

I JUST HAVE A BIT OF MEDICAL KNOWLEDGE.

...WE'LL HEAR YOUR TALE AT THE CASTLE.

COME ALONG!

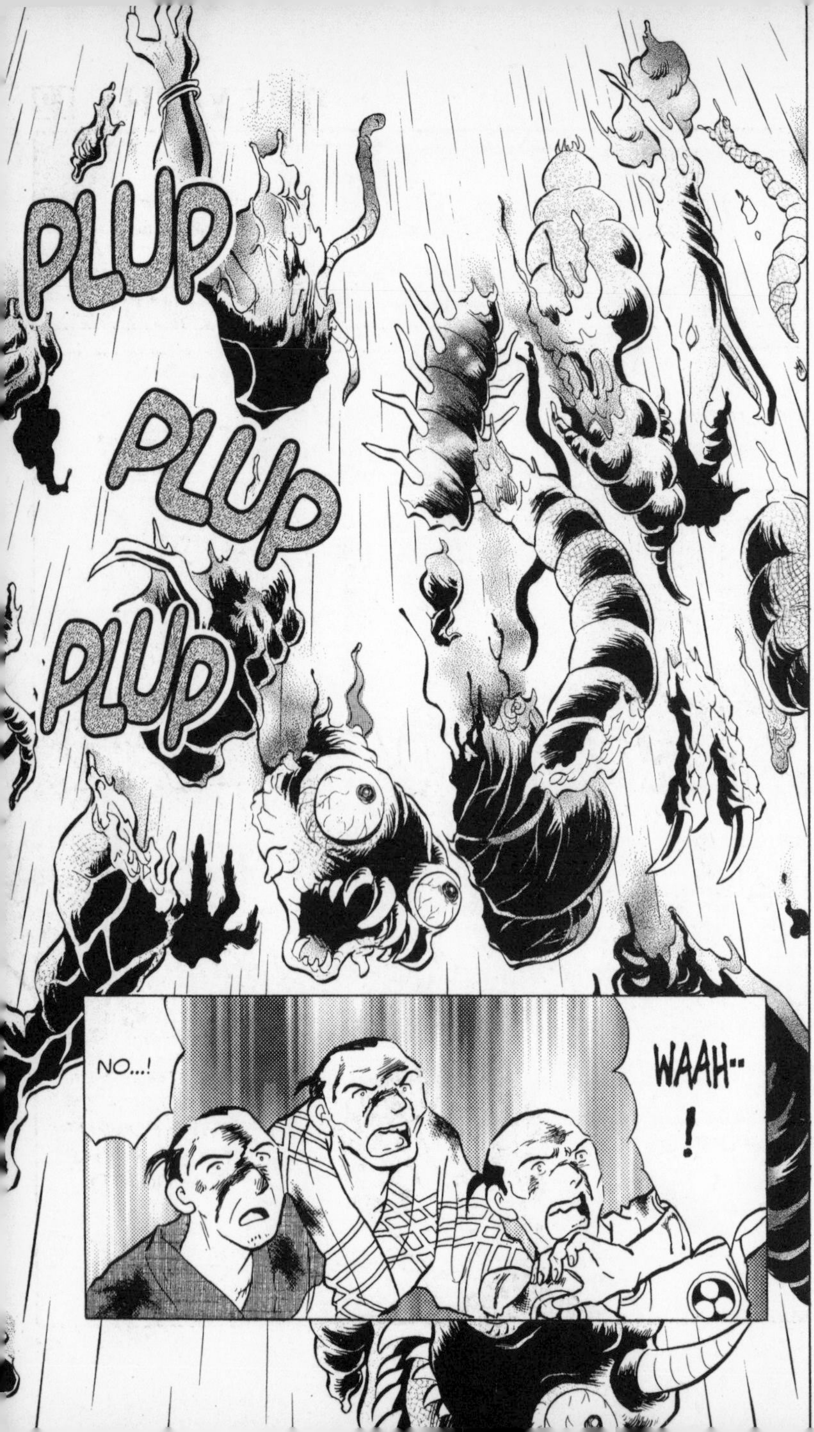
PLUP
PLUP
PLUP
NO...!
WAAH--!

IN ANY CASE...

I'VE ALREADY ACCEPTED THEIR PAYMENT.

NOW WE'RE OBLIGATED.

WHEN IN THE WORLD...

DON'T DO THINGS LIKE THAT!

KLANK

...

SANGO....

WHAT'S THE MATTER?

I WAS WONDERING...

IF THERE WERE ANY DEMONS OTHER THAN NARAKU... WHO COULD EMIT SUCH TERRIBLE WAVES OF EVIL.

...

OUR HITOMI CLAN LEADER LORD KAGEWAKI WAS BORN WITH A WEAK CONSTITUTION.

YESTERDAY, OUR PREVIOUS LORD PASSED AWAY AND HE SUCCEEDED TO THE TITLE...

AND THOUGH HIS BODY HAS BEEN FAILING HIM QUICKLY...

HE WON'T EVEN LET US, HIS RETAINERS, NEAR HIM.... MUCH LESS DOCTORS.

NO, I CANNOT!

I WAS TOLD TO LET NO ONE PASS...!

STAND ASIDE! STAND ASIDE, I SAY!

I BROUGHT A PRIESTESS WHO CAN CURE LORD KAGEWAKI'S ILLNESS!

THE LORD WILL NOT SEE ANYONE!

EH? THIS CASTLE...

THE RETAINERS, ALL MERE MORTALS, BUT...

WHA...

OH !

ZZZp

THE EVIL AURA THAT PERMEATES THE CASTLE...

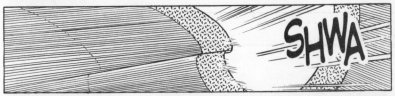

SHWA

SHHF...

EMANATES FROM *THIS* MAN...?!

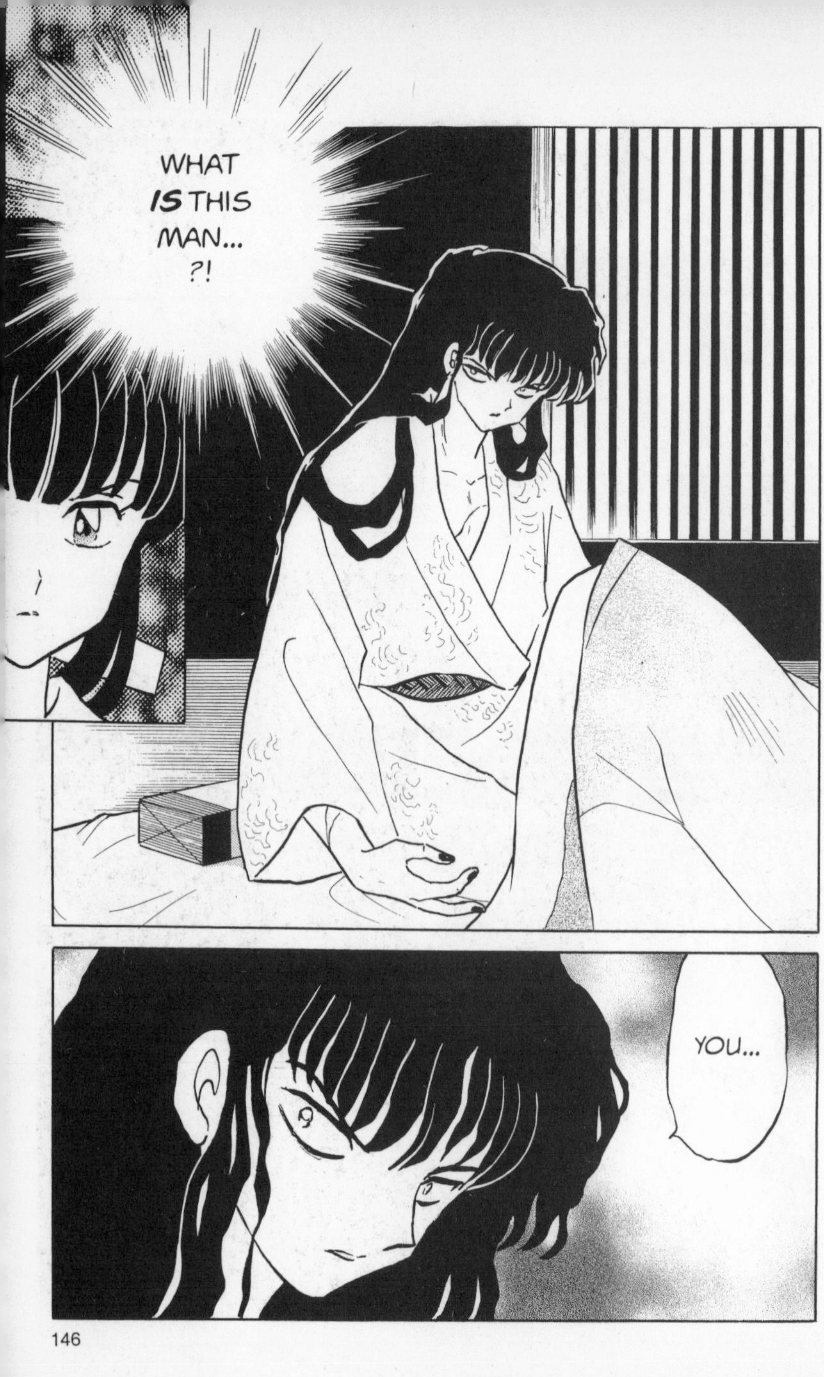
WHAT *IS* THIS MAN...?!
YOU...

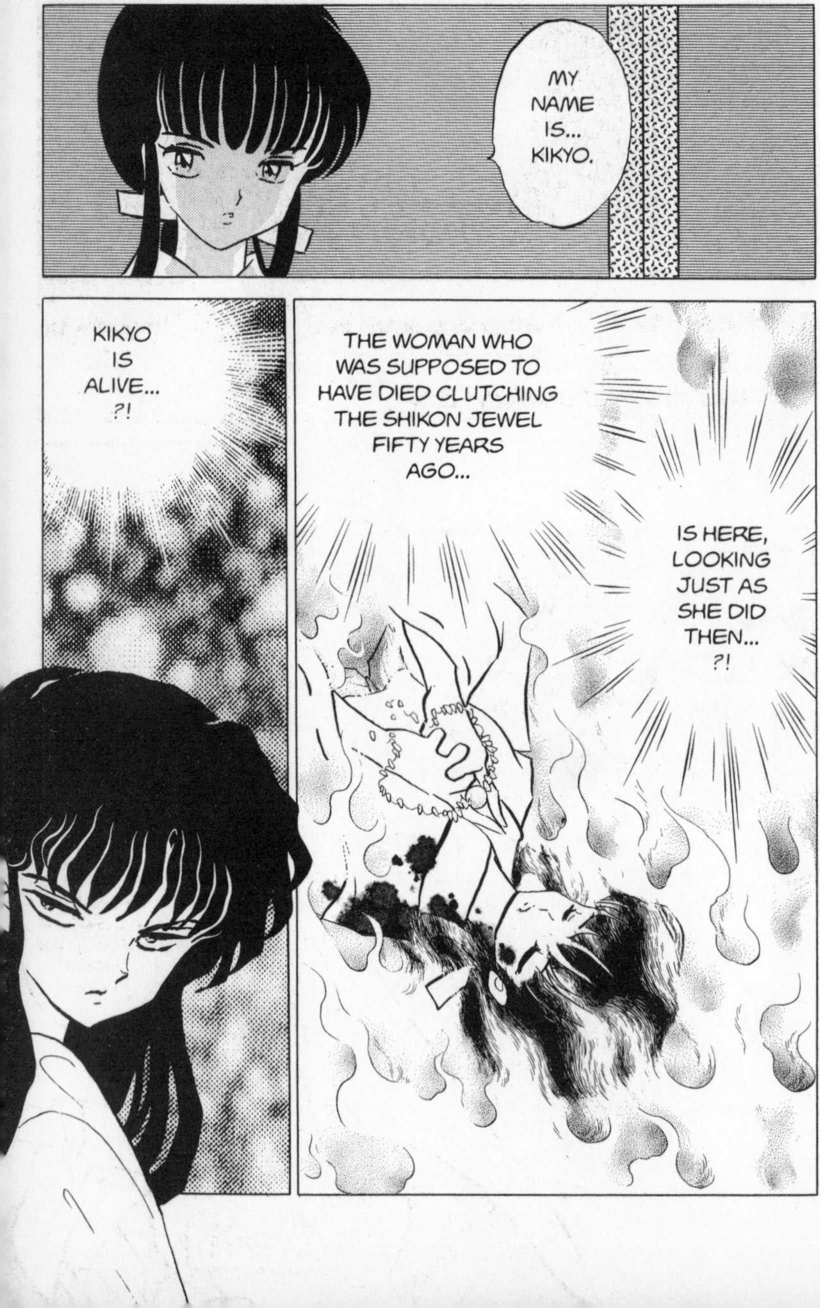
MY NAME IS... KIKYO.
KIKYO IS ALIVE... ?!
THE WOMAN WHO WAS SUPPOSED TO HAVE DIED CLUTCHING THE SHIKON JEWEL FIFTY YEARS AGO...
IS HERE, LOOKING JUST AS SHE DID THEN... ?!

WHO **IS** THIS WOMAN...?!

HWOOOOO

AREN'T WE CLOSE TO THE BORDER?

CLOSE ENOUGH.

THANKS TO THE POISONOUS VAPORS, NOT A TREE OR A BLADE OF GRASS CAN GROW HERE.

SHF

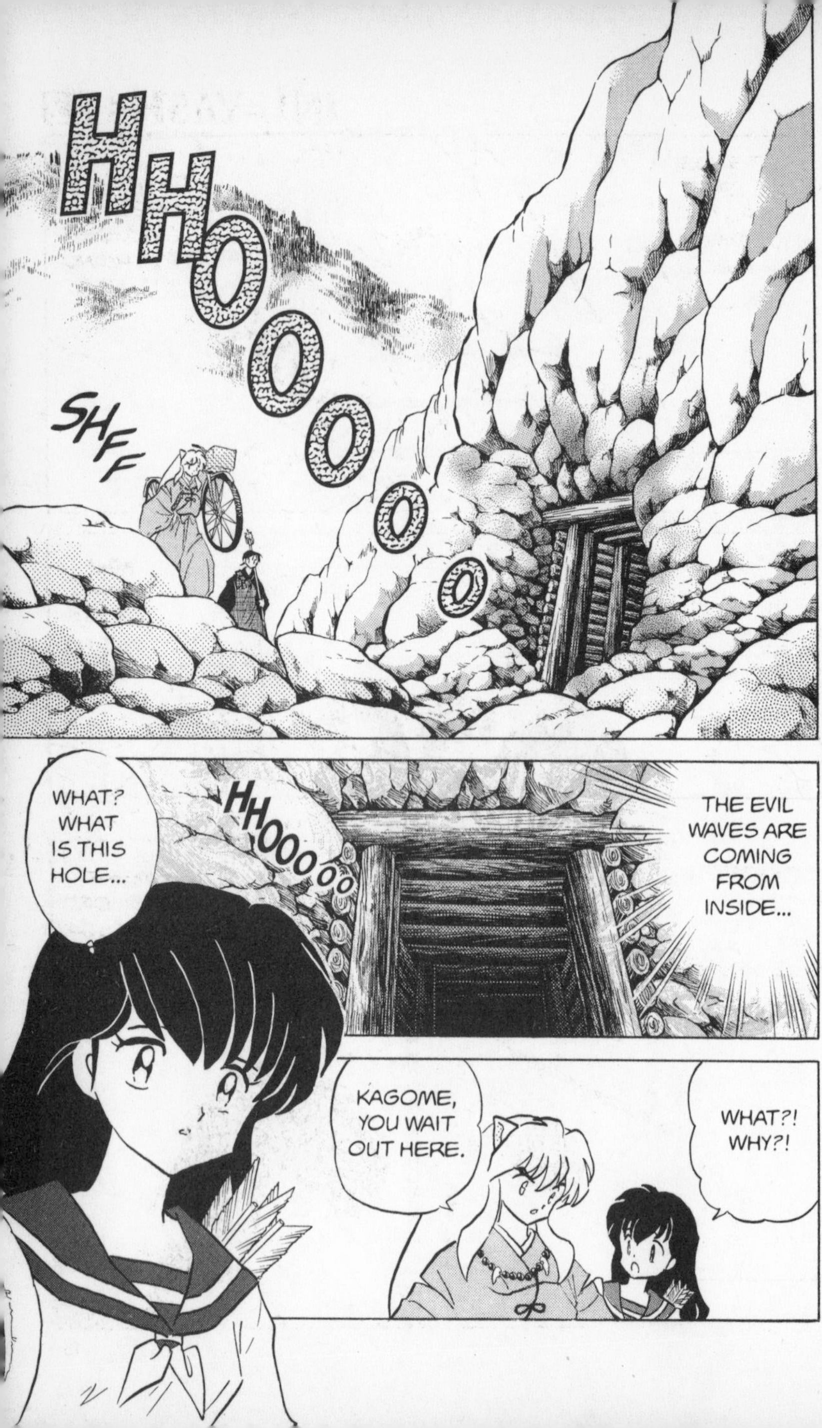
HHOOOOOO
SHFF
WHAT? WHAT IS THIS HOLE...
HHOOOOOO
THE EVIL WAVES ARE COMING FROM INSIDE...
KAGOME, YOU WAIT OUT HERE.
WHAT?! WHY?!

THERE IS AN EVER LARGER EVIL POWER ROILING ABOUT...

OUTSIDE THE CASTLE... TOWARD THE MOUNTAINS... THERE'S SOMETHING.

NOW, IF YOU'LL EXCUSE ME...

THE LORD HAS ORDERED US TO NOT LET YOU OUT OF THE CASTLE.

KIKYO... AFTER FIFTY YEARS... HUH.

I MUST LEARN THE TRUTH ABOUT THIS.

BUT WHETHER I LET HER LIVE OR KILL HER...

...SHE SHOULD PROVE TO BE A MOST USEFUL WOMAN...

SCROLL NINE

FULFILLMENT

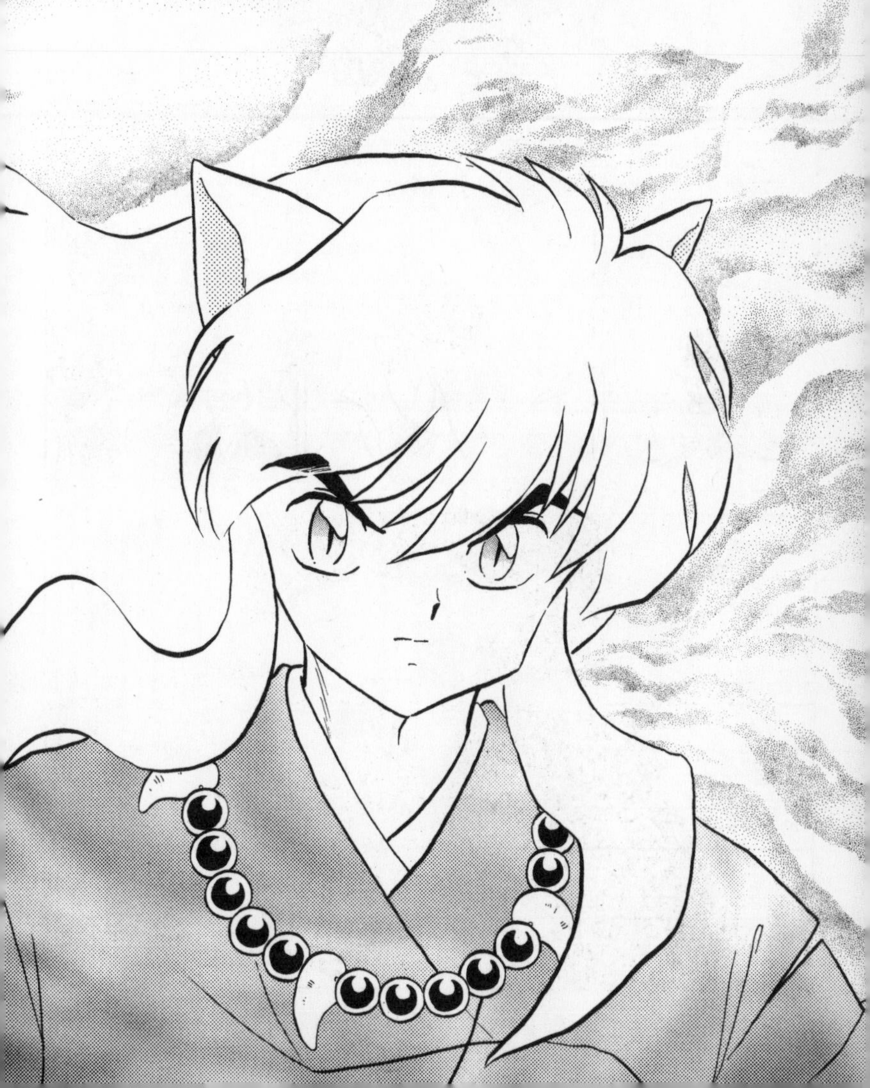

HHSS

THE EVIL AURA GROWS IN THE MOUNTAINS...

TONIGHT... THE FULFILLMENT WILL COME AT LAST....

GWOOOO

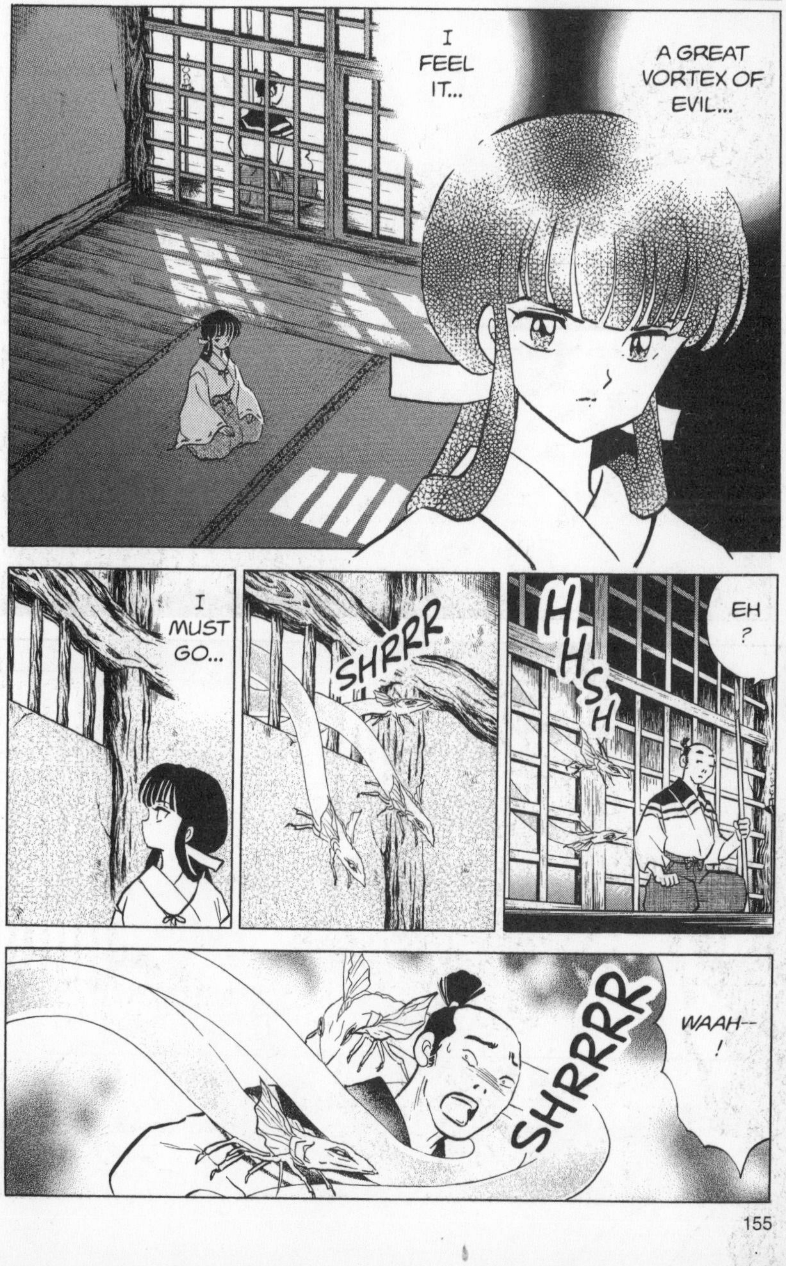
I FEEL IT...
A GREAT VORTEX OF EVIL...
I MUST GO...
SHRRR
HHHSH
EH ?
SHRRRR
WAAH-- !

KAGOME... HOW IS IT THAT YOU ARE SO UN-AFFECTED?

KNOCK WOOD.

I'M FINE TOO.

GLOW

THE AURA MUST BE MORE POWERFUL INSIDE...

WOOOO

YEAH... PROBABLY....

I HOPE INU-YASHA AND LORD MIROKU ARE OKAY....

...

BLEHHH

DO YOU HAVE TO DO THAT, MIROKU?

IT'S EMBAR-RASSING.

SH-SHUT UP.

ONLY MY YEARS OF TRAINING MAKE IT POSSIBLE FOR ME TO KEEP GOING IN THE FACE OF SUCH AN EVIL MIASMA.

A NORMAL MAN WOULD BE DEAD BY NOW.

BOOM

THERE'S SOMETHING UP AHEAD!

AND NOT JUST ONE...!

WAFT

WE'RE GOING IN!

LIGHT?!

GLEEM

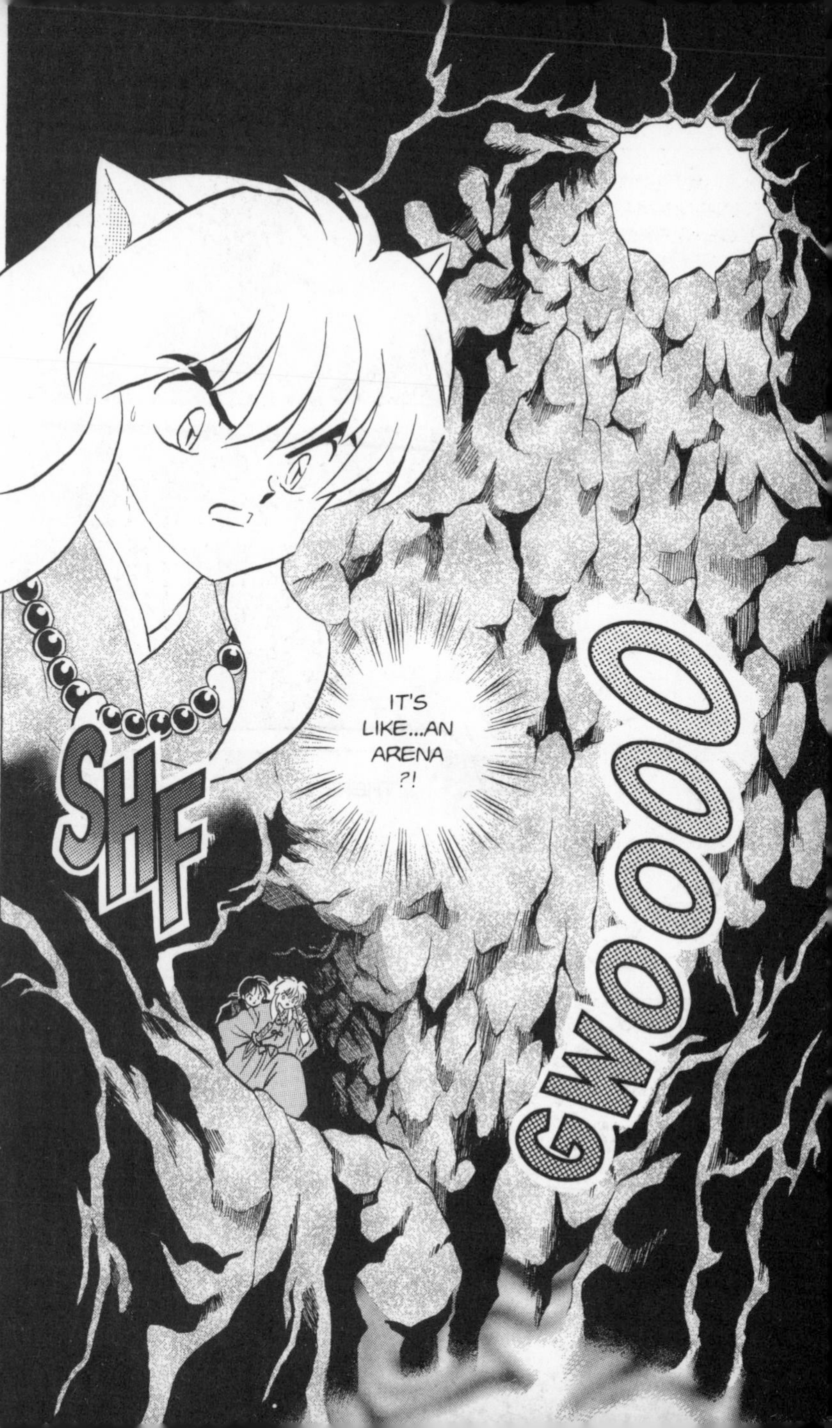
SHF
IT'S LIKE...AN ARENA ?!
GWOOOO

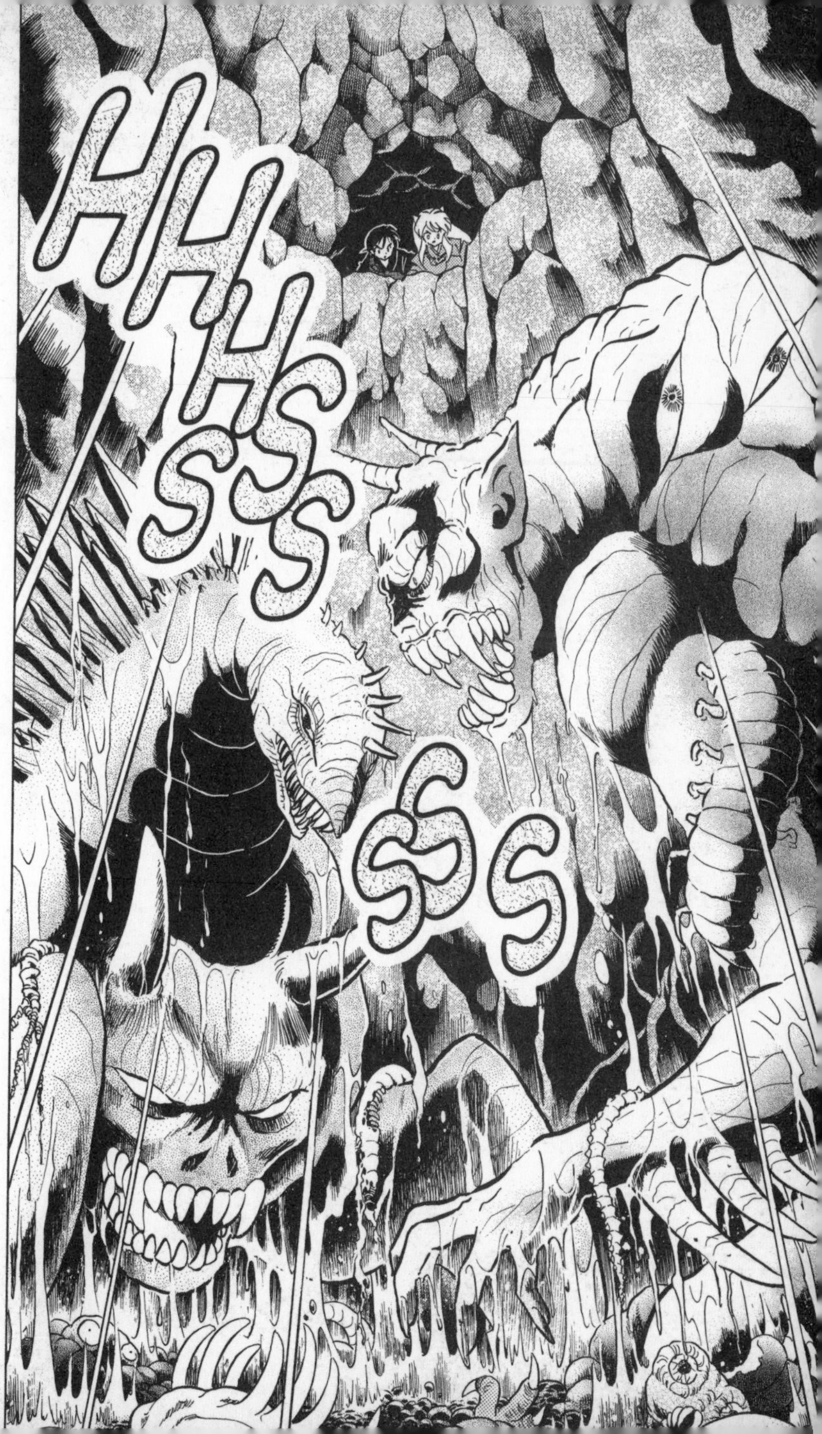
HHHHSSS
SSS

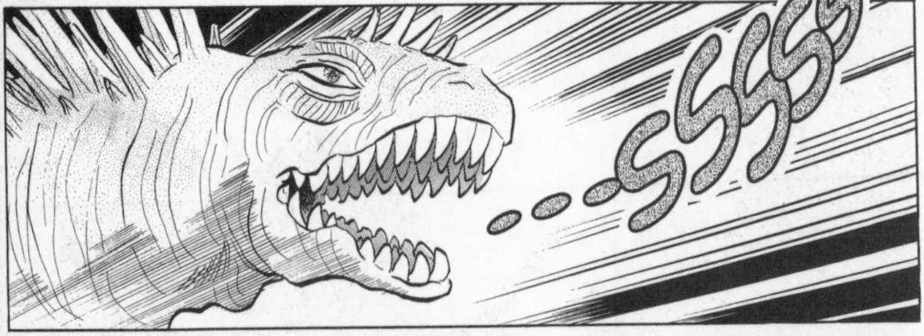
...SSSSS
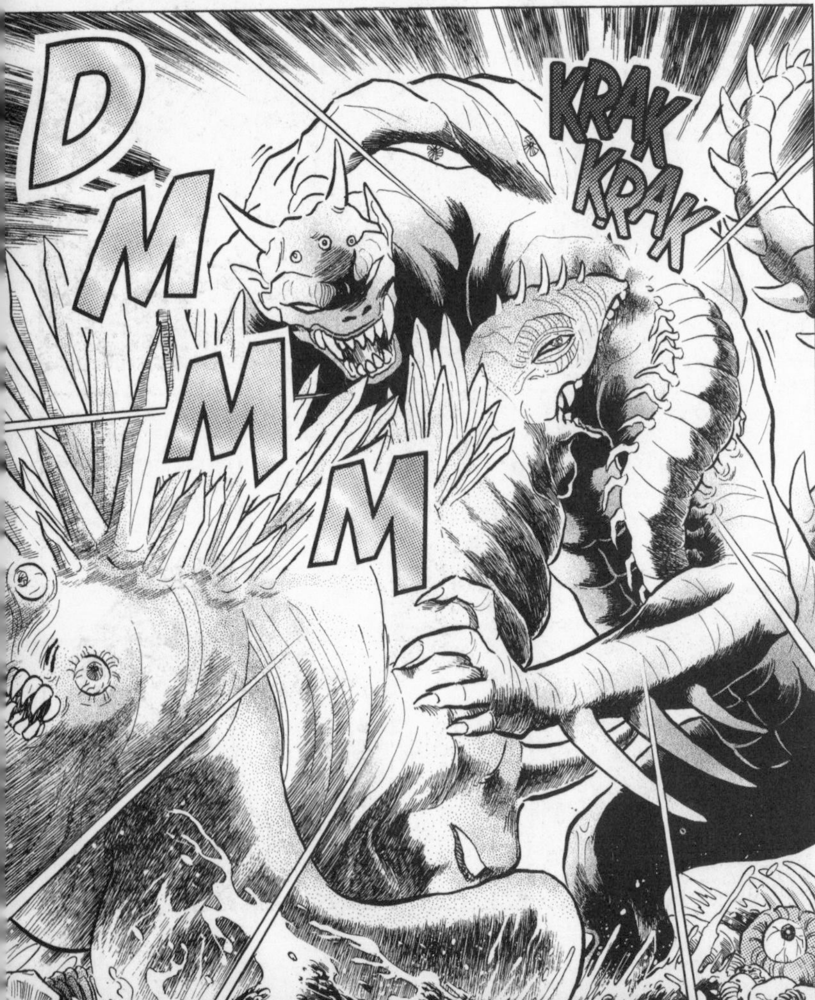
DMMMM
KRAK KRAK KRAK

THEY'RE BATTLING...

IT SEEMS... THERE WERE HUNDREDS OF DEMONS HERE AT ONE TIME...

YEAH.

THOSE CORPSES ARE THE LOSERS.

SSSHHH

GUBBB

THEN IT WAS PIECES OF THESE CORPSES THAT RAINED ON THE VILLAGE WE PASSED....

MOST LIKELY EXPELLED FROM THAT HOLE UP THERE...

BUT WHAT ON EARTH...

COULD BE THE PURPOSE OF THIS... ?

163

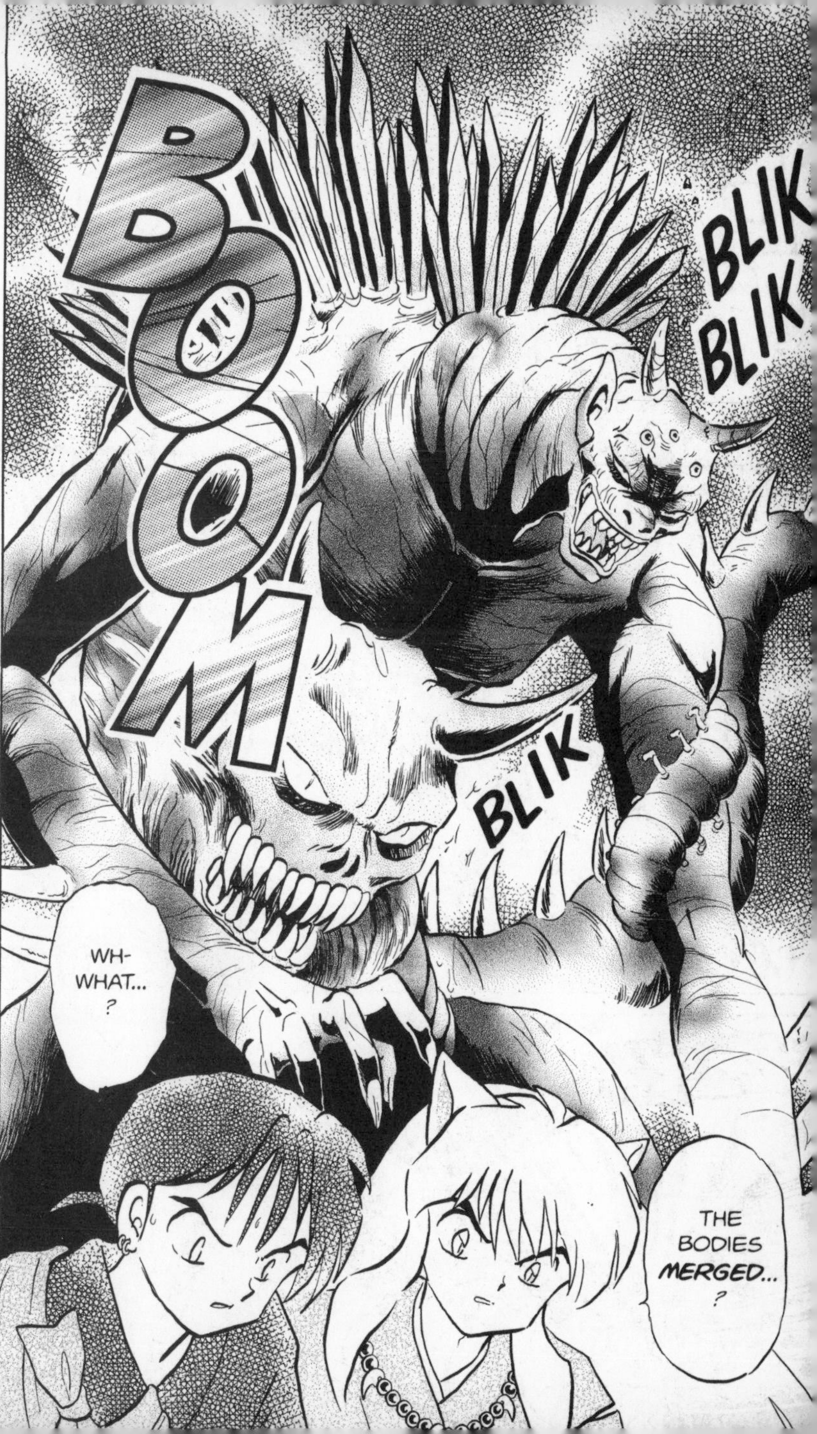
BOOOM
BLIK BLIK
BLIK
WH-WHAT... ?
THE BODIES MERGED... ?

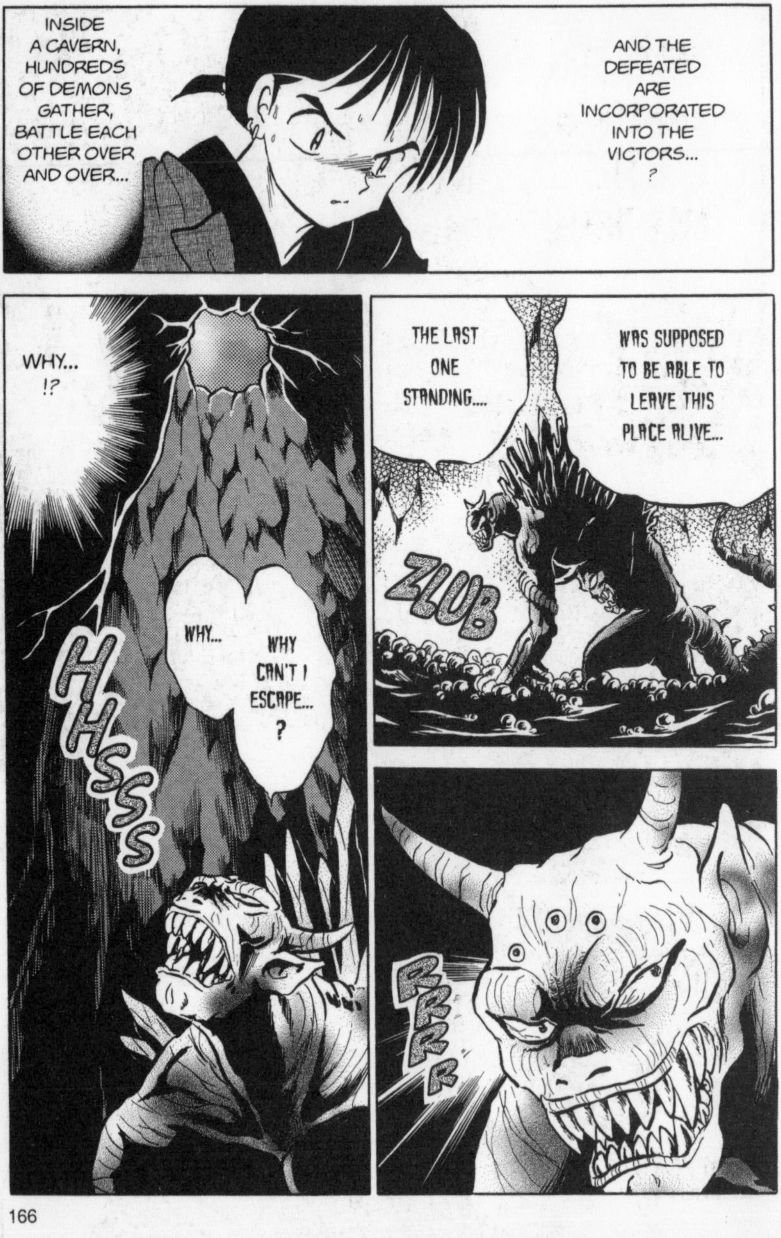
INSIDE A CAVERN, HUNDREDS OF DEMONS GATHER, BATTLE EACH OTHER OVER AND OVER...
AND THE DEFEATED ARE INCORPORATED INTO THE VICTORS... ?
WHY... !?
HHSSS
WHY...
WHY CAN'T I ESCAPE... ?
THE LAST ONE STANDING....
WAS SUPPOSED TO BE ABLE TO LEAVE THIS PLACE ALIVE...
ZLUB
RRRRR

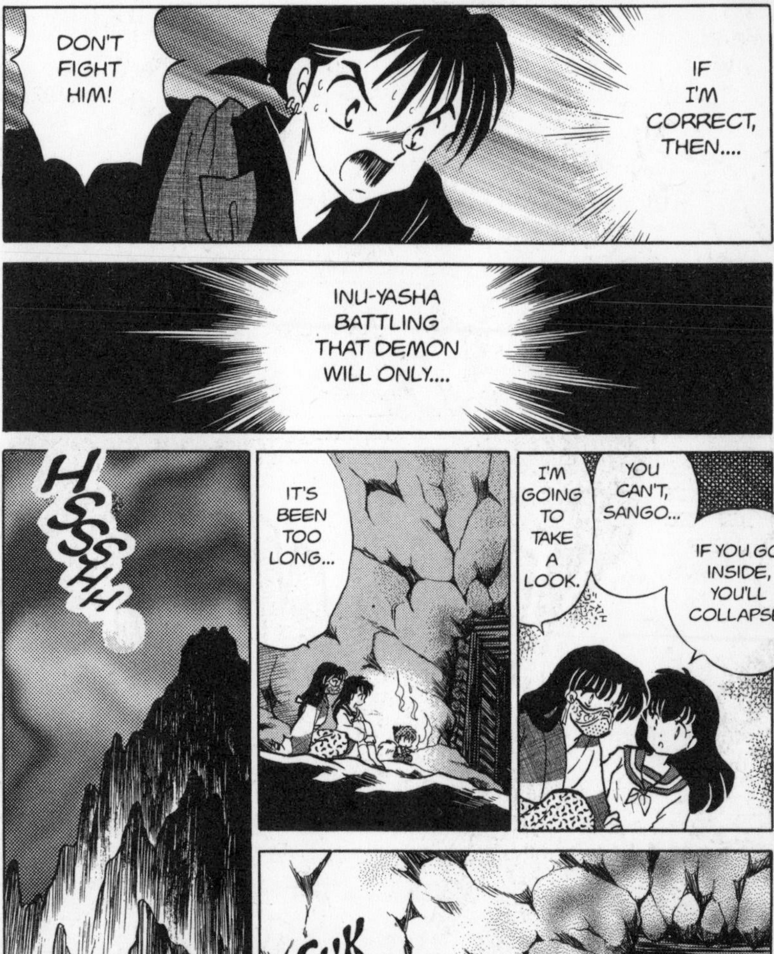
DON'T FIGHT HIM!
IF I'M CORRECT, THEN....
INU-YASHA BATTLING THAT DEMON WILL ONLY....
HSSSHH
IT'S BEEN TOO LONG...
I'M GOING TO TAKE A LOOK.
YOU CAN'T, SANGO...
IF YOU GO INSIDE, YOU'LL COLLAPSE.
SHK

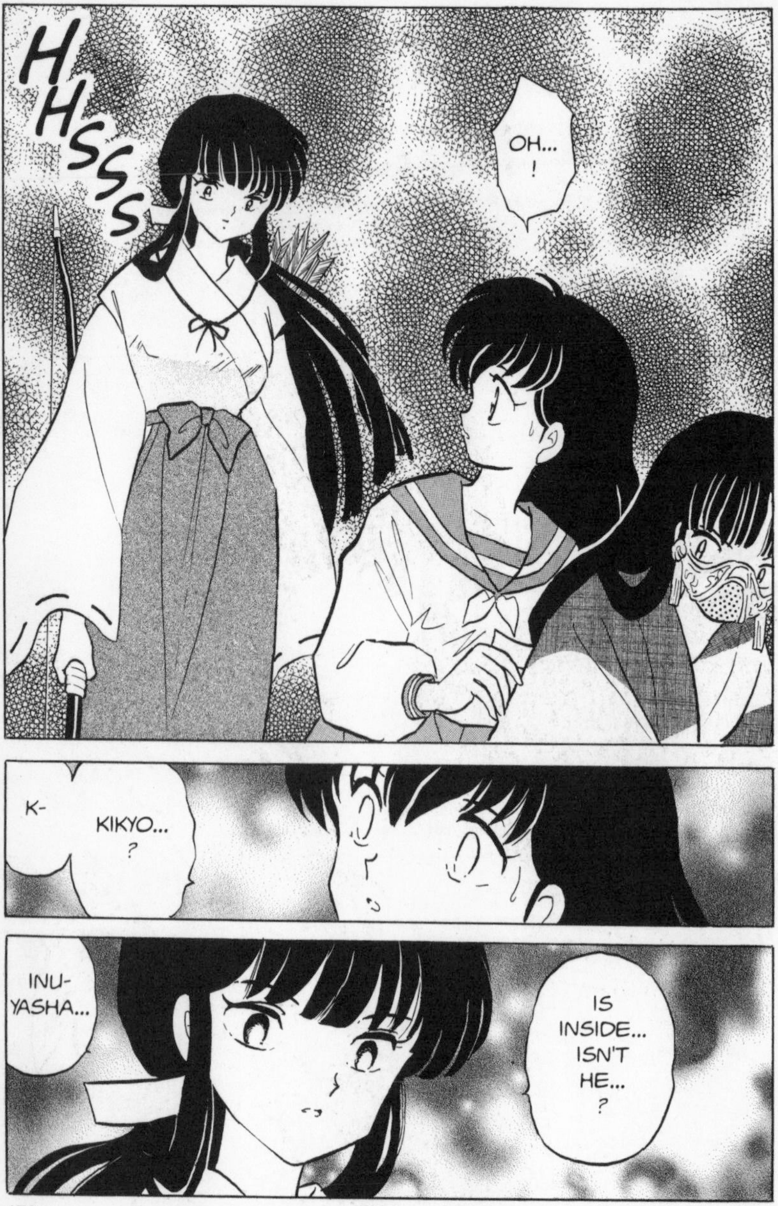
HHSSSS
OH... !
K-
KIKYO... ?
INU-YASHA...
IS INSIDE... ISN'T HE... ?

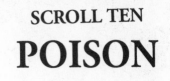

SCROLL TEN
POISON

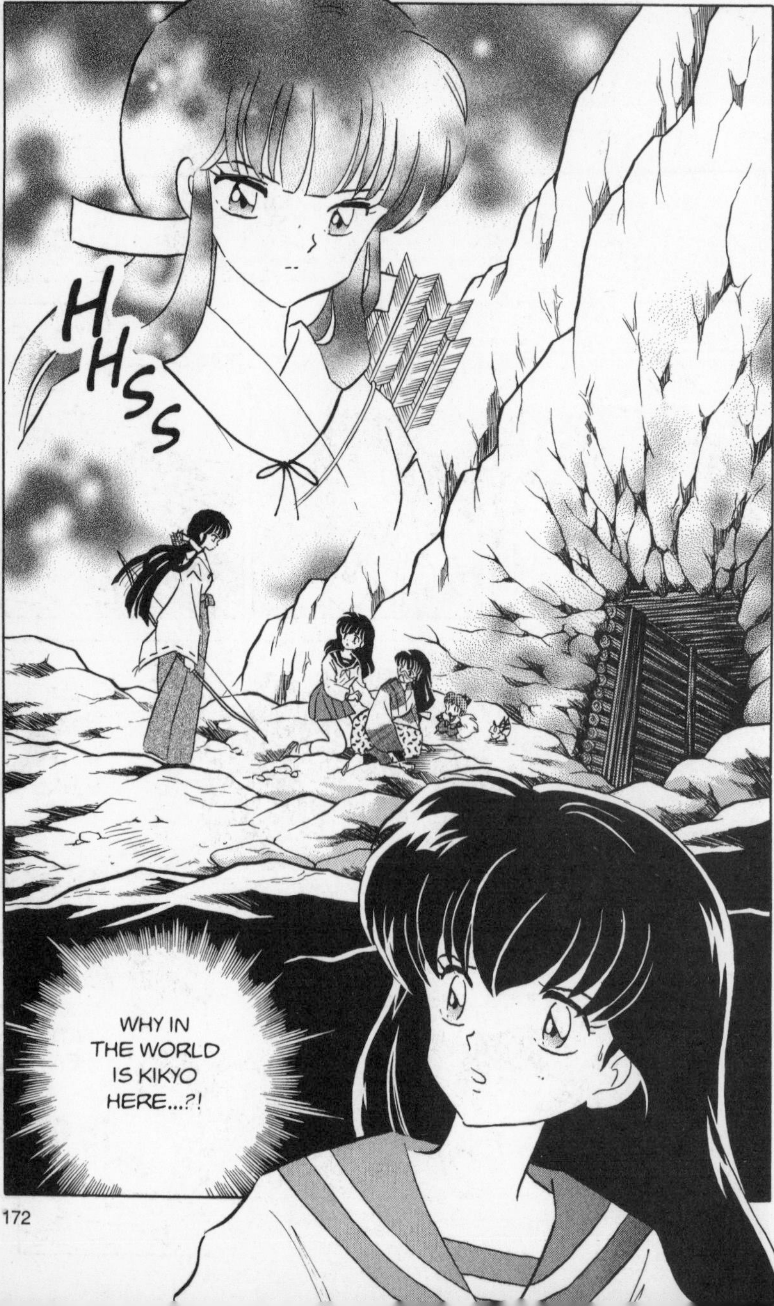
HHSSS
WHY IN THE WORLD IS KIKYO HERE...?!

THAT PRIEST-ESS...

IS KIKYO.

THE WOMAN INU-YASHA USED TO LOVE... A LONG TIME AGO.

SHF

HWOOOO

THE DEAD SOULS INSIDE ME ARE TRYING TO GET OUT.

ARE THEY DRAWN TO THE EVIL AURA IN THIS CAVE...?

HHHSSSS

AND...IS INU-YASHA IN THERE... ?

HWOOOOO

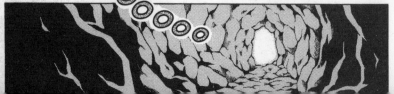

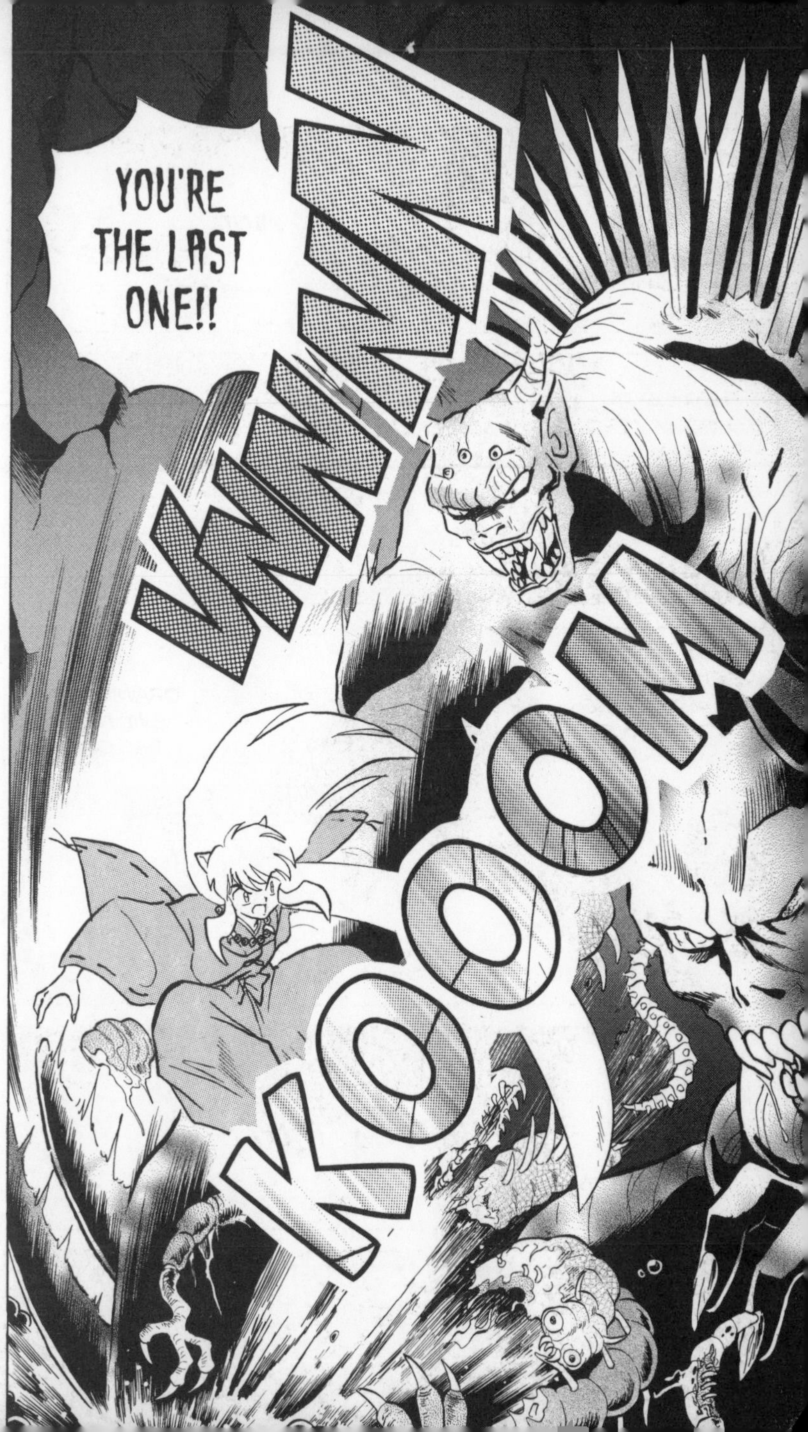
YOU'RE THE LAST ONE!!
VMMMM
KOOOOM

THIS IS JUST LIKE A DARK PRIEST'S SPELL.

IT'S THE SAME MAGIC THAT MAKES A POISON IMP!

HUH--?

HE'S LOSING IT AGAIN...

I ALONE...

...WILL LEAVE HERE ALIVE!

FSSH

INSIDE A SINGLE VESSEL, YOU PLACE VENOMOUS INSECTS, LIZARDS, FROGS, OR OTHER ANIMALS...

AND LET THEM KILL EACH OTHER! WITH THE PROPER SPELL, THE LAST ONE LEFT ALIVE BECOMES A POISON IMP!

THIS CAVE...

...IS A HUGE POISON-IMP VESSEL!

IF YOU SHOULD DEFEAT THAT DEMON...

HIS BODY WILL BE ABSORBED INTO YOURS, WHETHER YOU LIKE IT OR NOT!

HHSSS

SO LONG AS YOU FIGHT IN THIS ARENA, NO MATTER WHO WINS, YOUR BODIES WILL BECOME ONE!

FEH...

HRRRR....

KRAK

HYAH!

WOOOM

THEN, NO MATTER HOW YOU LOOK AT IT... THE ONLY CHOICE IS TO FIGHT!

HYAH

GWOOOOO

THERE'S NOWHERE TO HIDE !!

WE NEED OUT....

IF WE COULD ONLY BREAK THE SPELL THAT WAS LAID ON THIS PLACE...

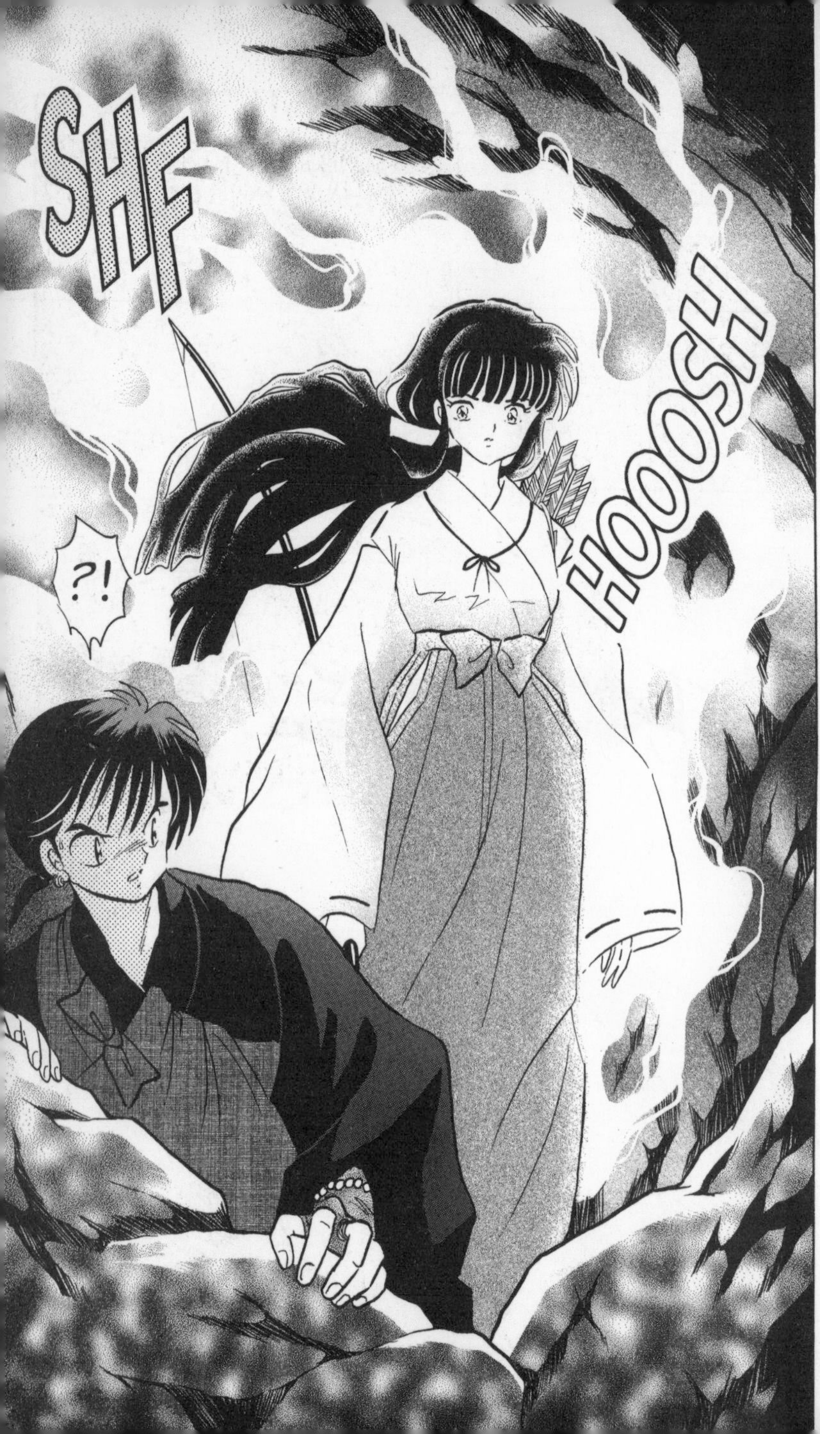
SHF
?!
HOOOSH

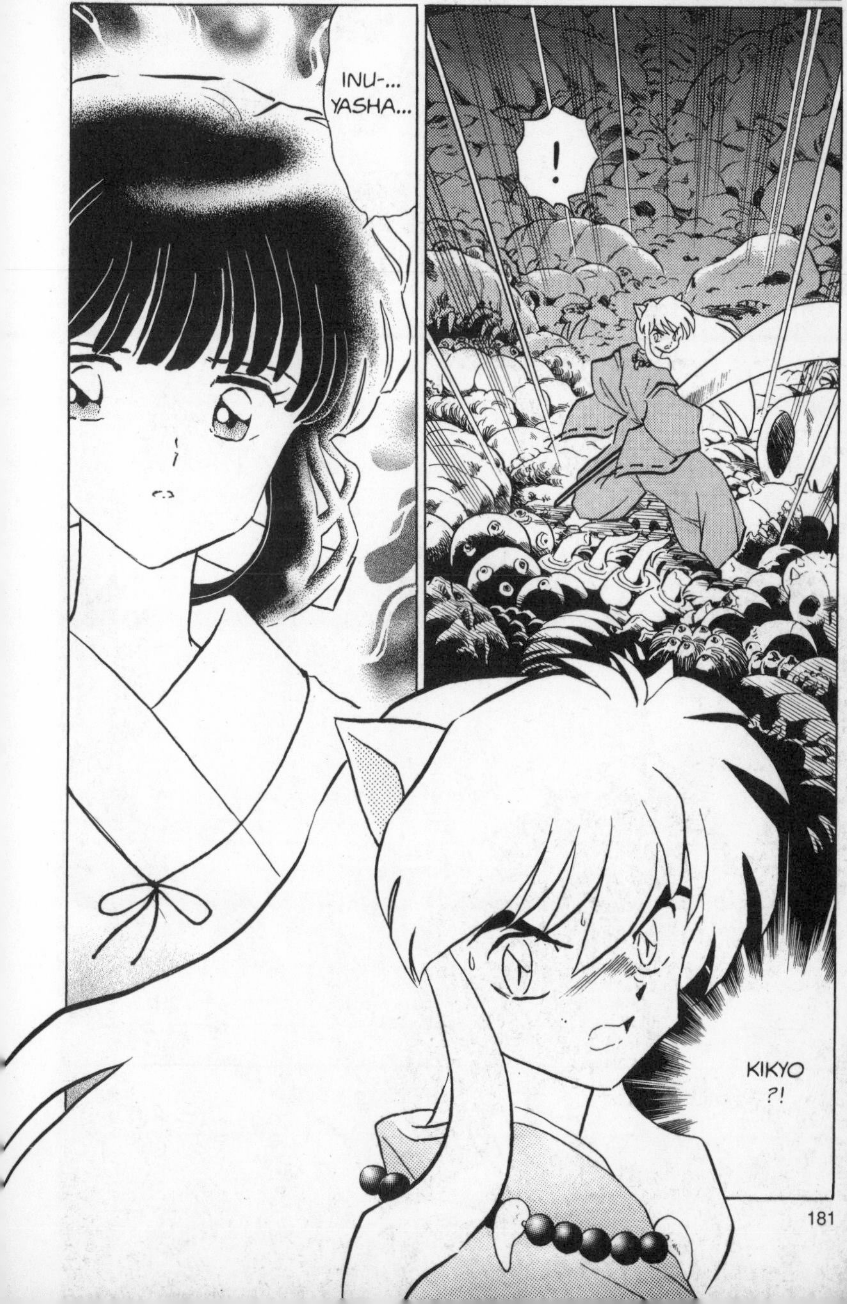
INU-... YASHA...
!
KIKYO ?!

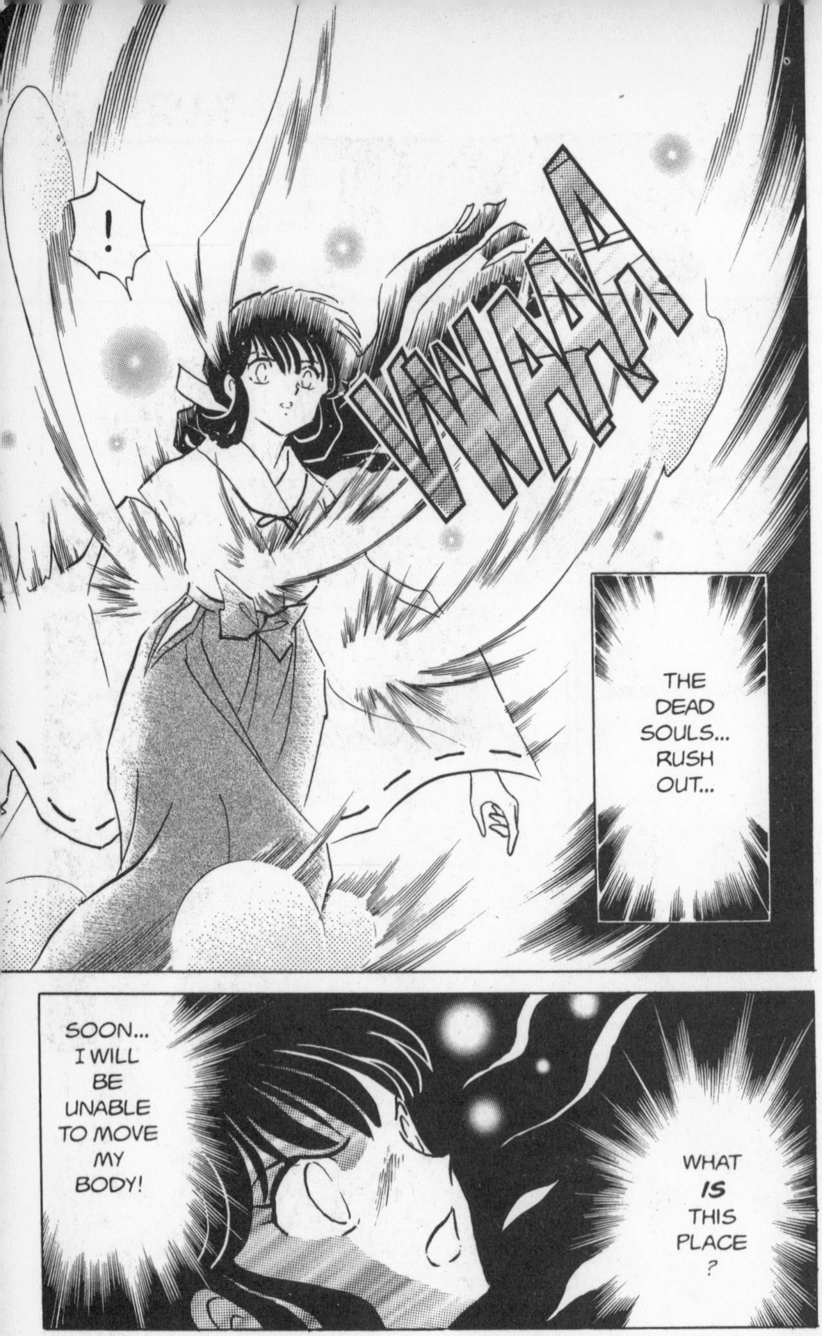
!
THE DEAD SOULS... RUSH OUT...
SOON... I WILL BE UNABLE TO MOVE MY BODY!
WHAT *IS* THIS PLACE?

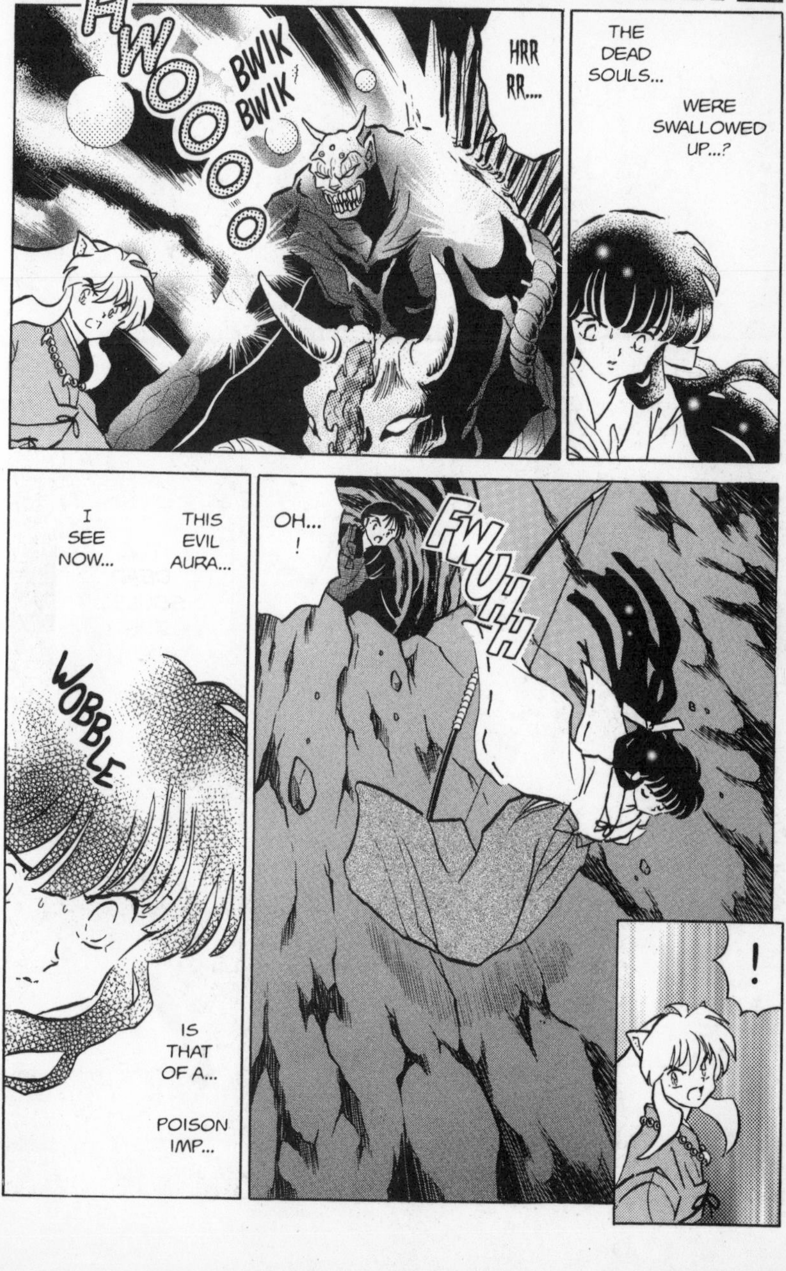
HWOOOOO
BWIK BWIK
HRR RR....
THE DEAD SOULS...
WERE SWALLOWED UP...?
I SEE NOW...
THIS EVIL AURA...
WOBBLE
IS THAT OF A...
POISON IMP...
OH... !
FWUHH
!

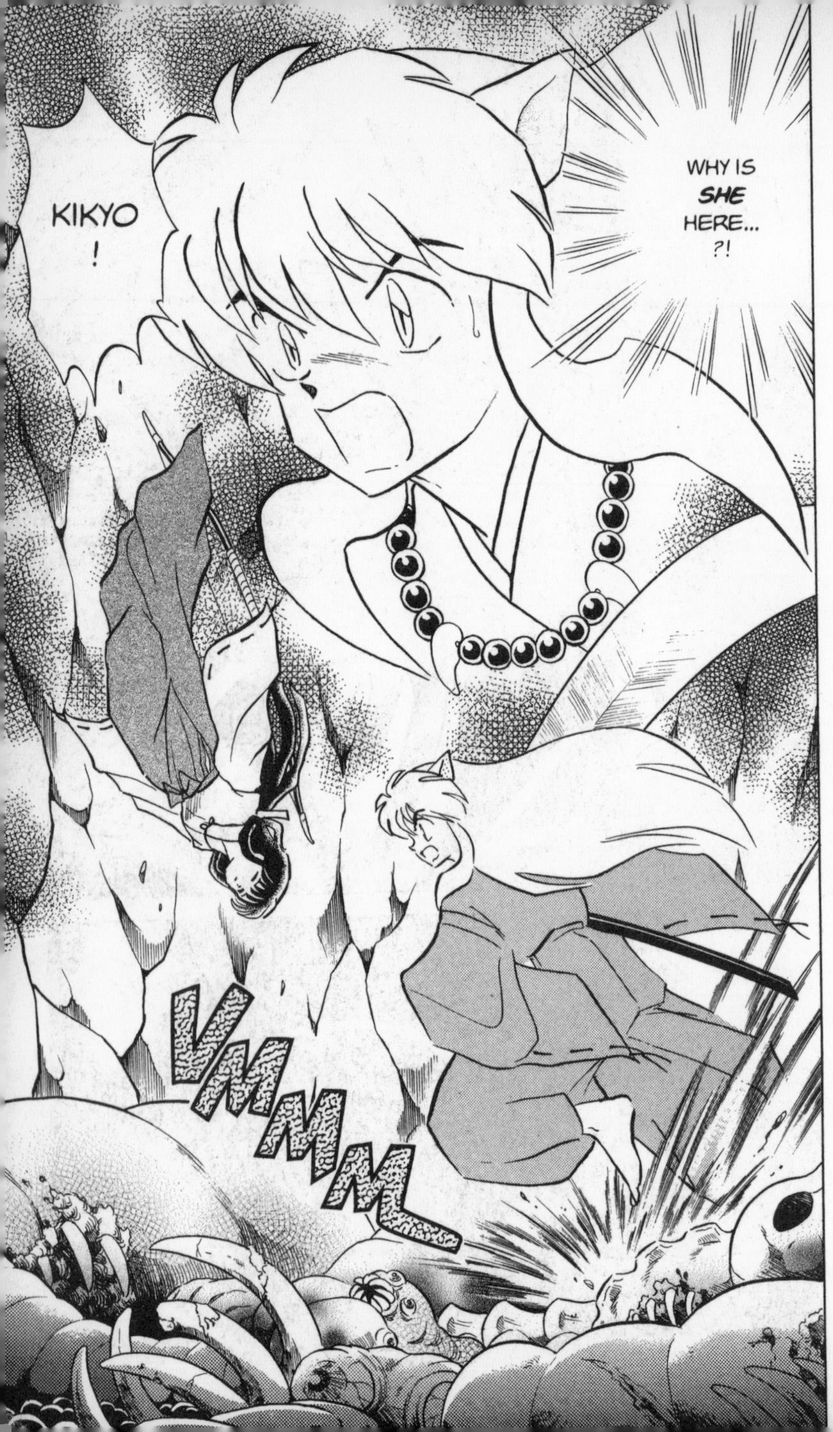

KIKYO !
WHY IS SHE HERE... ?!
VMMML

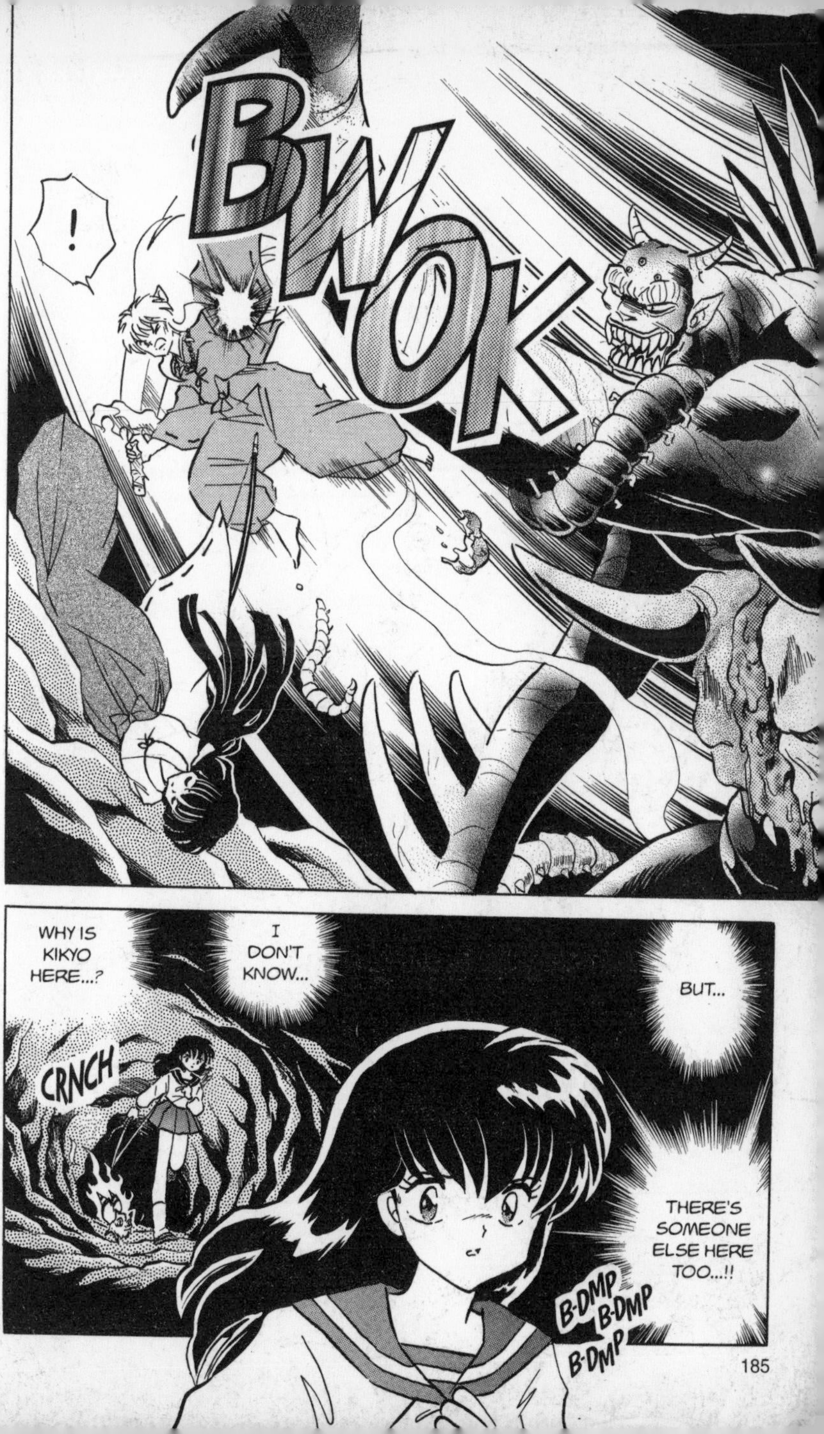
!
BWOK
WHY IS KIKYO HERE...?
I DON'T KNOW...
BUT...
CRNCH
THERE'S SOMEONE ELSE HERE TOO...!!
B-DMP
B-DMP
B-DMP

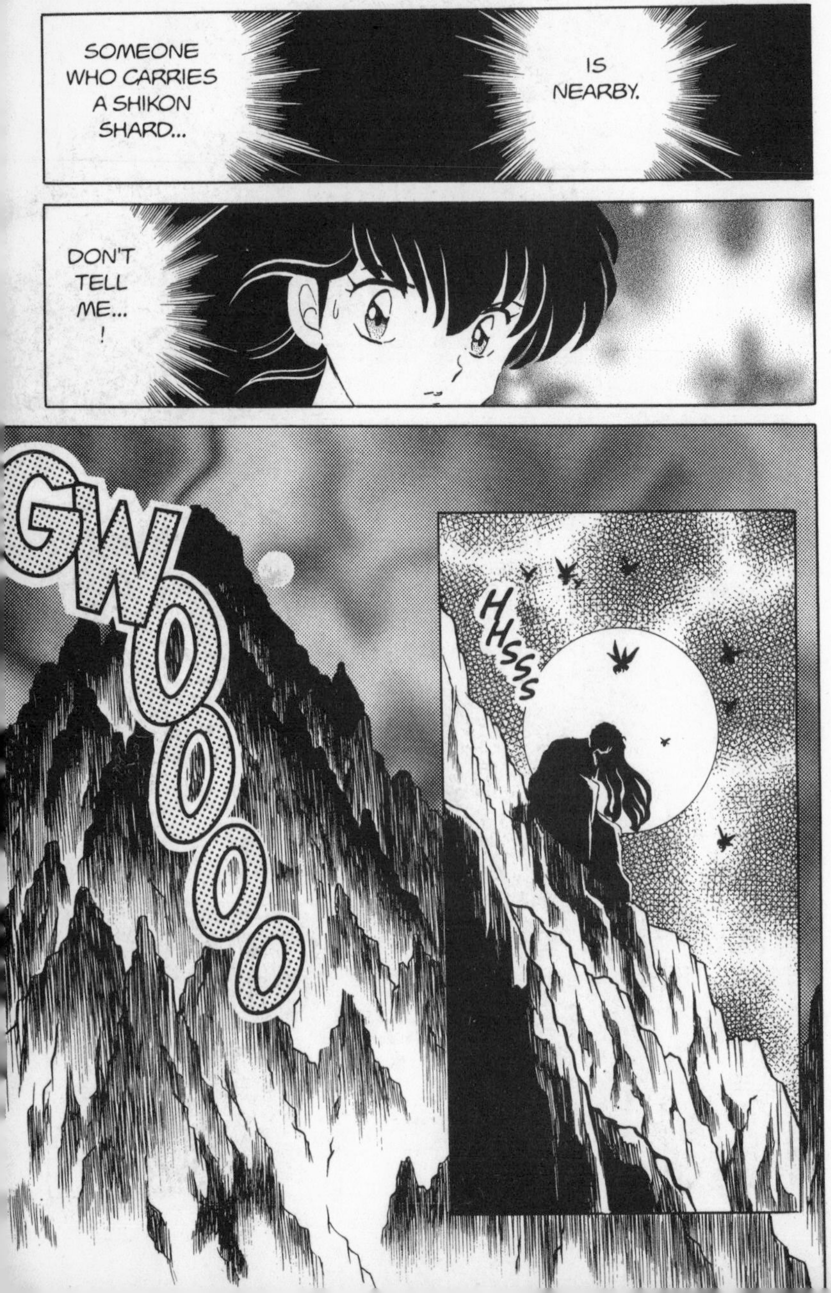
SOMEONE WHO CARRIES A SHIKON SHARD...
IS NEARBY.
DON'T TELL ME... !
GWOOOOO
HHSSS

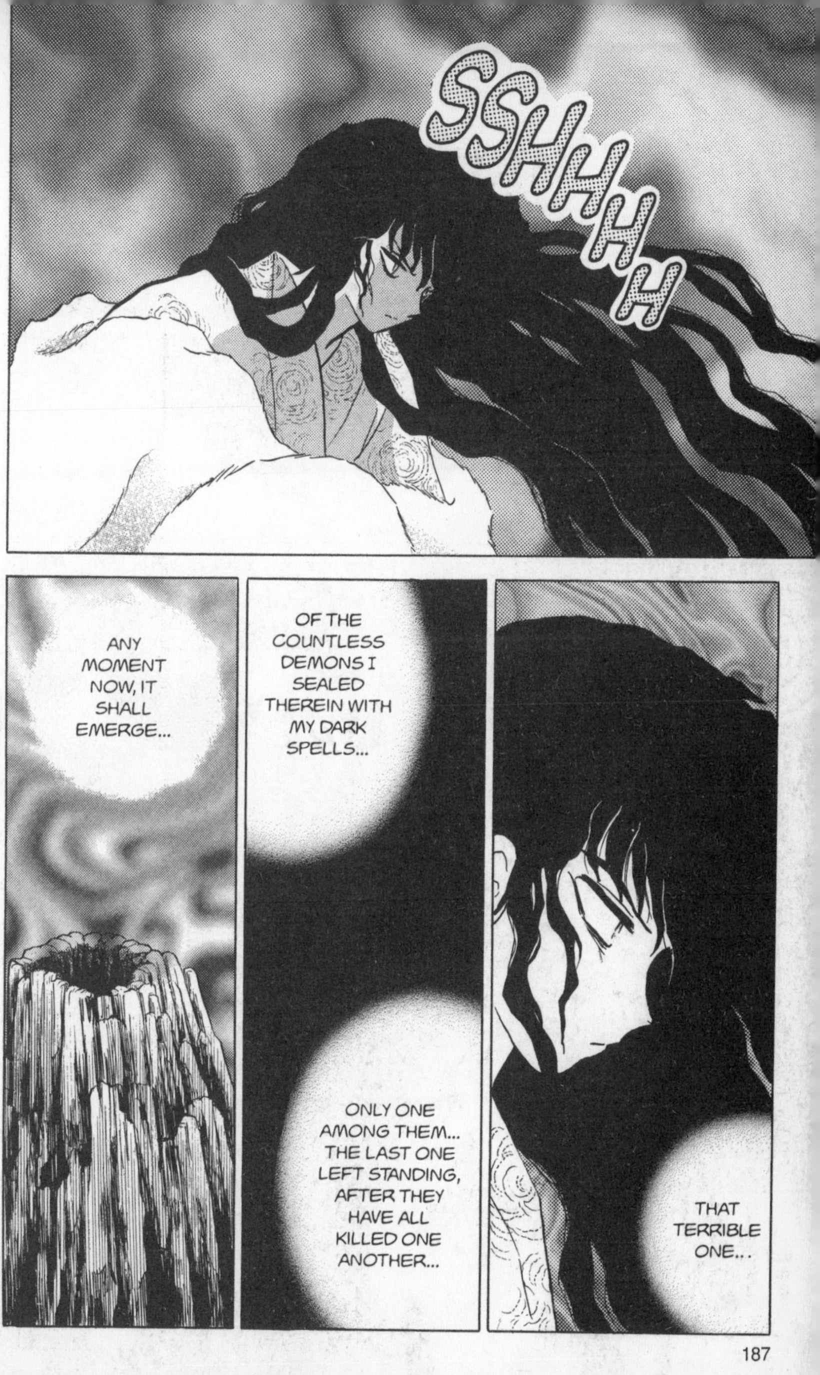
SSHHHH
ANY MOMENT NOW, IT SHALL EMERGE...
OF THE COUNTLESS DEMONS I SEALED THEREIN WITH MY DARK SPELLS...
ONLY ONE AMONG THEM... THE LAST ONE LEFT STANDING, AFTER THEY HAVE ALL KILLED ONE ANOTHER...
THAT TERRIBLE ONE...

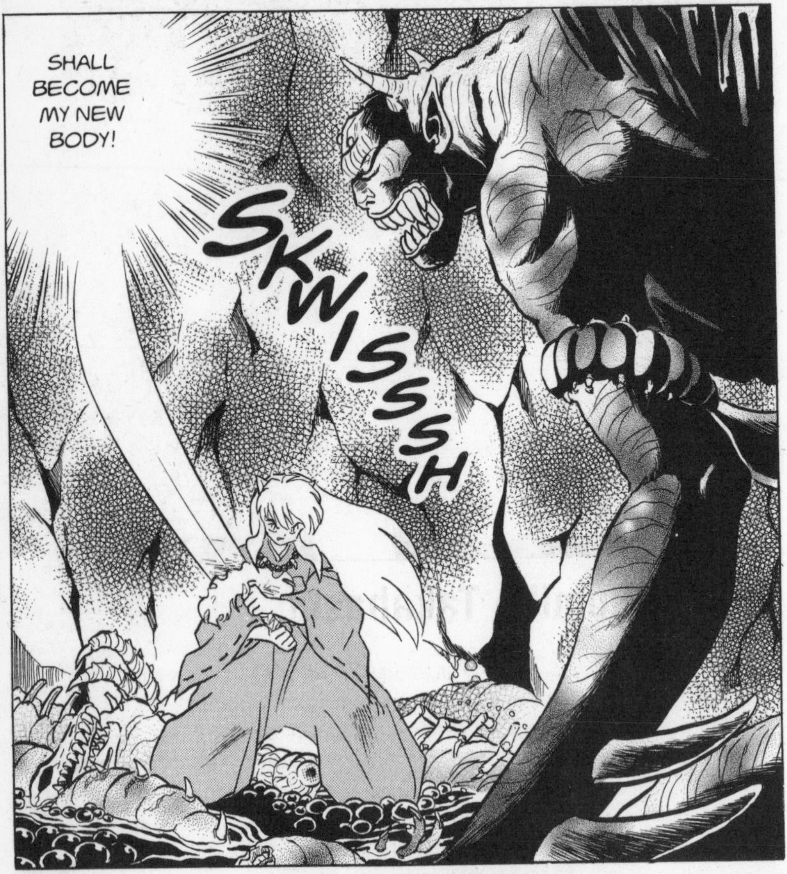
SHALL BECOME MY NEW BODY!
SKWISSSH
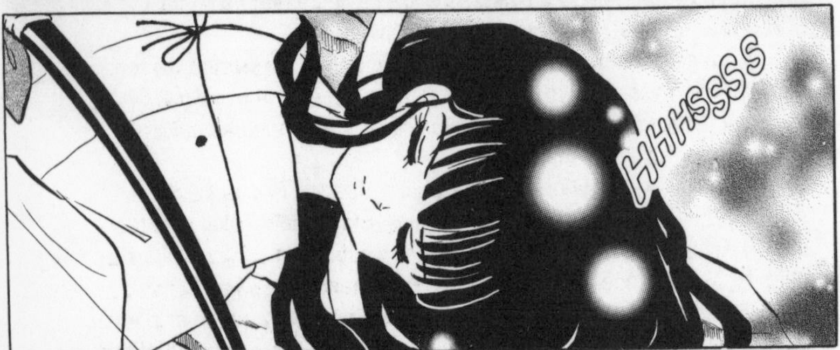
HHHSSSS

TO BE CONTINUED...

About Rumiko Takahashi

Born in 1957 in Niigata, Japan, Rumiko Takahashi attended women's college in Tokyo, where she began studying comics with Kazuo Koike, author of CRYING FREEMAN. She later became an assistant to horror-manga artist Kazuo Umezu (OROCHI). In 1978, she won a prize in Shogakukan's annual "New Comic Artist Contest," and in that same year her boy-meets-alien comedy series URUSEI YATSURA began appearing in the weekly manga magazine SHÔNEN SUNDAY. This phenomenally successful series ran for nine years and sold over 22 million copies. Takahashi's later RANMA 1/2 series enjoyed even greater popularity.

Takahashi is considered by many to be one of the world's most popular manga artists. With the publication of Volume 34 of her RANMA 1/2 series in Japan, Takahashi's total sales passed *one hundred million* copies of her compiled works.

Takahashi's serial titles include URUSEI YATSURA, RANMA 1/2, ONE-POUND GOSPEL, MAISON IKKOKU and INUYASHA. Additionally, Takahashi has drawn many short stories which have been published in America under the title "Rumic Theater," and several installments of a saga known as her "Mermaid" series. Most of Takahashi's major stories have also been animated, and are widely available in translation worldwide. INUYASHA is her most recent serial story, first published in SHÔNEN SUNDAY in 1996.

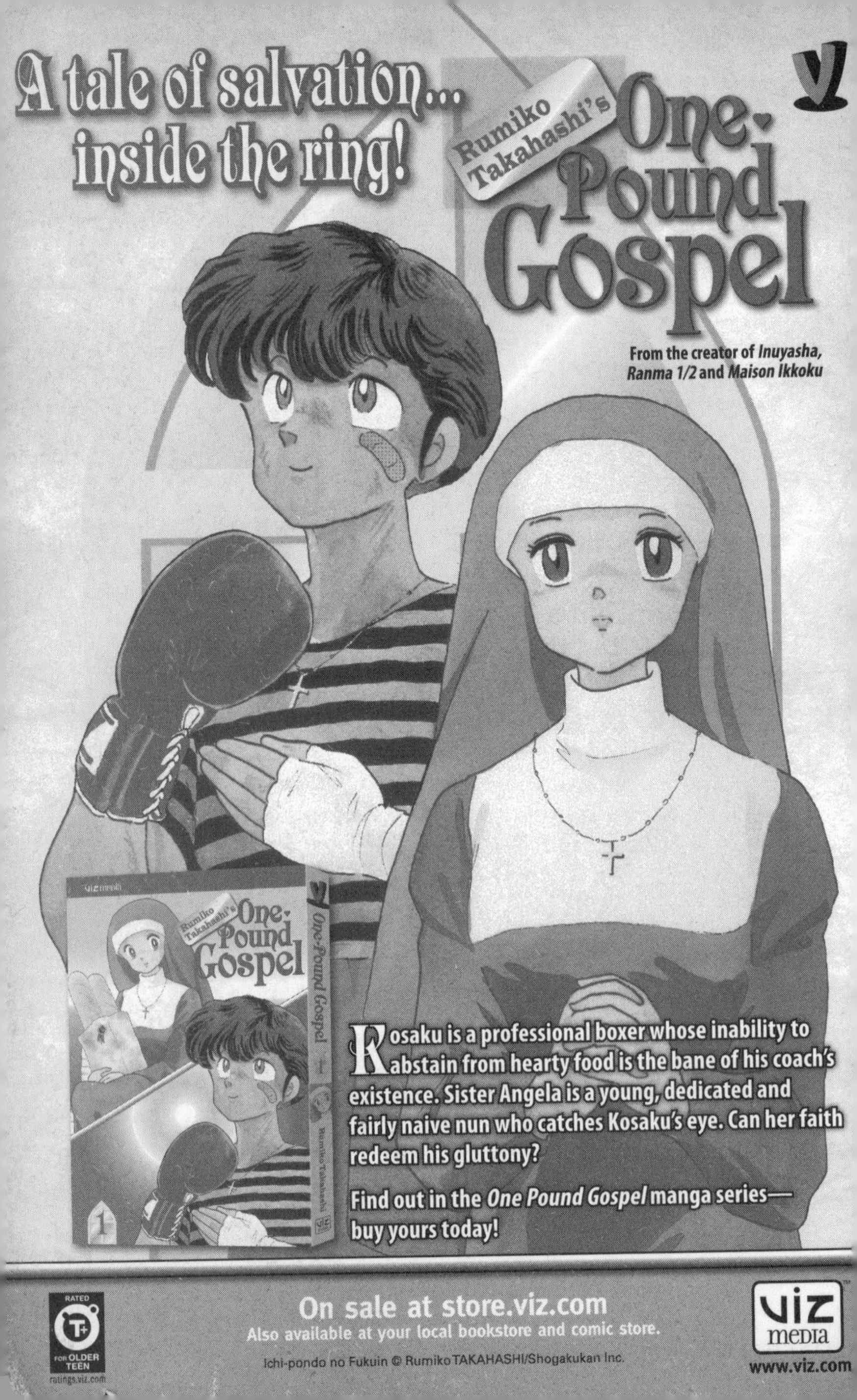
A tale of salvation...
inside the ring!
Rumiko Takahashi's
One-Pound Gospel
From the creator of *Inuyasha*, *Ranma 1/2* and *Maison Ikkoku*
Kosaku is a professional boxer whose inability to abstain from hearty food is the bane of his coach's existence. Sister Angela is a young, dedicated and fairly naive nun who catches Kosaku's eye. Can her faith redeem his gluttony?
Find out in the *One Pound Gospel* manga series—buy yours today!
RATED T+ FOR OLDER TEEN
ratings.viz.com
On sale at store.viz.com
Also available at your local bookstore and comic store.
Ichi-pondo no Fukuin © Rumiko TAKAHASHI/Shogakukan Inc.
viz media
www.viz.com

LOVE MANGA?
LET US KNOW WHAT YOU THINK!

OUR MANGA SURVEY IS NOW
AVAILABLE ONLINE. PLEASE VISIT:
VIZ.COM/MANGASURVEY

HELP US MAKE THE MANGA
YOU LOVE BETTER!